Preparing Globally Minded Literacy Teachers

This textbook brings together internationally renowned scholars to provide an overview of print and digital literacy instruction for pre-service teachers and teacher educators. It examines historical and cultural contexts of literacy practices around the globe, and addresses issues that teachers need to consider as they teach children from diverse world cultures, languages, and backgrounds.

Organized into three Parts—Early Literacy, Intermediate to Adolescent Literacy, and Case Studies—the text highlights key practices around the world to provide literacy educators and students with a broader view of effective practices as well as strategies for overcoming challenges faced by literacy educators worldwide. The global case studies present complex issues and allow readers to discuss what it means to be globally minded, as well as how to implement best practices in literacy instruction. All chapters include consistent elements for ease of use, such as vignettes, historical and cultural contexts, implications for future research, and discussion questions.

Grounded in current research and theory, this book is designed for foundational courses in literacy education and literacy methods, as well as courses in comparative and multicultural education.

Jan Lacina is Professor of Literacy in the College of Education at Texas Christian University, USA.

Robin Griffith is Associate Professor of Literacy in the College of Education at Texas Christian University, USA.

Preparing Globally Minded Literacy Teachers

Knowledge, Practices, and Case Studies

Edited by Jan Lacina and
Robin Griffith

Routledge
Taylor & Francis Group

NEW YORK AND LONDON

First published 2020
by Routledge
52 Vanderbilt Avenue, New York, NY 10017

and by Routledge
2 Park Square, Milton Park, Abingdon, Oxon, OX14 4RN

Routledge is an imprint of the Taylor & Francis Group, an informa business

Library of Congress Cataloging-in-Publication Data
A catalog record for this title has been requested

ISBN: 978-0-367-02784-1 (hbk)
ISBN: 978-0-367-02786-5 (pbk)
ISBN: 978-0-429-39779-0 (ebk)

Typeset in Bembo
by Swales & Willis, Exeter, Devon, UK

For Caroline and Grace ~ J.L.
and
For Katherine, Zachary, and William ~ R.G.

Contents

Illustrations

Figures

Tables

Foreword

James Hoffman

The chapters in this edited volume advance international research on literacy in ways that are profoundly important to scholars, practitioners and policy makers around the world. I would invite readers coming to this volume to consider the wealth of expertise represented and the rich perspectives on literacy that are being explored. This volume comes at a critical moment in time with respect to global understandings and perspectives on literacy. It has been my impression that the literacy research community is largely unaware of the issues that are of concern in international contexts and, more importantly, unaware of the impact that research conducted in northern/western countries is having on literacy teaching, literacy research, and literacy policy around the globe.

As I read these chapters I made immediate connections to two recent publications: Tierney's (2018) "Toward a Model of Global Meaning Making" and the International Literacy Association's (2019) *¡Ya Basta! Con EGRA: Humanizing International Support for Literacy Development.*

Tierney's essay explores many different dimensions of global perspectives on literacy and, the often, oppressive effects of western/northern perspectives on the world scene. I think particularly relevant to the chapters in this volume are Tierney's concerns over the absence of attention to the contributions of international scholars to our deliberations. Tierney argues for the benefits to all in opening up our scholarship to diverse voices – rather than silencing or ignoring the alternate epistemologies that surround us. Tierney subscribes to the belief that: "Western research has achieved a monopoly through protectionism that inhibits global knowledge development" (p. 400). The chapters in this volume represent a range of research methods and epistemologies. The authors are grounded in their local context and offer a glimpse of what our literacy community might look like if we embraced the voices of others.

The *¡Ya Basta!* essay is a position paper published by the International Literacy Association that calls for an end to literacy development work that ignores and disparages local expertise and the capacity of our international colleges to address the literacy challenges they face in schools. The position paper uses the example of EGRA (formerly Early Grade Reading Assessment and now Early Grade Reading Activity) that has been promoted by USAID, the World Bank, and private donors like the Gates Foundation to call attention to the devastating ways in which hundreds of millions of dollars are being used to export a version of "DIBELS" from the United States into emerging countries. The position paper argues for a more humanizing approach to support literacy initiatives that values local expertise, positions all children as capable, and embraces a broad view of literacy as culturally embedded meaning making. The chapters in this volume offer insight into local problem-posing and contextually rich inquiry into literacy that could become the foundation of international development work.

I am a literacy teacher educator working in a university-based teacher preparation program in the United States. I have been fortunate, over the past 25 years, to work in literacy development projects in South Africa, Malawi, and other African countries. Most recently, Misty Sailors and I have been working in Mozambique on a seven-year project supported by the Canadian government designed to improve elementary teacher preparation in the area of literacy.

Across these contexts, I have gained understandings that have helped me rethink and redesign my own literacy teacher preparation program. International experiences can be expansive for everyone if we stay open to the idea of partnerships, collaboration, and dialogue. Sadly, this is not the stance taken by many who engage in international work.

- I have sat in lectures in these contexts where Bloom's taxonomy was offered as the essential tool for teaching – with me trying to recall the last time I heard of Bloom's taxonomy set as the centerpiece of literacy teacher preparation.
- I have sat in seminars in these same contexts where the "simple view" of reading was described as established science that should guide all teaching and policy development surrounding literacy instruction.
- I have seen external consultants from the United States present to Ministry's of Education with guaranteed success in learning to read for **all children** if the 45 "research-based" lessons they have prepared are taught with high fidelity.
- I have witnessed high quality children's literature authored by local teachers for use in the teaching of literacy be revised to conform to EGRA standards for decodable texts intruding on the authors' word choices for their own students.

At the same time and in the face of these oppressive and colonizing practices, I have witnessed amazing professionalism, imagination, and commitment at the local level for doing what is best for children in the moment.

- I worked with a primary grade teacher who orchestrates powerful literacy instruction in a single classroom with over 150 students (and she walks 10 kilometers to and from school each day).
- I work with a teacher educator who guides an entire literacy mentoring program with over 100 preservice teachers and primary students – all on her volunteer time.
- I have collaborated with local colleagues on research around first and second language acquisition and how to support students into literacy in complex linguistic environments.
- I have authored children's books with teachers who write around with passion around the kinds of lived experiences that their students can connect to in their daily lives.

These are not exceptions or anomalies. These are examples that represent the working lives of the vast majority of professional educators in developing economies who are committed to serving their students and working under challenging circumstances. I have to believe that it is the local, represented in these kinds of cases, that will inform the global and not the continuation of colonizing practices that currently dominate international work. Through the kind of work offered in this volume we can begin to work internationally in ways that not only assist others but in ways that grow our own teaching as well.

References

Hoffman, J.V., Bloch, C., Pallais-Downing, D., Goodman, K., & Makalela, L. (2019). ¡Ya Basta! Con EGRA: Humanizing International Support for Literacy Development. Newark, DE: International Literacy Association.

Tierney, R. (2018). Toward a model of global meaning making. Journal of Literacy Research, 50(4) 397–422.

Contributors

Fatima Hasan Bailey is an Assistant Professor in the College of Education at Zayed University in the United Arab Emirates. As a teacher educator, she prepares culturally responsive "classroom ready" pre-service teachers. Fatima is a recipient of the prestigious Gordon Allport Prize for Outstanding Papers on Intergroup Relations and a RIF Research Grant.

Celeste C. Bates is an Associate Professor of Literacy Education and the Director of the Clemson University Reading Recovery. She has a Ph. D. in Language and Literacy from Georgia State University in 2003. Previously, Bates earned her M.A.T. in Early Childhood at the University of South Carolina. Her work has been published in *The Reading Teacher*, *Young Children*, and *The Journal of Digital Learning in Teacher Education*. Her research agenda focuses on the use of digital tools to enhance and deliver professional development for reading interventionists and K-2 classroom teachers, which stems from her ongoing inquiry into the teaching of children who are having difficulty learning to read and write.

Connie Briggs is a Professor and Reading Recovery trainer at Texas Woman's University. She continues to tutor primary grade students in order to inform her practice and research. Dr. Briggs has served as president of both the North American Trainers Group and the Reading Recovery Council of North America, and is currently editor of *The Journal of Reading Recovery*.

Patricia A. Crawford is Associate Professor and acting chair of the Department of Instruction and Learning at the University of Pittsburgh. Her work focuses on the ways that literacy learning and early childhood education intersect, with specific attention to the role of children's literature. She is co-editor of *Early Childhood Education Journal*.

Julia Douetil was the first director of the International Literacy Centre at the University College London Institute of Education. Although retired, she continues to work closely with Reading Recovery teacher leaders and teachers around the world.

Mary Anne Doyle is a Professor Emerita in the Neag School of Education at University of Connecticut where she was a Professor, Reading Recovery Trainer, and Department Chair of Curriculum and Instruction. She is widely known as an outstanding scholar, on a national and international level, and, in particular, in the area of Reading Recovery, a program aimed at improving the reading skills of at-risk first-graders.

Ann Ebe has worked as a bilingual teacher, reading specialist, and school administrator in the United States and Hong Kong. She served as Director of Bilingual Education and Associate Professor of Literacy Education at Hunter College in New York City. She is now an educational consultant living in Mexico City.

Beryl Exley is a Professor of English Curriculum and Literacies Education with the School of Education and Professional Studies at Griffith University in Queensland, Australia. Beryl adopts a socio-cultural approach to curriculum planning and pedagogical implementation and is interested in the affordances of social media for advancing this learning.

Ana Ferreira is a Senior Lecturer in English language and literacy education with the School of Education at the University of the Witwatersrand, Johannesburg, South Africa. Ana's work is positioned at the interface of pedagogy, identity/subjectivity, and textuality, and is underpinned by social justice education in global contexts of diversity.

Douglas Fisher is Professor and Chair of Educational Leadership at San Diego State University and a leader at Health Sciences High & Middle College having been an early intervention teacher and elementary school educator. He has published numerous articles on reading and literacy, differentiated instruction, and curriculum design as well as books, such as *Building Equity*.

Nancy Frey is Professor and Chair of Educational Leadership at San Diego State University and a leader at Health Sciences High & Middle College having been a special education teacher. She has published numerous articles on reading and literacy, differentiated instruction, and curriculum design as well as books, such as *All Learning is Social and Emotional*.

Murray Gadd is a New Zealand-based literacy facilitator, researcher, and teacher who works across the country and around the world on ways of engaging students as developing writers. He is affiliated to the University of Auckland as an honorary academic and lives on Waiheke Island, Auckland.

Virgilia Pérez García is a Zapotec Indigenous language primary school teacher at the Luz y Progreso Intercultural Bilingual Elementary School in Soledad Salinas, Oaxaca, México. Virgilia currently teaches first grade and promotes and advances Zapotec literacy development by co-creating books with and for her students.

Robin Griffith is an Associate Professor of literacy in the College of Education at Texas Christian University and co-editor of the journal *The Reading Teacher*, published by the International Literacy Association. Her research focuses on teaching decisions in literacy instruction.

James Hoffman is a Professor of Language and Literacy at The University of North Texas and currently serves as the Meadows Endowed Chair for Literacy. Dr. Hoffman is a former editor of *The Reading Research Quarterly* and *The Yearbook of the National Reading Conference*. He has served as President of the National Reading Conference and as a member of the Board of Directors of the International Reading Association. Dr. Hoffman was an affiliated scholar with both the National Reading Research Center and the Center for the Improvement of Early Reading Achievement. He was elected to the Reading Hall of Fame in 2002 and served as President of this organization from 2008 to 2010. He has been active in international literacy projects in Central American, Africa, and Asia. Dr. Hoffman has published more than 150 articles, books, and chapters on literacy related topics.

Frances Hoyte is a Research Assistant in Education at Griffith University in Queensland, Australia. She is researching pedagogies for language development and literacy learning in the context of the Australian Curriculum. Her research explores the role of relationships and oral language opportunities in children's literacy development.

Evelyn Jepkemei has worked extensively in the education sector in Kenya in different capacities. She is currently the Education Advisor for the World University Service of Canada in Kenya after transitioning recently from Tusome Early Grade Reading program at RTI International in Kenya. She holds a Doctor of Philosophy in Education Management and Policy Studies.

Felipe Ruiz Jiménez is a Zapotec Indigenous language teacher at the Ramón López Velarde Intercultural Bilingual Elementary School in Soledad Salinas, Oaxaca, México. Felipe currently teaches third grade and as a published poet, promotes and advances Zapotec literacy development through his own Zapotec poetry and by co-creating and performing plays with his students.

Hwawei Ko's research interest is in reading Chinese. With evidence from eye movement studies, she and her lab members have advocated teaching student words and concepts instead of teaching characters only. Ko also ran PIRLS in Taiwan and mobilized elementary school teachers to attend to reading literacy and reading strategies.

Jan Lacina serves as Professor of Literacy and Interim Dean within the College of Education at Texas Christian University. Jan is the U.S. Ambassador for the

United Kingdom Literacy Association (UKLA). She is co-editor of the journal *The Reading Teacher*, published by the International Literacy Association. She began her career in education as a Texas public school teacher.

Marta Larragueta is a Ph.D. candidate on children's literature at Universidad Camilo José Cela, in Madrid (Spain). She has a Master's degree in International Education and Bilingualism and has been working for several years as a kindergarten and primary teacher in different schools in Spain and the United Kingdom.

Soyoung Lee is an Assistant Professor at Konkuk University in Seoul, Korea, in the Department of General Studies. She received her degree from UC Berkeley's Graduate School of Education. Before moving back to her home country Korea, she served as Associate Professor of Education Studies at Skidmore College in New York. Her research interests lie at the intersection of language and literacy education for linguistic minorities, English as a Second Language, and the sociocultural context of literacy education.

Jamie Lipp, Ph.D., is a Reading Recovery Trainer at the Ohio State University. Dr. Lipp has 15 years of experience as a classroom teacher, Reading Recovery Teacher, Literacy Specialist, Curriculum Specialist and college instructor. Jamie does research in primary education, teaching methods, and teacher education. She has been published previously in *The Reading Teacher* and *Reading Horizons*.

Natalia Kucirkova is Professor of Early Childhood Education and Development at the University of Stavanger, Norway. Natalia's research concerns innovative ways of supporting children's book reading, digital literacy, and exploring the role of personalization in early years.

Allyson Matczuk, Ph.D., is an early literacy consultant and a Reading Recovery Trainer/Co-ordinator at Western Canadian Institute of Reading Recovery.

Cheryl McLean is an Associate Professor of Literacy Education and English Education at the Graduate School of Education, Rutgers University. Her research on adolescent learners and immigrant youth focuses on culture and identity, digital and multimodal literacy, and redefining writing composition to contemporize English Language Arts.

John Potter is Associate Professor (Reader) in Media in Education at the University College London Institute of Education. His research, teaching, supervision, and publications are in the fields of: media education, new literacies, creative activity, and learner agency; the changing nature of teaching and learning in response to the pervasive use in wider culture of media technologies in formal and informal settings.

Lorena de Poza Gutiérrez is a teacher of Hearing and Language and Therapeutic Pedagogy with a Bachelor's degree in Kindergarten Education. In 2015 she was awarded the Extraordinary Award in the Master's in Psychology and Educational Sciences Research from the University of León (Spain). She started her profession in Cantabria and currently works in a school in León.

Steve Daniel Przymus is an Assistant Professor of Bilingual/Multicultural Education at Texas Christian University. Steve researches language ideologies and their impact on the educational experiences of emergent multilingual students in U.S. and Mexican schools. Steve prepares future teachers to serve culturally and linguistically diverse youth with a translanguaging stance.

Sherron Killingsworth Roberts serves as the Heintzelman Literature Scholar at University of Central Florida. Her research examines literacy as social practice and content analyses of children's literature. Her work is in *Reading Teacher, Journal of Teacher Education, Journal of Research in Childhood Education, Teaching and Teacher Education*, and *Journal of Reading Education* among others.

Jennifer Rowsell is Professor of Literacies and Social Innovation at the University of Bristol in the United Kingdom. In addition to authoring and editing books and collections, she is Co-Editor of the *Routledge Expanding Literacies in Education* series with Cynthia Lewis and she is the Department Editor of Digital Literacies for *The Reading Teacher*.

Joanna Schaefer is a history teacher and academic coach at Health Sciences High & Middle College. Ms. Schaefer is a nationally board certified teacher who is focused on building students' academic and disciplinary literacy.

Annette Torres-Elias, Ph.D., is an Associate Professor and Reading Recovery/Descubriendo la Lectura Trainer in the Department of Reading at Texas Woman's University. She believes that the main goal of an instructor should be to create critical thinkers and lifelong learners. One of her passions is supporting in-service teachers and administrators by providing high quality professional development in her many areas of expertise.

Linda-Dianne Willis is Lecturer in Curriculum Studies at the University of Queensland, teaching English and Literacy and Humanities and Social Sciences courses. She uses sociological concepts such as agency to conduct educational research in: initial teacher education, coteaching, cogenerative dialoguing, innovative pedagogies, inquiry curriculum, parent engagement, and principal leadership.

Chapter 1

Introduction
A Global Perspective to Literacy Teaching and Learning

Jan Lacina and Robin Griffith

To reach real peace in the world, we will have to begin with the children—Gandhi

As Gandhi eloquently describes in the quote above, everything in life begins with children. For our world to become free from war and violence, we must prioritize the education of our world's children. Educating children encourages better understanding of others across the globe who may have different views, values, and beliefs. Educating children helps them understand and learn from history, including the mistakes of the past as well as successful moments in history. Educating children provides opportunities for socioeconomic prosperity they may otherwise not have.

In 1989, the United Nations adopted the Convention on the Rights of the Child, a historical and important commitment to children that contains 54 principles. These principles include the most widely ratified human rights treaty in history, which influenced governments to change laws and policies to protect children and to prioritize children and their needs. Eradicating illiteracy among children is one of these rights. Despite the progress made throughout the world since 1989, children continue to face illiteracy. In some countries, children's schooling is cut short, and in other countries, girls still do not receive the same rights for an education as boys receive. A new generation of educational leaders must come forward with a similar commitment, like the world leaders in 1989 who led the Convention on the Rights of Children. In schools across the world, teachers are still making a difference in the literacy lives of children.

Preparing globally minded teachers involves a better understanding of others across the globe and how we can learn from each other. With this book, we focus on literacy across the globe, and how teachers from diverse backgrounds are implementing innovative and culturally relevant pedagogical practices in their own communities. In some countries, teachers have the opportunity to ask questions, challenge curriculum, and vote for political leadership to influence educational changes. With these opportunities, educators should also offer alternatives to educational practices (Hoffman, Sailors, & Aguirre, 2016), and serve as a voice for the educational profession. This text offers examples of teachers who offer such alternatives as they shape literacy practices in developing nations as well as in industrialized nations worldwide. The book provides examples of teachers, schools, and curricula that are changing lives through literacy practices and instruction.

Literacy Rates

Why is it important to consider literacy at the global level? According to data from UNESCO Institute of Statistics (2016), there are 758 million adults 15 years and older who still cannot read a simple sentence; close to two-thirds of those individuals are female. Although literacy rates worldwide continue to rise, the literacy rates of young women, particularly in sub-Saharan Africa, remain dismally low at 65%. Literacy rates in such countries as Afghanistan, Guinea, Mali, and South Sudan remain below 30%. Literacy is clearly a global concern.

Disparity continues between the research of best practices for literacy instruction and students' experiences in the classroom (Applebee & Langer, 2011; Boudreau Smith, 2017). Teachers often know the work of pedagogy theorists and practitioners (Graves, 1983; Jago, 2014); however, there may be multiple reasons as to why best practices are not always implemented in the classroom. Lack of relevant resources, pressures for testing and accountability, and, in some cases, lack of professional development to support teachers all contribute to the disconnect between theory and practice. Yet, literacy educators around the world are finding ways to overcome these challenges.

Literacy practices, as well as literacy achievement, differ worldwide. For aspiring teachers, and inservice teachers, it is important to know how literacy may be assessed and publicized in the media, and ways in which policy-makers evaluate the success and failure of educational policy (Dixon et al., 2013). The Progress in International Reading Literacy Study (PIRLS) is an international comparative assessment that measures student learning in reading (PIRLS, 2016). PIRLS has been documenting trends internationally since 2001 in the reading knowledge of 4th graders, and school and teacher practices related to instruction. The design of the test is completed by an international group of experts, and, after test development, the test is translated into many languages, and reviewed at the international level to ensure that all groups are fairly tested (Strietholt & Rosén, 2016). The 4th graders complete a reading assessment and questionnaire assessing their attitudes towards reading and their reading habits. Additional questionnaires are collected from teachers and school principals documenting students' school experiences in developing literacy.

PIRLS 2016 trends indicated an increase in good readers internationally, with eleven countries showing improved scores from 2011 to 2016 (PIRLS, 2016). The 2016 data also indicated that girls on average are better readers than boys in 48 out of the 50 PIRLS countries administering the assessment. Additional trends in high test scores indicate that good readers have home environments that support literacy learning, which includes more resources, such as books, more digital devices, as well as parents who noted that they like to read. PIRLS data also indicates that good readers learn to read early in preprimary schools; these children's parents were engaged in their early literacy activities. Those students who scored well on PIRLS attended, on average, more affluent schools, attended school regularly, and were not tired or hungry. Most interesting from this data is that those students who performed well on the PIRLS also came from international schools where reading instruction was a high priority at the primary level. From these schools, 27% of the instructional time is allocated for language instruction, and 18% is dedicated to reading instruction. Reading instruction includes access to libraries and weekly digital learning activities (PIRLS, 2016).

Many researchers question the validity of the PIRLS, and note the exam may be biased towards wealthier nations. Other researchers note the deficiency of these rankings in improving educational practice (Dixon et al., 2013), and those countries with lower scores were not necessarily propelled to make educational changes. Despite the controversy, scholars who support the use of PIRLS note that with such international rankings may be a lever for improvement of educational standards (Strietholt & Rosén, 2016). Literacy scholars can use PIRLS data to demonstrate the importance of resources, such as the significance of children having qualified teachers, involved parents, financial resources, and prioritized literacy instruction, especially at the primary level.

Critical Sociocultural Theory

We approached the formation of this book with a critical sociocultural mindset. Nieto (2018) explains that sociocultural theory assumes that social relationships and political realities are intertwined. Sociocultural theory enables teachers to better understand others, and most importantly, to better teach students from diverse linguistic, racial, and cultural backgrounds. Critical sociocultural theory aims to better address issue of power, identity, and agency as it relates specifically to literacy learning and practice (Lewis, Enciso, & Moje, 2007). The chapters in this book demonstrate how research and literacy practice make visible the ideological foundations of historical and cultural contexts within which teachers and children are situated. Cultural history activity theory, a strand of sociocultural theory, includes such elements as subject, object, rules, community, signs, or tools—grounded within cultural and historical tradition (Bazerman & Russell, 2003; Lewis et al., 2007). With this in mind, activities within a school or classroom are viewed as social practices positioned within a community, with specific norms and values for those literacy practices. The chapter authors in this book draw on a variety of theoretical perspectives, while connecting to literacy practices within their home country and offering ideas for globally minded literacy teachers.

Literacy around the World

Literacy practices worldwide differ based on the expectations of educational systems, government requirements, and what individual countries and cultures view as best practices. In many countries, research literature explains best practices for reading and writing instruction. Best practices for reading instruction includes teaching using a wide selection of literature, teaching using a comprehensive word study program, teaching reading for authentic, meaning-making purposes, as well as using assessment to inform instruction (Morrow, Gambrell, & Pressley, 2003); best practices for writing instruction include process writing instruction, like a writer's workshop, and using literature as a model for writing instruction (Lacina, 2018; Lacina & Griffith, 2017; Troia, Lin, Cohen, & Monroe, 2011). Across the globe, literacy instruction approaches vary. For example, teachers in some Asian countries do not commonly implement the reading or writing process in their classrooms since good teaching in some schools is viewed through a Confucian lens. Instructional practices may vary based on macro-level aspects, such as the government and educational policies of individual countries (Ping Hsiang & Graham, 2016). With such variance in educational practices between western and eastern parts of the world, educators as well as aspiring teachers must keep in mind social practices situated within a community, and the norms and values for those literacy practices.

Literacy practices also differ across the globe based on government expectations, testing, and teacher preparation. In a study that compared writing instruction in Portugal to Brazil, both Portuguese-speaking countries, researchers found that middle school teachers spent little time teaching writing, nor did they often teach strategies (Simão, Malpique, Lourdes, & Marques, 2016). However, these teachers viewed writing as a shared responsibility, and viewed writing instruction as the responsibility for all teachers. While schools have the autonomy to decide on their own educational methods and curriculum to some extent, some school systems must adhere to the government attainment targets to receive financial support. In summary, literacy practices differ based on a variety of factors, such as expectations of educational systems and government requirements.

Literacy practices are further influenced by the economic, social, cultural, and historical contexts in which children live (Singh, Han, & Woodrow, 2012), and it is important to take into consideration this background. It is imperative that teachers, and preservice teachers, have the opportunity to read about teachers, schools, and communities across the globe that are successful, and how they face their challenges, when faced with varied economic support systems. It is important for educators to study similarities and differences in instructional practices worldwide, and to reflect on literacy in the context of social practices situated within a community, with specific norms and values for those literacy practices. Just as important, in this text you will read of the current renaissance within education globally as international language scholars have been exploring the flow of language, literacy, transnationalism, and technology, around the globe.

How to Read This Book

Based on the review of research, as well as the documented need for books that highlight global literacy practices, we set out to gather literacy scholars from around the world who could help globally minded teachers learn about the challenges and innovative literacy practices employed in different countries. The authors are internationally and/or nationally known for their scholarship in literacy education. They work in developing nations, industrialized nations, and in some cases with indigenous communities. The authors are outstanding scholars and teachers who care deeply about literacy and children.

The book is divided into three parts: (1) Early Literacy; (2) Intermediate to Adolescent Literacy; and (3) Case Studies. The goal of this book is to provide literacy educators with a better understanding of literacy practices worldwide as well as examples of teachers who face challenges, and find ways to solve those problems while meeting the literacy needs of the children they teach. We believe that these chapters deserve careful consideration, as they provide emerging research in the field of literacy within our globalized society. We hope you will not only enjoy reading this book, but that you will use the text with preservice and inservice teachers to discuss literacy practices around the world.

Chapter Outline: Chapters 1–11

Each chapter includes the following elements to provide fluidity among chapters.

- **Summary of Chapter**: The author provides three bullet points that describe in one sentence each of the major goals of the chapter.
- **Vignette**: A vignette begins each chapter, which shows the reader a literacy practice in action in a classroom from the author's home country. The vignette offers a best practice for literacy connected to the research presented in the chapter.
- **Historical and Cultural Context**: This section provides an overview of best practices for literacy from a cultural standpoint. The author describes education in the context of his/her home country and culture, including the historical background and trends in education within their

country in the present day. What are teachers expected or required to teach; what philosophical underpinnings influence their teaching practices?

- **Theory and Research Base**: The author provides current research of best practice to support the topic covered in the chapter.
- **Implications for Future Research**: In this section the author describes implications for future research. Why is this research important for teachers, and to the children they teach?
- **Recommendation for Globally Minded Literacy Teachers**: The chapter author provides recommendations on how teachers can serve as globally minded literacy teachers, based on the research presented in this chapter. What do teachers need to keep in mind as they teach children from diverse world cultures, languages, and backgrounds?
- **Discussion Questions and Application**: In this section the author provides discussion questions and applications in which readers of the text can apply what they learned in the text to their classroom, and to think about critical issues.
- **References**.

Case Study: Chapters 12–16

Each case identifies a teacher (or teachers) who must solve a problem or challenge related to literacy instruction. The case evaluates the problem and possible solutions while encouraging the reader to think critically and analytically. Last, the author provides discussion questions and applications in which readers of the text can apply what they learned in the case to their classroom, and to think about critical issues.

Acknowledgements

We want to thank the entire team of chapter authors who worked tirelessly to complete this edited book. Your work inspires us, and we are thankful for your amazing contributions. We would also like to thank Madison Grantham and Delaney Paul who served as research assistants for us, and helped us tremendously with this project and other projects during the academic year. Thank you to Karen Adler, our Routledge editor, who encouraged and supported us throughout the process. Most importantly, we thank our children—who inspire us each day as we teach and write. You make us want to make the world a better place. Thank you to Caroline, Grace, Katherine, Zachary, and William. We also thank our husbands, Pete and Scott, for their support and encouragement throughout this project.

References

Applebee, A. N., & Langer, J. A. (2011). A snapshot of writing instruction in middle schools and high schools. *English Journal, 100*(6), 14–27.

Bazerman, C., & Russell, D. R. (Eds.). (2003). Writing selves/writing societies: Research from activity perspectives. WAC clearinghouse perspectives on writing. [Online]. Available: https://wac.colostate.edu/books/perspectives/selves-societies/

Boudreau Smith, N. (2017). A principled revolution in the teaching of writing. *English Journal, 106*(5), 70–75.

Dixon, R., Arndt, C., Mullers, M., Vakkuri, J., Engblom-Pelkkala, K., & Hood, C. (2013). A lever for improvement or a magnet for blame? Press and political responses to international educational rankings in four EU countries. *Public Admin, 91*, 484–505.

Graves, D. H. (1983). *Writing: Teachers and children at work.* Portsmouth, NH: Heinemann Educational Books.

Hoffman, J. V., Sailors, M., & Aguirre, S. H. (2016). Thinking globally in literacy instruction: Making a difference in the world. *The Reading Teacher, 70*(2), 143–148.

Jago, C. (2014). Writing is taught, not caught. *Educational Leadership, 71*(7), 16–21.

Lacina, J. (2018). Literacy leadership: Global leaders call for the teaching of writing. *English Journal, 107*(4), 59–63.

Lacina, J., & Griffith, R. (2017). Teaching writing: Literacy coordinators' views. *New England Reading Journal, 52*(2), 11–19.

Lewis, C. J., Enciso, P., & Moje, E. B. (Eds.). (2007). *Reframing sociocultural research on literacy: Identity, agency, and power.* Mahwah, NJ: Lawrence Erlbaum Associates.

Morrow, L. M., Gambrell, L. B., & Pressley, M. (2003). *Best practices in literacy instruction* (2nd ed.). New York, NY: Guilford Press.

Nieto, S. (2018). *Language, culture, and teaching: Critical perspectives* (3rd ed.). New York: Routledge.

Ping Hsiang, T. P., & Graham, S. (2016). Teaching writing in grades 4–6 in urban schools in the greater China region. *Reading and Writing, 29*(5), 869–902.

Progress in International Reading Literacy Study. (2016). PIRLS. *What makes a good reader: International findings from PIRLS 2016.* Retrieved from Lynch School of Education at Boston College website: http://pirls2016.org/download-center/

Simão, A. M. A., Malpique, A. A., Lourdes, F. M. B., & Marques, A. (2016). Teaching writing to middle school students in Portugal and in Brazil: An exploratory study. *Reading and Writing, 2*(5), 955–979.

Singh, M., Han, J., & Woodrow, C. (2012). Shifting pedagogies through distributed leadership: Mentoring Chilean early childhood educators in literacy teaching. *Australasian Journal of Early Childhood, 37*(4), 68–76.

Strietholt, R., & Rosén, M. (2016). Linking large-scale reading assessments: Measuring international trends over 40 years. *Measurement, 14*(1), 1–26.

Troia, G. A., Lin, C. S. J., Cohen, S., & Monroe, B. W. (2011). A year in the writing workshop linking writing instruction practices and teachers' epistemologies and beliefs about writing instruction. *The Elementary School Journal, 112*(1), 155–182.

United Nations. (1989). *Convention on the rights of the child.* New York, NY: Author.

United Nations Educational, Scientific and Cultural Organization. (2016). *UNESCO: United Nations Educational, Scientific and Cultural Organization.* Paris, France.

Part I

Early Literacy

Chapter 2

Reading Recovery
Transcending Global Boundaries

*Celeste C. Bates, Connie Briggs, Mary Anne Doyle,
Annette Torres-Elias, Allyson Matczuk, Julia Douetil,
and Jamie Lipp*

Summary of the Chapter

This chapter explores the early literacy intervention, Reading Recovery®, found across multiple continents, to highlight the

- collaborative work as an international community,
- consistency and structure of the intervention across all boundaries, and the
- positive impact for student and teacher learning worldwide.

Vignette

Rashid eagerly reads the story, "The Hungry Giant," by Joy Cowley. It is one of his favorites. He smiles as he finishes and turns to tell his teacher proudly, "That sounded like a reader!" Not long ago, Rashid felt differently about his abilities to read and write. Later in the lesson, Rashid decides to write about the mean giant in the story. He hesitates when it is time to write the word *looked*. "That's a word you can read," encourages his teacher. Rashid perks up and quickly writes *looked* into his story. "Let's check it in the book," his teacher suggests. Rashid's lesson, like all others, is a continual ebb and flow of an observant teacher offering a careful scaffold to build a confident and capable child who takes risks in reading and writing. Together, Rashid and his teacher have embarked on a shared journey of literacy discovery.

Historical, Cultural, and Political Context

Morrell (2017), in the last line of an important and timely essay, states, "teachers, researchers, policy makers, and advocates across the globe must come together as a community" for change to occur (p. 461). The change

Morrell is addressing relates to equity and diversity in literacy, research, policy, and practice. Further, he questions "Can such calls for change be collaborative rather than competitive?" (p. 455). Since 2001, the Reading Recovery community, a network of literacy researchers and learners, has worked collaboratively to transcend global boundaries and further thinking around literacy practice and professional learning.

Reading Recovery is a highly successful, short-term, early intervention designed to reduce both the numbers of children in their second year of schooling who find learning to read and write most difficult and the costs of these learners to education systems (Burroughs-Lange, 2008; May, Sirinides, Gray, & Goldsworthy, 2016; Pinnell, Lyons, Deford, Bryk, & Seltzer, 1994; Schwartz, 2005). Founded by Marie M. Clay, a developmental psychologist, the first national implementation of Reading Recovery occurred in New Zealand in 1983 and continues today. It is unusual for an innovative literacy intervention to last 35 years and even more unusual for an educational intervention to have transferred to systems in seven other countries and maintain outstanding results. Currently, Reading Recovery is implemented in Europe, Canada, Australia, New Zealand, and the United States, with each entity holding its own trademark, granted by Marie Clay to indicate adherence to quality assurances.

As the intervention was expanded to other countries, Clay founded the International Reading Recovery Trainers' Organization (IRRTO), a global infrastructure, to support both the quality and effectiveness of the research-based teaching and training procedures across nations. The mission of IRRTO is to maintain the quality, uphold the integrity, improve the efficiency and effectiveness, and support change and growth in Reading Recovery through international collaboration, research, and resource development. IRRTO members, who are international Reading Recovery trainers, are responsible for ensuring that the Reading Recovery implementations sustain their effectiveness and continue to evolve in response to new research and developments in measured, thoughtful ways. The international trainers meet every 18 months and hold an international institute, which rotates to different countries every three years. In addition to the group at large who serve on one of three standing committees, an executive board with equal representation from participating countries works alongside the committees to help guide, "research and development, training of trainers, funding, communications, and system design" (Schmitt, Askew, Fountas, Lyons, & Pinnell, 2005, p. 22).

The international implementation of Reading Recovery is unique given that education systems vary from country to country. Challenges in one geographic location may not be present in another and attention to individual settings and their educational histories is paramount to the implementation. Clay (2015) stated that the, "central tenets of Reading Recovery have been tentativeness, flexibility, and problem-solving" (p. 298). Clay applied these tenets at a variety of levels including the ways in which teaching addresses the needs of individual children, the modes in which teachers are trained, and the manner in which Reading Recovery is implemented. Tentativeness, flexibility, and the willingness to problem-solve have allowed Reading Recovery to be implemented in distinctive settings while at the same time providing a measure of consistency. Across international implementations the measure of consistency is seen not only in the stable and dependable outcomes of students, but in the initial and ongoing training of Reading Recovery professionals. Reading Recovery teachers use a universal language, based on Clay's (2015) literacy processing theory, to describe children's reading and writing behaviors and the interactions and experiences around them.

IRRTO, the international network, focuses on specific areas that support implementation. The areas include guidelines for delivery, the training of teachers, the lesson components, and practice that is grounded in a complex theory of literacy learning and development (Clay, 2009). Through this support, "Reading Recovery professionals have learned how to hold fast to principles, practices, and rationales while at the same time allowing for variability in the education practices and beliefs, and change over time in society" (Clay, 2015, p. 298). These areas are consistent across unique contexts and define and conceptualize literacy teaching and learning.

There are several reasons for the success of Reading Recovery in these very different international settings. One reason is that Clay constructed the intervention as a "problem-solving approach to an unstructured problem" (Watson & Askew, 2009, p. 221); and therefore, each new international setting was approached with tentativeness and flexibility as educators collaborated to ensure success. Crucial factors for continued success include: guidelines for delivery, training of teachers, lesson components, and the complex theory of literacy learning and children's development (Watson & Askew, 2009). An overarching reason for international success is that the implementation of Reading Recovery works from a systems approach supporting the notion that systems must change and adapt to support educational innovations. In their book, *Learning to Improve: How America's Schools Can Get Better*, Bryk, Gomez, Grunow, and LeMahieu (2015) define a system as, "An organization characterized by a set of interactions among the people who work there, the tools and materials they have at their disposal, and the processes through which these people and resources join together to accomplish its goals" (p. 198). Reading Recovery professional development has been shown to impact educational systems. Through shared beliefs, understandings, and language about literacy processing the international Reading Recovery community builds cohesion and impacts the learning of not only those children most at-risk of literacy failure at the onset of formal reading instruction, but also other students the teachers trained in Reading Recovery theory and methods teach (Bryk et al., 2015;

Fullan & Quinn, 2016; McNaughton, 2011; Patterson, Holladay, & Eoyang, 2013; Sharratt & Fullan, 2009; Sharratt & Fullan, 2012; Sharratt & Harild, 2014).

Historical and Philosophical Underpinnings

In times of austerity, with many competing pressures on education systems, decision makers at every level must ensure that resources are used to achieve the best possible outcomes. The international implementation of Reading Recovery is perhaps unique in that every practitioner, in every country and at every level of operation, both contributes to and is informed by the accountability processes through which Reading Recovery provides evidence of impact. Beginning with the individual teacher, lesson records provide daily checks that teaching is effectively addressing this child's literacy learning needs. Each school has information to ensure that the resource is appropriately targeted and efficiently meeting the needs of its cohorts. Each education system collects and analyzes data to ensure the investment in teacher professional learning is positively impacting school practice. Governments have the information to make policy decisions, to direct spending, and to support or challenge change. Internationally, implementations can share research using parallel and combined data sets to learn from practice around the world.

All Reading Recovery interventions use Clay's observational assessment tools (Doyle, 2009), which provide sensitive quantitative and qualitative measures from the earliest glimmer of understanding and awareness of literacy, through to the fully fledged young reader and writer. These assessments have been standardized in different national settings, and tested for reliability (Watson & Askew, 2009). Thus, at every level in a system, a child's progress in literacy can be reliably compared with that of other children.

Clay's assessments also provide diagnostic information, which enables the teacher to identify barriers to learning for each child and strengths upon which to build. This qualitative data is a powerful resource for the development of professional understanding through research, ranging from small scale action research among a group of schools operating as a community of professional learners, to high level academic research, disseminated through scholarly journals.

In addition to Clay's assessments, each international setting uses and reports additional local measures. This systematic monitoring supports quality assurance and student outcomes; engineering the implementation into the local context, assessing the impact of implementation decisions, and advocating for vulnerable children.

Initial screening identifies children in the greatest need of intervention and can also provide a snapshot of strengths and weaknesses in the system at that point. For example, in England data revealed that a government led focus on phonics meant that, among the lowest attaining pupils, decoding and word knowledge had increased but understanding about how books work was in a steady decline across the country (Burroughs-Lange, 2008). Reporting this information at the national level led to a shift in government policy.

Over the past 25 years and across all major national settings, consistently around eight out of ten children who complete the lesson series make accelerated progress, attaining age appropriate levels of literacy, within 20 weeks of instruction. Few if any educational initiatives can point to this level of replication of outcomes both across diverse settings and from year to year.

The compelling consistency of outcomes can substantively change expectations of what is possible throughout an education system. In the United Kingdom, children who completed Reading Recovery demonstrated an average of four months' progress in reading age for each month of tuition. This evidence shaped a requirement in the United Kingdom referred to as the National Literacy Strategy, which stated that any intervention should be able to demonstrate at least half that rate of progress in order to be considered beneficial (Burroughs-Lange, 2008).

Children in certain groups, for example indigenous peoples, Travelers, or summer-born children, can fall through the evidence net because they represent a very small or very thinly spread population. Evidence of what typically supports, or disadvantages learners may be unreliable in these cases because it does not adequately represent their group. The aggregation of Reading Recovery data at the national and international level can provide a substantial sample of these relatively small or thinly spread populations, leading to a better understanding of how to support these students. Meticulous data collection is an integral part of every Reading Recovery implementation and because of the global network these data are able to inform decisions at the local, national, and international level.

Immigration and Literacy Learning

Reading Recovery teachers across global contexts work with the lowest achieving children as determined by *An Observation Survey of Early Literacy Achievement* (Clay, 2013). From the inception on the intervention, Reading Recovery has not denied children entry into the intervention. In fact, Clay stated that

> exceptions are not made for children of lower intelligence, for second-language children, for children with low language skills, for children with poor motor coordination, for children who seem immature, for children who score poorly on readiness measures, or for children who have been categorized by someone else as learning disabled.

> (Clay, 1991, p. 60)

This inclusive approach includes immigrant children. Reading Recovery lessons are individually designed and delivered based upon the child's unique strengths. Further, the close relationship between teacher and child that is characteristic of the one-to-one instruction may provide additional support for children who are assimilating into a new country.

Language Learning

In response to the diverse linguistic and cultural needs in various countries where Reading Recovery is implemented, the intervention has been reconstructed to serve children in multiple contexts and languages (e.g., English, Spanish, French, and Danish).

This section will share information about Descubriendo la Lectura®, the reconstruction of Reading Recovery to Spanish currently implemented in dual language education programs in the United States, and Intervention Préventive en Lecture-Écriture®, the redevelopment of Reading Recovery in French for Canada. Both interventions were originally designed for students in grade one having difficulty learning to read and write in their native language. Now, they are also available for students who are receiving literacy instruction in a language other than English whether Spanish, French, or Danish is the child's first language, or the child is in a language immersion program offering a second language. While many aspects of literacy must be addressed in the reconstruction of the intervention, the theoretical foundation of all programs is the same as Reading Recovery and is underpinned by Clay's theories of emergent literacy and literacy processing (Doyle, 2019).

The collaborative work of Reading Recovery in Spanish began in 1989 with the reconstruction of *An Observation Survey of Early Literacy Achievement* (Clay, 2013) with the guidance and support of Marie Clay. The *Instrumento de Observación de los Logros de la Lecto-Escritura Inicial* (Escamilla, Andrade, Basurto, Ruíz, & Clay, 1996) accounts for the unique features of the Spanish language and provides opportunities to observe the early literacy behaviors of a child whose understandings about reading and writing are the product of a bilingual and bicultural environment.

Teaching procedures originally published in the *Early Detection of Reading Difficulties* (Clay, 1985) were reconstructed to Spanish and examples from bilingual students provided. This work was shared with Descubriendo la Lectura teachers for trial and further development. The refinement of teaching procedures for Descubriendo la Lectura is an ongoing process. The Descubriendo la Lectura trainers work in close collaboration with teacher leaders and teachers to review the procedures to match the revisions in the most current edition of *Literacy Lessons Designed for Individuals* (Clay, 2016). Descubriendo la Lectura sites collect and report data on every child served in the program. Research studies confirm that Descubriendo la Lectura has positive results similar to those of Reading Recovery (Escamilla, 1994; Escamilla, Loera, Ruíz, & Rodríguez, 1998; Neal & Kelly, 1999; Rodríguez & Rodríguez, 2006).

The international reconstruction of Reading Recovery in Canada, Intervention Préventive en Lecture-Écriture, was the result of a collaboration with Marie Clay and Gisele Bourque to redevelop Reading Recovery in French. Canada has two official languages with both French first-language schools and French immersion programs offered across the country. This made the implementation of Reading Recovery in both English and French a necessity. As with Descubriendo la Lectura, the initial work for the reconstruction was the adaptation of *An Observation Survey of Early Literacy Achievement* (Clay, 2013) to French, which resulted in the publication of the assessment, *Le Sondage d'Observation en Lecture-Écriture* (Bourque, 2001).

Several educational institutions in Canada collaborated in the development of Intervention Préventive en Lecture-Écriture: The Nova Scotia Department of Education initiated the efforts, and the Canadian Institute of Reading Recovery/Institute Canadien d'Intervention Préventive en Lecture-Écriture worked on refining the reconstruction and conducted validity and reliability studies for *Le Sondage d'Observation en Lecture-Écriture* in the provinces of Nova Scotia, Manitoba, Alberta, and Ontario in 2001. The Conseil Scolaire Acadien Provincial conducted the first pilot implementation in French first-language schools in 2003 followed by French immersion schools in 2005 (Clay, 2003; Schmitt et al., 2005).

The experiences of the reconstruction of Reading Recovery to Spanish and French provides evidence that a good starting point to adapting Reading Recovery to other languages is the redevelopment of the observation tasks of *An Observation Survey of Early Literacy Achievement* and the reconstruction of instructional procedures that consider the linguistic and cultural diversity of the students. To date, *An Observation Survey of Early Literacy Achievement* has also been reconstructed in Danish, Irish, and Welsh in addition to Spanish and French. If this is done carefully and in collaboration with the pertinent educational institutions who serve the students "then the window of opportunity for an early intervention in literacy learning appears to be able to cross language barriers and remain effective" (Watson & Askew, 2009, p. 243).

Theory and Research Base

Around the world, the design and delivery of Reading Recovery instruction is based on theoretical perspectives of learners and learning that have been shown to be robust and is grounded upon two important hypotheses. The first hypothesis is that a detailed series of lessons is designed for an individual after a close and detailed observation period that documents the ways in which that child responds to written language. The teacher identifies the child's reading and writing strengths and focuses on how the child is able to problem-solve with increasing proficiency and speed. The second hypothesis is that it is economical to draw on the reciprocal nature of reading and writing to accelerate literacy learning. A child's series of lessons is shaped daily by teacher analysis of the learner's oral reading behaviors gradually moving up a gradient of difficulty to create opportunity to lift performance in literacy processing.

Reading Recovery instruction is based on Clay's (2015) literacy processing theory, a theoretical perspective resulting from her extensive, empirical investigations of children acquiring initial reading and writing abilities. Clay defined reading as

> a message-getting, problem-solving activity, which increases in power and flexibility the more it is practiced. It is complex because within the directional constraints of written language, verbal and perceptual behaviors are purposefully directed in some integrated way to the problem of extracting sequences of information from texts to yield meaningful and specific communications.
>
> (Clay, 2015, p. 1)

Theoretical explanations rest on understandings of both the specific verbal and perceptual behaviors involved in reading and writing acquisition and explanations of the integration of complex cognitive processes. Therefore, "[t]he teaching is directed to a curriculum of psychological processes (perceptual and cognitive), linguistic competencies and social practices necessary for working with written language" (Clay, 2016, p. 15).

Clay's literacy processing theory reflects an interactive parallel processing model defined by Rumelhart (2013). Clay also related the theoretical discussions of Holmes (1953, 1970) and Singer (1994) to her theory. Specifically, she found the concept of literacy processing involving the child's brain assembling the processing system needed to complete a particular task descriptive of the reading work that she discovered among emergent readers (Doyle, 2019).

Clay's literacy processing theory is predicated on the constructive child. From opportunities to read and write continuous text with appropriate scaffolding from the teacher, each learner gains neurological networks for reading and writing. The child is the constructor of this working system. The teacher can only observe reading behaviors (as on a running record or oral reading task) and infer how the system is developing. The teacher remains tentative in her conclusions and plans instruction to meet hypothesized needs. Clay (2015) describes the new system as a self-extending system. Thus, constructive learners are capable of independently "pushing the boundaries of their own knowledge" (Clay, 2015, p. 301), and the result is more and more proficient literacy behaviors observed in reading and writing. In Reading Recovery instruction, teachers work from the child's known skills, building on existing strengths.

To construct the "in the head" perceptual/cognitive processing systems, or working systems, necessary to read for meaning, learners must be reading meaningful, continuous text. This allows the learner to develop internal working systems "to manage the different types of information" (Clay, 2015, p. 128) found in text and to problem solve while reading for meaning. Studying words in isolation does not allow this construction to occur.

Learning to read and write involves continuous change. Literacy processing strategies become more proficient over time, and the reader presented with new challenges is able to problem solve texts of increasing difficulty. Teachers must observe closely and change their instructional foci on an ongoing basis in order to provide the most powerful learning experiences.

An additional aspect of the Reading Recovery teacher's theoretical perspective is the reciprocal nature of reading and writing. What is learned in writing words and sentences can be applied in reading, and what is learned in reading can be revisited in writing. By understanding the reciprocity between reading and writing, teachers can impact literacy development positively by connecting new learning from one experience to the other.

International communities of literacy researchers offer varying definitions of literacy. The perspective held by our international set of Reading Recovery professionals is reflected in Clay's summary of alternative views:

> Even though a simpler theory may suffice for most children, *I am certain that a view of complexity is the kind of understanding required to deliver results in an early intervention program aiming to prevent subsequent literacy difficulties in as many children as possible.*
>
> (Clay, 2015, p. 138, Italicized in the original text)

The shared understanding of Clay's literacy processing theory underpins the work of Reading Recovery across unique contexts.

Implications for Future Research

Professionals involved in any aspect of Reading Recovery require specialized training in order to design and deliver lessons to children with unique learning and literacy profiles. Principles guiding professional development in Reading Recovery are based on Clay's (1966) original research and on implementation factors that lead to optimal learning for children, training for teachers, teacher leaders, and trainers anywhere in the world Reading Recovery is implemented.

Globally minded teachers grounded in these understandings are empowered to change the learning trajectories of young readers and writers, bringing them in a short time to acceptable levels of literacy independence for their age regardless of their global context (Burroughs-Lange, 2008; May et al., 2016; Pinnell et al., 1994; Schwartz, 2005). Reading Recovery began with a focus on children and needs to continue to maintain that focus through the connection of theory and practice in professional learning. "Children's needs will always be implicit in every research project, every refinement of implementation, and every individual lesson. Ultimately, to ensure the important benefits of instruction, teachers' professional development is key" (Doyle, 2009, p. 290).

Recommendations for Globally Minded Literacy Teachers

Regardless of the professional's role in Reading Recovery, teacher, teacher leader, or trainer, a year of professional learning is required in order to complete the appropriate qualifications. Principles guiding the development of the training, available in each of the countries implementing the intervention, reflect evidence and research-based practices. Reading Recovery is an investment in teacher knowledge and expertise and this is evident in the training requirements. "Studies of the initial training for teachers has a powerful effect on the individuals involved" (Schmitt et al., 2005, p. 97). The teacher is pivotal in Reading Recovery since there is no fixed set of materials and no prescriptive sequences. Teachers are required to sensitively observe and analyze children's current literacy development in order to determine the most powerful, contingent teaching decisions that will foster the child's construction of an ever changing and self-extending literacy processing system.

In every country implementing Reading Recovery, professional learning begins in a group context. The elements of the professional model require the process of articulating the cognitive process which is sometimes described as a cognitive apprenticeship (Brandt, Farmer, & Buckmaster, 1993; Rogoff, 1990; Wertsch, James, & Tulviste, 1990). Consistent with Reading Recovery's constructivist view of children's learning, the professional learning of Reading Recovery teachers, teacher leaders, and trainers also adopts a constructivist paradigm. Central to this paradigm is a practice of learning through live interactions with students and teachers, known as *behind-the-glass*. Behind-the-glass utilizes a one-way mirror to observe, inquire, discuss, and reflect on teaching and learning (Rodgers & Rodgers, 2007). Behind-the-glass includes both a pre-brief and debrief conversation in addition to the observation of the lesson and is an essential professional learning practice found in all forms of Reading Recovery's initial and ongoing training around the world.

Among all educational settings, from the local to the global level, student achievement is of utmost importance. Investing in teacher improvement has been noted as the most beneficial expenditure positively impacting student achievement (Darling-Hammond, 2010). Therefore, working in support of student achievement means it is critical to consider the kinds of professional development that directly support teacher improvement. Recently, the Learning Policy Institute released a research brief (Darling-Hammond, Hyler, Gardner, & Espinoza, 2017) identifying specific elements of effective professional development. The elements were derived from a meta-analysis that examined 35 professional development initiatives. From the analysis seven elements were identified and the report concluded that professional development should:

1. Focus on content
2. Incorporate active learning utilizing adult learning theory
3. Support collaboration, typically in job-embedded contexts
4. Use models and modeling of effective practice
5. Provide coaching and expert support
6. Offer opportunities for feedback and reflection
7. Be of sustained duration (p. 1).

These seven elements unify the teaching and professional development across our international contexts. As part of the policy brief, Darling-Hammond and colleagues recognize Reading Recovery as a model of effective professional development and as "an example of one program that possesses all seven elements and has been found to generate positive student gains" (Darling-Hammond et al., 2017, pp. 4–5).

With this in mind, Reading Recovery's systems approach to professional development and support has implications for teacher education in general, as well as the potential to strongly support the development of globally minded teachers. The seven key features identified in *Effective Professional Development* (Darling-Hammond et al., 2017) and validated through Reading Recovery's professional development model can be used to reimagine teacher professional learning beyond the borders of any one specific country. Because the professional development model of Reading Recovery does not vary due to country or continent, it is evident that the effectiveness recognized within this model could support professional development models elsewhere. Reading Recovery's model of professional development is a central tenet to the program's effectiveness, and thus, has grand implications for training and professional development globally.

Discussion Questions and Application

- In what ways can Clay's literacy processing theory extend from early intervention to support classroom instruction globally?
- How can reading and writing as reciprocal processes support global literacy learning across all contexts?
- What current professional development structures and supports are in place to support teacher learning, and which ones may be missing?

Conclusion

Working collaboratively as part of an international learning community towards a collective goal enriches the understandings of individual contexts. The commitment to ongoing inquiry into teaching and professional learning is a reflection of Clay's initial question about "what is possible" for young readers and writers in their first years of school (Clay, 2004). Marie Clay brought a unique perspective to the study of early literacy acquisition and instruction. Her deep inquiry has contributed greatly to teacher knowledge and development and that has translated into opportunities for millions of children to learn and become productive citizens of the world. Reading Recovery as an organization continues to ask "what is possible" as it seeks to transcend global boundaries in the areas of early literacy intervention and teacher professional development.

References

Bourque, G. (2001). Redevelopment of reading recovery in French: Intervention preventiveen lecture-écriture. *The Journal of Reading Recovery*, *1*(1), 25–26.

Brandt, B. L., Farmer, J. A., Jr, & Buckmaster, A. (1993). Cognitive apprenticeship approach to helping adults learn. *New Directions for Adult and Continuing Education*, *1993*(59), 69–78.

Bryk, A. S., Gomez, L. M., Grunow, A., & LeMahieu, P. G. (2015). *Learning to improve: How America's schools can get better at getting better*. Cambridge, MA: Harvard Education Press.

Burroughs-Lange, S. (2008). *Comparison of literacy progress of young children in London schools: A Reading Recovery follow up study*. London: Institute of Education,University of London.

Clay, M. M. (1966). *Emergent reading behavior*. Unpublished doctoral thesis. Auckland: The University of Auckland.

Clay, M. M. (1985). *The early detection of reading difficulties: A diagnostic survey with recovery procedures*. Auckland, New Zealand: Heinemann.

Clay, M. M. (1991). *Becoming literate: The construction of inner control*. Portsmouth, NH: Heinemann.

Clay, M. M. (2003). *Le sondage d'observation en lecture-écriture*. Toronto: Les Editions de la Chenelière.

Clay, M. M. (2004). Simply by sailing in a new direction you could enlarge the world. In C. M. Fairbanks, J. Worthy, B. Maloch, J. V. Hoffman, & D. L. Schallert (Eds.), Fifty-third yearbook of the National Reading Conference (pp. 60–66). Oak Creek, WI: National Reading Conference.

Clay, M. M. (2009). The Reading Recovery research reports. In B. Watson, & B. Askew (Eds.), *Boundless horizons: Marie Clay's search for the possible in children's literacy* (pp. 37–100). Rosedale, New Zealand: Pearson Education.

Clay, M. M. (2013). *An observation survey of early literacy achievement* (3rd ed.). Portsmouth: NH: Heinemann.

Clay, M. M. (2015). *Change over time in children's literacy development*. Auckland, New Zealand: Global Educations Systems Ltd.

Clay, M. M. (2016). *Literacy lessons designed for individuals: Why? when? and how?* (2nd ed.). Portsmouth, NH: Heinemann.

Darling-Hammond, L. (2010). *The flat world and education: How America's commitment to equity will determine our future.* New York, NY: Teachers College Press.

Darling-Hammond, L., Hyler, M. E., Gardner, M., & Espinoza, D. (2017). *Effective professional development.* Palo Alto, CA: Learning Policy Institute.

Doyle, M. A. (2009). A dynamic future. In B. Watson, B. Askew, & M. (Eds.), *Clay's search for the possible in children's literacy: Boundless horizons* (pp. 287–308). Rosedale, NZ: Pearson Education New Zealand.

Doyle, M. A. (2019). Marie M. Clay's theoretical perspective: A literacy processing theory. In D. E. Alvermann, N. J. Unrau, M. Sailors, & R. B. Ruddell (Eds.), *Theoretical models and processes of reading* (pp. 84–100). New York: Routledge.

Escamilla, K. (1994). Descubriendo la lectura: An early intervention literacy program in Spanish. *Literacy, Teaching and Learning: an International Journal of Early Literacy, 1* (1), 57–70.

Escamilla, K., Andrade, A. M., Basurto, A. G., Ruíz, O. A., & Clay, M. M. (1996). *Instrumento de observación de los logros de la lecto-escritura inicial.* Portsmouth, NH: Heinemann.

Escamilla, K., Loera, M., Ruíz, O., & Rodríguez, Y. (1998). An examination of sustainingeffects in Descubriendo la Lectura programs. *Literacy Teaching and Learning: AnInternational Journal of Early Reading and Writing, 3*(2), 59–81.

Fullan, M., & Quinn, J. (2016). *Coherence: The right drivers in action for schools, districts, and systems.* Thousand Oaks, CA: Corwin Press.

Holmes, J. A. (1953). *The substrata-factor theory of reading.* Berkeley, CA: California Book.

Holmes, J. A. (1970). The substrata-factor theory of reading: Some experimental evidence. In R. B. Ruddell, M. R. Ruddell, & H. Singer (Eds.), *Theoretical models of processes of reading* (pp. 187–197). Newark, DE: International Reading Association.

May, H., Sirinides, P. M., Gray, A., & Goldsworthy, H. (2016). Reading recovery: An evaluation of the four-year i3 scale-up.

McNaughton, S. (2011). *Designing better schools for culturally and linguistically diverse children.* New York, NY: Routledge.

Morrell, E. (2017). Toward equity and diversity in literacy research, policy, and practice: A critical, global approach. *Journal of Literacy Research, 49*(3), 454–463.

Neal, J. C., & Kelly, P. R. (1999). The success of reading recovery for English language learners and Descubriendo la Lectura for bilingual students in California. *Literacy Teaching and Learning, 4*(2), 81–108.

Patterson, L., Holladay, R., & Eoyang, G. (2013). *Radical rules for schools: Adaptive action for complex change.* Circle Pines, MN: Human Systems Dynamics Institute.

Pinnell, G. S., Lyons, C. A., Deford, D. E., Bryk, A. S., & Seltzer, M. (1994). Comparing instructional models for the literacy education of high-risk first graders. *Reading Research Quarterly, 29*, 9–39.

Rodgers, A., & Rodgers, E. (2007). *The effective literacy coach: Using inquiry to support teaching and learning.* New York, NY: Teachers College Press.

Rodríguez, Y., & Rodríguez, C. (2006). *An overview of Descubriendo la Lectura.* Worthington OH: Reading Recovery Council of North America.

Rogoff, B. (1990). *Apprenticeship in thinking: Cognitive development in social context.* New York: Oxford University Press.

Rumelhart, D. E. (2013). Toward an interactive model of reading. In D. E. Alvermann, N. J. Unrau, & R. B. Ruddell (Eds.), *Theoretical models and processes of reading* (pp. 719–747). Newark, DL: International Reading Association.

Schmitt, M. C., Askew, B. J., Fountas, I. C., Lyons, C. A., & Pinnell, G. S. (2005). *Changing futures: The influence of Reading Recovery in the United States*. Worthington, OH: Reading Recovery Council of North America.

Schwartz, R. M. (2005). Literacy learning of at-risk first-grade students in the Reading Recovery early intervention. *Journal of Educational Psychology, 97*(2), 257.

Sharratt, L., & Fullan, M. (2009). *Realization: The change imperative for deepening district-wide reform*. Thousand Oaks, CA: Corwin Press.

Sharratt, L., & Fullan, M. (2012). *Putting FACES on the data*. Thousand Oaks, CA: Corwin Press.

Sharratt, L., & Harild, G. (2014). *Good to great to innovate: Recalculating the route to career readiness, K-12+*. Thousand Oaks, CA: Corwin Press.

Singer, H. (1994). The substrata-factor theory of reading. In R. B. Ruddell, M. R. Ruddell, & H. Singer (Eds.), *Theoretical models of processes of reading* (pp. 895–927). Newark, DE: International Reading Association.

Watson, B., & Askew, B. (2009). *Boundless horizons: Marie Clay's search for the possible in children's literacy*. Rosedale, New Zealand: Pearson Education.

Wertsch, J. V., Tulviste, P., & Hagstrom, F. (1993). A sociocultural approach to agency. In E. A. Forman, N. Minick, & C. A. Stone (Eds.), *Contexts for learning: Sociocultural dynamics in children's development* (pp. 336–355). New York: Oxford University Press.

Chapter 3

Early Literacy in Australia

Teaching Teachers to Grow Children's Global Mindedness Through Multimodal Text Production

Beryl Exley, Linda-Dianne Willis, and Frances Hoyte

Summary of Chapter

- This chapter recounts our ways of working in teacher education to develop preservice teachers' pedagogical practices for working with multimodal text to promote children's global mindedness.
- We also focus on the importance of language and literacy as socially and textually produced practices (Janks, 2010) so that children can more fully explore topics that build their global mindedness.
- As Dooley, Exley, and Comber (2013) assert, without the capacity to receive and express ideas through language and literacy across a range of modes and media, children remain limited in their participation as learners and citizens of the here-and-now and into the future.

Vignette

In this chapter, we recount an early years inquiry Miss Erin set up for her preparatory year students (aged four and a half years of age). Miss Erin posted a photo of her recent overseas holiday on the class social media site. She invited the children to share photos and descriptions of their favourite holiday destinations as well. With the help of their families, the children responded with posts of their recent holidays. Throughout the process, the children listened, talked, and learnt from one another, recounting family experiences, activities, connections, histories, memories, and the traditions they enjoyed in diverse contexts. Miss Erin subsequently assisted each child to write about their special place. Next, all of the children used the iPads to type their descriptions and draw an accompanying picture. The children were taught how to use the audio-recording function and when the children were each satisfied with their efforts, Miss Erin posted their work on the social media site. Parents responded enthusiastically to seeing their child's work on the class social media site.

Historical, Cultural, and Political Context

Historical and Philosophical Underpinnings

We three authors are experienced classroom practitioners, having each spent at least a decade teaching in elementary schools. We have all since moved in and out of a number of other leadership and research positions and into our roles as teacher educators and mentors of preservice and early career teachers. In the current era, teacher education in Australia is charged with the responsibility of preparing early career teachers who are deemed to be 'classroom-ready from their first day as a teacher' (Teacher Education Ministerial Advisory Group, 2014, p. 6). Whilst much contention exists over the constitution of the different lenses of 'classroom readiness' (see Alexander, 2018), we are nonetheless active within this space (see Lytle, 2013). We each attempt to support teachers to have the determination to situate curriculum learning in approaches that enable children to engage with themes that have global relevance (Cox & Robinson-Pant, 2011), and to do so in ways that allow children to develop understandings and skills to work with others.

When we introduce case studies of other teachers' practices that we have collected through our research work, the focus is on building a rich and an abiding account of the contexts of the learning and teaching. We do so through written and video narratives, some of which have been published (Exley, 2007; Ridgewell & Exley, 2010; Tierney & Willis, 2015), and others that have been turned into teaching resources. At other times, we take the adult learners into the classrooms of exemplary teachers (Dooley, Exley, & Comber, 2013) and draw on this shared experience in reflective discussions with the adult learners. Our modus operandi is a carefully unfolding pedagogy of metalogue, a strategy we have used and written about previously (see Willis, Grimmett, & Heck, 2018). At a descriptive level, Bateson (1972) explains metalogue as 'a conversation about some problematic subject' (p. 12). Whilst we do not construct teacher professional learning as a 'problem' *per se*, our approach is centered within a 'conversation' about something that we should not take for granted. In this way, we encourage the adult learners to hone in on something worthy of investigation, examination, analysis, critique, reflection and/or explanation. The conversations are hosted in such a way that 'each person's voice is respected (e.g. through equal turn taking and not talking over one other); ideas are shared and built upon; judgement is suspended; debate without necessarily reaching consensus occurs; and differences are valued' (Willis & Exley, 2016, p. 78). Metalogue encourages adult learners to adopt an open disposition to learn with and from the case studies as well as from one another and from us as teacher educators (see, for example, Willis, 2019). Our shared goal is to nurture generations of teachers who think deeply about the children who are passing through their classrooms as well as the communities to which they belong, the overarching role of global mindedness (New London Group, 2000) and the import of literacy knowledge and skills as an essential foundation for advancing children's learning and life choices within the future world (Janks, 2010). Put another way, we shun pedagogical practices that simply tell aspiring and practicing teachers how to teach, instead embracing opportunities for the adult learners to move back and forth across the theory/practice divide to heighten their skills for observing, discovering, abstracting, thinking and theorising and thus reflecting and refining the delivery of their own pedagogical practice (Dooley, Exley, & Comber, 2013).

In the Australian context we work with adult learners who are implementing the inaugural Australian Curriculum (Australian Curriculum, Assessment and Reporting Authority [ACARA], 2018a). The opening statement in the overview asserts that the 'Australian Curriculum is designed to help all young Australians to become successful learners, confident and creative individuals, and active and informed citizens' (2018a). The Australian Curriculum is structured into eight Learning Areas of English, Mathematics, Science, Health and Physical Education, Humanities and Social Sciences, The Arts, Technologies, and Languages. The latter four Learning Areas have been written to include multiple subjects, reflecting custom and practice in the discipline. In each Learning Area, Content Descriptions specify what young people will learn, and Achievement Standards describe the depth of understanding and the sophistication of knowledge and skill expected of children at the end of each year level. The three-dimensional design of the curriculum recognises the importance of the eight Learning Areas, alongside seven General Capabilities and three Cross-curriculum Priorities. The seven General Capabilities play a significant role in 'equipping young Australians to live and work successfully in the twenty-first century' (ACARA, 2018b). The seven General Capabilities are Literacy, Numeracy, Information and Communication, Critical and Creative Thinking, Social and Personal Capability, Ethical Understanding, and Intercultural Understanding. The three Cross-curriculum Priorities give children 'the tools and language to engage with and better understand their world at a range of levels' (ACARA, 2018c) and include developing knowledge, understanding and skills relating to Aboriginal and Torres Strait Islander Histories and Cultures, Asia and Australia's Engagement with Asia and Sustainability.

Together the eight Learning Areas, seven General Capabilities and three Cross-curriculum Priorities are intended to promote global mindedness in Australian children for now and the future. Whilst the nomenclature of global mindedness is not used explicitly, particular points of reference are noteworthy. Whilst space precludes an exhaustive list, the following points are highlighted. For example, the Intercultural Understanding General Capability 'assists young people to become responsible local and global citizens, equipped through their education for living and working together in an interconnected world' (ACARA, 2018d). The Intercultural Understanding General Capability seeks to cultivate children's 'values and dispositions such as curiosity, care, empathy, reciprocity, respect and responsibility, open-mindedness and critical awareness, and supports new and positive intercultural behaviours' (ACARA, 2018d). The Ethical Understanding General Capability scaffolds children in 'building a strong personal and socially oriented ethical outlook that helps them to manage context, conflict and uncertainty, and to develop an awareness of the influence that their values and behaviour have on others' (ACARA, 2018e). The Ethical Understanding General Capability identifies that 'technologies bring local and distant communities into classrooms, exposing children to knowledge and global concerns as never before' (ACARA, 2018e). Reference is also made to the stages of schooling supporting children's knowledges and skills for future encounters with navigating 'a world of competing values, rights, interests and norms' (ACARA, 2018e). The reference to future encounters is note-worthy, suggesting that even in the elementary years, children should have a focus on active citizenship (see Cox & Robinson-Pant, 2011).

By definition, in Australia, curriculum documents do not specify peda-gogical practice. Instead learning and teaching frameworks are developed at the State (Department), System (e.g. Government or Public schools, or Catholic System Schools) or School level. Due to the requirements of the ethical permission contract to which we authors are bound as we collected data on two case study classrooms, we do not identify the schooling system, the schools, the teacher or the children specifically. Where a personal men-tion is needed, we offer a pseudonym. Direct quotes and references to the learning and teaching framework used at the two case study classrooms are also not provided. Instead, we paraphrase and reword elements of the learn-ing and teaching framework so as to highlight the main points but to dis-guise the traceable features. The point of departure of the learning and teaching framework is the notion that every child learner is in some respect like all other child learners whilst also being like no other child learner. Teachers are thus required to respond to this wide reaching breach with creativity, flexibility and a futures orientation. We take this to mean that individual children are the starting point of pedagogic practice, a foundation of Dewey's (1902/1968) original thinking. From this standpoint, we inter-pret this position to mean that different pedagogical framings have poten-tially different cognitive and social effects for different learners (Exley & Richard-Bossez, 2013; Smith, 2015). The learning and teaching framework that we've been privy to is centred on ideas of relationships, shared respon-sibility, visible, explicit and responsive pedagogies that are deemed to have the capacity to create equity and excellence for all learners. The framework also talks about learning as being personal, relational and communal, as well as visible, active and interactive. We note the use of the word active, another foundational principle of Dewey's (1902/1968) thinking. We also note the multiplicity of binaries here, and, by default, all things in between. It seems the learning and teaching framework advocates for a carefully crafted and deliberate 'weaving' of visible and invisible pedagogies (Exley & Richard-Bossez, 2013; Smith, 2015) so as to produce high quality and high equity outcomes for different students (see New London Group, 2000). We thus understand the learning and teaching framework guiding pedagogy in the case study schools as requiring effective teachers to have at the ready a sophisticated repertoire of practices that are carefully crafted and continually re-crafted to be fit-for-purpose (Smith, 2015).

Immigration and Literacy Learning

The task of developing globally minded literacy teachers also requires a conception of literacy as a rich and varied set of skills, both traditional and contemporary (see Janks, 2010). It particularly requires that teachers have the mindset and skills to support immigrant and domestic children alike to use and produce multimodal texts (New London Group, 2000). In Australia, the population of immigrants is growing. By way of background, the 2016 Australian Census identified that 28.5 per cent of Australia's resident population was born overseas (Australian Bureau of Statistics, 2017a), with the top six countries being the United Kingdom, New Zealand, China, India, Philippines, and Vietnam. In addition, the largest population growth categories include those born in Nepal (27 per cent), Pakistan (13.2 per cent), Brazil (12.1 per cent), India (10.7 per cent) and Bangladesh (8.9 per cent) (Australian Bureau of Statistics, 2017a). Data released by the Australian Government Department of Immigration and Border Protection (2017) identified that the humanitarian visa categories are now dominated by immigrants from Iraq, Syria, Burma, Afghanistan, Democratic Republic of Congo, Bhutan, Somalia, Iran, Ethiopia, and Eritrea. In addition, the Australian Indigenous population has increased. Australia's First Nations People, Aboriginal and Torres Strait Islanders, now represent 2.8 per cent of the people counted in the 2016 Census (Australian Bureau of Statistics, 2017b). This represents an increase of 2.5 per cent compared to the 2011 Census (Australian Bureau of Statistics, 2017b).

The Literacy General Capability of the Australian Curriculum supports children to 'become literate as they develop the knowledge, skills and dispositions to interpret and use language confidently for learning and communicating in and out of school and for participating effectively in society' (ACARA, 2018f). As reported by Mills and Exley (2014), the Australian Curriculum explicitly embraces a contemporary definition of texts, highlighting the ubiquity of digital formats and their circulation across modes and media (see also Exley & Cottrell, 2012). For example, Literacy is described as children 'listening to, reading, viewing, speaking, writing and creating oral, print, visual and digital texts, and using and modifying language for different purposes in a range of contexts' (ACARA, 2018f). Literacy as a General Capability is embedded in all Learning Areas (Scribner & Cole, 1981), providing the potential to also embrace the Information and Communication General Capability and focus on issues of global significance (like sustainability) and globally relevant ways of working (such as collaborative problem solving and multimodal communication).

Language Learning

The curriculum documents prepared by the Australian Curriculum, Assessment and Reporting Authority (ACARA, 2018d) for English, Mathematics, Science, Humanities and Social Sciences, The Arts, Technologies, Health and Physical Education, and Languages also focus attention on the diversity of students in our schools, in particular students with English as an Additional Language or Dialect (EAL/D). The Australian Curriculum defines EAL/D students as those 'whose first language is a language or dialect other than English and who require additional support to assist them to develop proficiency in English' (ACARA, 2018g). EAL/D students come from a range of backgrounds, including students:

- who were born overseas and immigrated to Australia;
- who were born in Australia but their first language is other than English;
- whose first language is an Aboriginal or Torres Strait Islander language, such as Torres Strait Creole or Aboriginal English.

There is no one-size-fits-all approach to developing the language outcomes of students from different linguistic and cultural backgrounds. Variation exists in terms of students' levels of competence and confidence in their first and additional languages. The variance comes about because of the different starting ages for using different forms of language for social and educational purposes (for example, family social communication compared to school content communication), as well as exposure to different modes of literacy communication (reading, writing, listening and speaking). In Australia, it is the teacher's responsibility to come to know their students' stages of learning Standard Australian English (SAE) and, from there, to determine the most effective content and pedagogy for literacy instruction. It is essential that the pedagogical orientation explicitly values and respects the students' linguistic competence in their first and additional languages and dialects and their cultural preferences for ways of working.

Theory and Research Base

This section provides an overview of two case studies of Australian teachers working with children in two schools from the same Catholic Education Diocese. Our description of the teachers' practices hone in on how they scaffold through a pedagogy of metalogue (see Willis, 2019) and support the children's global mindedness and the role of digital and multimodal text production (see Willis & Exley, 2018). We note commonalities whereby both teachers foreground global mindedness with an 'act locally, think globally' approach, encouraged by children's tendencies for oracy (see Hoyte, Torr, & Degotardi, 2014), whilst also finding authentic opportunities for children to engage with real-time outside-of-school virtual audiences. These are the sorts of case studies we use in our teacher education work so as to positively influence this generation of early career teachers.

We use the following codes when we present the classroom data. Direct quotes collected during the research cycles are presented in italics. Dots have been used to show where some words or sentences were removed from the transcript. This happened when a speaker repeated a word or made a false start, changed topics or said something that could not be used in this manuscript due to the ethical contract for participants to remain anonymous. Concepts that may not have been clear have been explained in rounded brackets. Square brackets have been used to provide information to the reader about a physical action (e.g. a student entering a group work session) or to summarise a longer quieter period without talk (e.g. when students were searching on the web).

'My Special Place' Inquiry

The first case study is from a collaborative inquiry project conducted in a Preparatory (Prep) Year classroom at a Catholic Education Diocese school where children were approximately four and a half to five and a half years of age. Fifteen children and their parents took part together with their teacher, Miss Erin (pseudonym). In total, 5 per cent of the children identified as Language Background Other than English (LBOTE) and 3 per cent of the children identified as Aboriginal or Torres Strait Islander. Miss Erin had taught in schools for more than a decade and volunteered to participate in the research. Data were collected as part of a larger study conducted by Beryl (Author 1) and Linda (Author 2) called EPIC – Engaging Parents in Inquiry Curriculum (see Willis & Exley, 2018). The means of engagement between the children, their parents, and Miss Erin was a freely available version of the digital application called Seesaw. Data comprised a planning session with Miss Erin, Beryl, and Linda, weekly 15-minute Skype or phone meetings with Erin and either Beryl or Linda, screen grabs and downloads of the children's work and online interactions between the children, their parents, and Miss Erin, and a concluding interview with Miss Erin, Beryl, and Linda.

Miss Erin set up a class specific website using Seesaw so only her children, their parents and herself could participate. Seesaw was selected by Miss Erin because of its built-in safety features for protecting children in the online space, availability of Seesaw on a range of online and mobile digital devices, the icon-driven platform which proved to be user-friendly for Prep children, the range of modalities of use (e.g., written, spoken, imaged, videoed, emoticons), and ease of sharing with others in and outside the class (e.g. blog posts). Seesaw enabled blog posts and learning artefacts to be private (among a single child, their parents and Miss Erin) or public (among all approved participants, including the whole class, the whole parent cohort and Miss Erin). Beryl and Linda were given access rights for research purposes. Any incoming media from the children or the parents needed to be approved by Miss Erin via a swiping process. When posts were approved for posting to a child's account, the child's parents' mobile devices beeped/pinged so they could engage in their child's learning in real time by swiping, and also, if they chose, to tap to include a written comment, emoji, and/or voice message.

Miss Erin taught for global mindedness by designing a unit of work on *place*, which drew content and concepts primarily from the Australian Curriculum Learning Areas such as English and Geography, together with the General Capabilities of Literacy and Intercultural Understanding (see Hamston & Murdoch, 1996). The Prep children investigated place using an inquiry approach driven by the two following questions:

- What places do you like to visit?
- Why are those places special?

The inquiry began with Miss Erin posting a photo of her recent overseas holiday on the class Seesaw site and inviting the children to share photos and descriptions of their favourite holiday destinations. With the help of their families, the children responded with posts of their overseas holidays to countries that included Hawaii, Sweden, and Thailand, and local Queensland places such as the Sunshine Coast. In an interview with Beryl and Linda, Miss Erin explained how the online posts were used as a resource for classroom learning:

> *I projected the post for the children and said, 'We've had a submission to our blog. Jane's mum has sent in a photo. Let's all have a look and Jane you might talk us through what's happening in this picture: Where are you? Why is this a special place?*
>
> (Miss Erin, Interview)

Throughout the process, the children listened, talked, and learnt from one another, recounting family experiences, activities, connections, histories, memories, and the traditions they enjoyed in diverse contexts. Miss Erin subsequently assisted each child to write about their special place. Embedded as part of daily literacy rotations, some children used Miss Erin's exemplar text about her special holiday place to independently write their own recounts using pencil and paper. Miss Erin subsequently conferenced with each child, helping them to proofread and edit their work. Other children discussed their ideas with Miss Erin and together they wrote a description of their special place. On these occasions, Miss Erin took on the role of scribe. Next, all of the children used the iPads to type their descriptions and draw an accompanying picture. The children were taught how to use the audio-recording function on Seesaw. Once satisfied with their initial written and visual texts, they produced a voice-over to match their written description. Miss Erin described the next part of text production:

> *And then they (children) can have that piece of work put up on the big screen for us all to look at and read and evaluate and, not so much critique ... but provide feedback to the child on the work they gave. For instance, 'Was their voice adequate? Was the volume adequate? Was the vocab (vocabulary) used correct? Was the grammar ...'. Then, look at their writing and their creating of the words and the text. Did they have a capital letter at the beginning, a full stop at the end, spaces in between? Did they use their knowledge of their sight words to write the piece of text?*
>
> (Miss Erin, Interview)

These focused whole-class sessions were continued by children in conversations with one another and Miss Erin as they returned to their work to make improvements based on class feedback. Miss Erin noted that sometimes when a child felt that their work was not of sufficient quality, they commented, '*Oh, I don't want to send that one home*'. On these occasions, Miss Erin confirmed, '*So, you don't want me to approve it? No, so okay, go back and have another go ...*' (Miss Erin, Interview). Only when the children were satisfied with the quality of their multimodal texts were these shared with their parents. Parents responded enthusiastically with positive written or emojied (e.g., love heart, applause) comments about their child's work.

Miss Erin followed a similar process when the inquiry focus shifted to include special places in the school. Following class discussions, the children took on the role of photographers and captured visual images on the iPads to share with the class. Commenting on the children's work during the interview, Miss Erin declared, '*... some of the photos they captured! They're better photographers than me! Some of them went into the garden and got up-close shots of beautiful plants in flower or vegetables growing on a bush ...*'. Speaking of explicit class lessons about text creation with still and moving images, she added, '*Well, I mean we hadn't even gone into that yet, but they experimented with focus to take up-close or panoramic shots or videos*' (Miss Erin, Interview). Miss Erin commented on the level of child engagement with text production, suggesting their innovative responses and motivation for producing high-quality work was due to '*the fact that their peers are giving feedback … they want theirs to be one of the best ones in the class, and also the fact that, "My mum's going to see this and my dad and maybe my grandparents"'* (Miss Erin, Interview 2).

The children used the social media channel to disseminate their draft and completed texts with one another and ultimately their parents. In teaching writing on the topic of place, Miss Erin oriented her Prep children towards global mindedness using pedagogies in which literacy is viewed as a sociocultural practice (McInerney, Smyth & Down, 2011). This was evident in her commitment to literacies as being 'multiple' and needing to be responsive to contemporary modes of practice. The multiliteracies approach, coined by the New London Group (2000), ensures learning and teaching responds to increasing globalisation, technological change, and cultural and social diversity by recognising the multiple ways literacy is practised in the twenty-first century. Kalantzis and Cope (2012) described this approach as necessary to meet contemporary literacy demands where previously-dominant written print texts no longer hold the privileged position they once occupied. In adopting a multiliteracies approach, Miss Erin's children learnt new ways to represent known texts while simultaneously attempting multiple new texts forms, especially those created through the digital and virtual modes (Marsh, 2013). Although many of these children were not yet fluent in print, they were still expanding their digital knowledge and skills for virtual text production. As noted, these children took photos, created images and moving images, uploaded photographs and videos, created voice-overs (voice narrations), selected digital icons and features to enhance meaning-making, and commented appropriately online on each other's work. They also used multimodality (New London Group, 2000), combining oral, visual, audio, gestural, and spatial elements to create increasingly sophisticated digital and virtual texts.

At the same time, they engaged in critical discussions and metalogues (see Willis, 2019) with Miss Erin and their classmates about the texts they were producing to communicate about their special places. These critical discussions and generative dialogues (Willis & Exley, 2016) assisted the children to make informed choices about language and literacy to suit different purposes (e.g., writing blog posts or capturing video images), contexts (e.g. school or home), and audiences (e.g. classmates or parents). These choices developed their knowledge and skills for not only moving between different social spaces (Marsh, 2010), but also *negotiating* language differences within and between these spaces (Janks, 2010). More often, they managed their own learning, worked cooperatively with others, spontaneously revisited their work to make improvements and were agentive in deciding when their work was ready for public release to the parent audience (Exley & Willis, 2016).

The 'Shark Dilemma' Inquiry Project

The second case study is from a collaborative inquiry project conducted in another school in the same Catholic Education Diocese. This school was located within easy driving distance of a number of sections of the expansive Australian eastern coast line that fronts the Pacific Ocean. The number of fatal and non-fatal shark attacks were on the rise. Common species included the Great White shark (up to 6 metres), the Thresher shark (up to 5.5 metres) and Grey Nurse sharks (up to 3.2 metres). These sharks were starting to hunt in areas that were typically shark free and frequented by swimmers, surfers and recreational fisher people. Bull sharks of up to 1.4 metres in length were also found hunting in the lower and upper streams of the city's main river, in local residential canals and in the bay waters surrounding local islands. Local media warned residents of the surge of sightings and attacks, encouraging humans to keep themselves and their pet dogs out of these waterways. This inquiry project was thus *place* based. The classroom teacher, Miss Olivia, an experienced educator, worked with approximately two dozen children who were approximately seven and a half to eight and a half years of age. Four per cent of the children identified as Language Background Other than English (LBOTE) and 1 per cent of the children identified as Aboriginal or Torres Strait Islander. Together all the children undertook an inquiry centred on the provocation 'Sharks: Dangerous or Misunderstood?' The children worked in small groups to undertake research to determine their position on this important topic and to produce a multimodal persuasive text to convince an external audience to adopt the same position.

As with the first case study, Miss Olivia used a free version of Seesaw to store the children's outputs and for the children to communicate between each other, Miss Olivia and their parents. Data included videos of lessons and group work, weekly fifteen-minute phone meetings between Miss Olivia, Miss Abigail (co-teacher) and Beryl (Author 1), screen grabs and downloads of the children's work and online interactions between the children, and between the children and their parents (collected by Frances, Author 3), and a concluding interview with Miss Olivia, Miss Abigail, and Beryl.

Miss Olivia and Miss Abigail designed the inquiry project to focus on both the receptive (reading and viewing) and expressive (composing and writing) requirements of the Australian Curriculum Learning Area of English. This chapter reports on the data collected from Miss Olivia's class only. The inquiry project assessment task involved the children working in small groups to compose a multimodal, persuasive presentation in response to the provocation question. During the inquiry project, Miss Olivia engaged the children in a variety of learning sequences. Some of these learning activities developed field knowledge about sharks, the place of sharks in the ecosystem, the social and economic consequences of upsetting the balance of food webs, and the social and economic significance of shark attacks on Australian beaches. The teachers and children from both classes participated in a two-day excursion to a local marine park, which included visiting animal exhibits, attending seminars delivered by marine experts, and camping overnight in an aquarium tunnel.

Once the children returned to school, Miss Olivia and the children prepared for the text production task. The preparation did not commence with a draft of the target text. Instead Miss Olivia started with an investigation of signs and news headlines and images. Miss Olivia and the children investigated the interplay between images and wordings. Miss Olivia taught the children the concept of intermodal coupling (see Exley & Cottrell, 2012), that is the combining of multiple modes such as words, colours and images together. The children disrupted existing texts (e.g. made a rainbow coloured danger sign) or augmented existing texts (e.g. adding bold font and red embellishments). Importantly, they were given the opportunity to talk and listen to each other's explanations. In the extract below, Miss Olivia gives a summary of the task and an invitation to the children to converse about their experimentation.

> *So children, the task which I gave you to do was to do a danger sign but for a creature that was not scary. So we are going to video some of you talking about the visual elements which you put into your sign for a creature that is not scary.*

Gilly's (pseudonym) pseudo-danger sign was triangular in shape and used a yellow and pink background with clear black lower case letters to spell out 'Warning: Teddy Bear's Picnic'. Gilly explained that she *'used my highlighter colours, maybe because they are bright and nice to see'*.

Another feature of Miss Olivia's pedagogy was the use of group work. The children spent considerable time in small groups preparing their arguments and multimodal presentations. Many pages in their presentations indicated the effectiveness of their learning about intermodal coupling. For example, one group decided to support the position that sharks are dangerous. The title, 'Monsters of the deep', was framed with a black background and a sharp angular line to separate the screen in two. On the other side of the screen was a shark rising out of the water with an open, tooth-filled red mouth. The shark picture was cut by a jagged line, parallel to the oblique line separating the page. The combination of colour, words, pictures, and lines created an effective composite message. Another group took the position that sharks are misunderstood and therefore should not be trapped with nets or culled. Their headline read 'Innocent Sharks Dead!!' with three photographs. Two photographs were of sharks trapped in nets, showing that humans were imposing on the life of sharks. The third photograph was of a shark swimming along the sandy bottom of the ocean, looking graceful and peaceful.

The group work provided multiple opportunities for the children to use child-to-child metalogues (Willis & Exley, 2016). These group conversations varied, sometimes focused on the field knowledge about sharks, and sometimes focused on the literacy skills that would be needed to communicate effectively with their audience. As an example, three boys, Harry, Jack and Sebastian (pseudonyms), worked together on their shared presentation. Each boy had a specific task, but they interacted to support each other, sharing their findings and refining their work. Below is the data from one episode of group work:

HARRY: *So we need a website or a video about someone rationalising about sharks.*

HARRY: *So let me read out what I've got first. 'Sharks are responsible for many deaths each year. These creatures of the deep are very dangerous. They can kill people. If that isn't dangerous, I don't know what is. They don't even need much provocation. (Something inaudible) Sharks are dangerous so we need strong nets to keep people safe. If sharks weren't dangerous, why would we need nets? And two thousand seven hundred people on average get fatally wounded by sharks every year. Is that good?'*

JACK: *You've got to write something more there (pointing to a part of the text).*

HARRY: *Yeah, well, we've just got to wait for the blog so I can get more ideas. In fact, there's a shark book inside that has lots of cool details about sharks. [Harry gets the book and looks through it briefly.]*

HARRY: *OK, so what I've thought of .... the reason that ... well, no one would make Jaws if sharks weren't dangerous 'cause (because), let's say if sharks weren't dangerous, and they were just a member of the ocean and doing nothing, why would people be scared of them? I'm going to write that.*

[While Harry is talking about and researching for writing, Jack is searching for music to accompany their presentation. Jack locates the Jaws theme music and then searches for a link that can be used to include the music in their presentation. Harry listens to the music that Jack found. Sebastian then comes into the video frame.]

SEBASTIAN: *So I've got a picture of a shark cage, so we can say 'Sharks are dangerous, because if the cage breaks ...'*

JACK: *I'll go on outlook and find some images ... [There is then some discussion about which image to use.]*

HARRY: *Oh is it this one? That's perfect.*

SEBASTIAN: *Yeah, but we might have to cut out the headline.*

In this episode of group work, Harry, Jack and Sebastian demonstrate their achievement of the Australian Curriculum General Capability of Information and Communication. Specifically they are searching, selecting and editing. Harry, Jack and Sebastian also demonstrate their achievement of the

Australian Curriculum General Capability of Personal and Social Capability, specifically being able to share tasks and work together to achieve a common goal, stay on task and refocus after a distraction.

After a few weeks, the children's presentations were delivered to a real-life audience of parents during school time and also on the class Seesaw portal as a digital text. The comments from the online parents provided some supportive feedback, but also encouraged some critical reflection:

> *This presentation was very engaging right from the start. It captured my attention by asking if anyone had been bitten by a shark and letting me know that I was more likely to be injured by a vending machine.*

> *Those images made the sharks look very scary and dangerous and your statistics were very impressive.*

> *I thought you were successful in your counterargument about people believing sharks are misunderstood ....*

> *Girls this was excellent. I especially loved the movie ... It's clear you all feel pretty passionate about conservation ...*

Discussion of Case Studies

These two case studies highlight how two teachers structure their teaching to draw on multiple dimensions of the Australian Curriculum (Hamston & Murdoch, 1996). These two teachers also demonstrate a contemporary understanding of literacy and a commitment to providing two sets of children with rich opportunities for conversation, as well as rich opportunities for authentic multimodal text production. In doing so, the teachers maximised learning and engagement through collaborative group work whilst also allowing the children to address a global issue connected to *place*. In the case of Miss Erin's class, the place was some place special to each child. In the case of Miss Olivia's class, the place was where humans and animals interacted. We also drew attention to the way that both teachers taught about multimodal digital and virtual texts. Both teachers were clear about the need for the children to understand the kinds of literacy practices that circulate around communities and across the globe (Exley & Willis, 2016; Marsh, 2010) and the purposes for these practices (Janks, 2010). Another crucial concept that both teachers made available through these inquiry projects was that of multimodality (New London Group, 2000). Multimodality considers how meanings are made when two or more modes are used in the one text

(New London Group, 2000). Multimodality explains how the meanings communicated via multiple modes could be combined to support, enhance or even contradict each other (Exley & Cottrell, 2012). An understanding of the subtle interplay of visual images, wordings and even audio and gestural meanings is central to comprehending the sophisticated multimodal texts that populate children's lives (Janks, 2010) and for creating the texts required for effective participation in these inquiry projects (Willis, 2019).

Implications for Future Research

Our attempts to take social media into early years classrooms to provide a platform for investigations around place provided some hurdles. Ethics approval for using social media with young children was heavily scrutinised by the University Ethics Committees as well as the school systems ethics committee. We don't make light of this matter, for reasons of student safety, but also for reasons attached to timelines for research projects.

Future research should also consider the affordances of engaging parents as learning partners, especially parents who are immigrants who might be feeling somewhat disconnected from the mainstream education system on offer in Australia, but who are rich resources of global information.

We're also keen to know how sharing these two case studies with our preservice teachers implicates the projects they'll plan in their own classrooms when they become early career teachers. We think a mechanism for collecting data in a few years when our preservice teachers have started their teaching careers will produce some interesting findings. Whilst we're hopeful that these case studies impact our preservice teachers in positive ways, we're also mindful of the competing agendas and early career teachers' propensity for tackling one hurdle at a time when starting out. We'd like to get a stronger sense of the priority our early career teachers give to globally minded inquiry projects.

Recommendations for Globally Minded Literacy Teachers

These two case studies facilitated inquiry projects that were inherently about global mindedness; the children developed their knowledge, skills, and confidence for operating effectively in a changing, complex, and ever more globalised world. We use exemplar case studies such as these in our work in preservice and inservice teacher professional learning. Through our own practices of metalogue, our preservice and inservice teachers can discover for themselves how teachers like Miss Erin and Miss Olivia further developed global mindedness by connecting the literacy practices of school to the lives of the children and to ongoing real-time and virtual conversations with their parents. Opening the inquiry with the invitation to share with each other and their families their special places (case study one) or their position on the relationship between sharks and humans (case study two) positioned the children as experts in knowledge creation (see Exley & Willis, 2016). The children consequently built their dispositions towards global mindedness throughout the inquiry project with content that was relevant to them and their families. Miss Erin and Miss Olivia, in the role of teachers, identified the opportunities to build the children's appreciations of the importance, significance, and value of place to others, cultural connections to places locally and globally, understandings of how perceptions influence people's sense of connectedness to place, the interconnectedness of people, animals and places, and the need to protect and preserve places for others to enjoy. In addition, Miss Erin and Miss Olivia, in the role of teachers, identified the opportunities to build the children's knowledge and skills with multiple modes of digital and virtual text production. The hallmark of both projects was the role of participating parents and the use of the Seesaw social media app for bridging children's out-of-school literacy practices and home connections to school knowledge building tasks (Willis & Exley, 2018). Knowing their parents were active participants in their school learning was also powerfully felt by the children in Miss Erin's class. We noted the children's persistence with developing texts with which they were satisfied. We also noted the mutually reinforcing relationship whereby parents' participation value-added to the knowledge that was shared whilst also value-adding to the children's sense of responsibility for producing texts that were deemed to be of sufficient quality. In Miss Olivia's class, the parents provided encouragement and critical feedback. In this way, authentic literacy practices deepened the knowledge, understanding, and skills pertaining to the topic of special places (case study one) and human/shark interactions (case study two), and to the knowledge, understanding and skills of digital and virtual text production. Sharing their individual work in the group space enabled the children to recognise commonalities and differences between themselves and how others experienced and interacted with their special places and the multiple positions held on the topic of human/shark interactions. Calling on authentic literacy practices for learning about writing and text production about place thus engendered global mindedness by laying a foundation for Miss Erin's and Miss Olivia's children to live and work empathetically, respectfully, and responsibly with others in the future. For all of these reasons, these case studies serve our preservice and inservice teachers particularly well.

Discussion Questions and Application

1. Can social media be used with young children in your learning and teaching context? Are there any legislative considerations before you can begin setting up a social media site for classroom use?
2. What is a critical social issue in your context of learning and teaching?
3. What do your children know about this critical social issue and would they be motivated to explore it further?
4. How is the critical social issue similar or different to critical social issues in other parts of the world?

References

Alexander, C. (2018). Conceptions of readiness in initial teacher education: Quality, impact, standards and evidence in policy directives. In C. Wyatt-Smith & L. Adie (eds.). *Innovation and accountability in teacher education: Setting directions for new cultures in teacher education.* Pp. 97–114. Sydney: Continuum.

Australian Bureau of Statistics. (2017a). 3412.0—Migration, Australia, 2015–16. Retrieved from www.abs.gov.au/ausstats/abs@.nsf/lookup/3412.0Media%20Release12015-16.

Australian Bureau of Statistics. (2017b). Census: Aboriginal and Torres Strait Islander population. Retrieved from www.abs.gov.au/ausstats/abs@.nsf/MediaRealesesByCatalogue/02D50FAA9987D6B7CA25814800087E03?OpenDocument.

Australian Curriculum, Assessment and Reporting Authority. (2018a). Overview. Retrieved from www.australiancurriculum.edu.au/f-10-curriculum/learning-areas/.

Australian Curriculum, Assessment and Reporting Authority. (2018b). General capabilities. Retrieved from www.australiancurriculum.edu.au/f-10-curriculum/general-capabilities/.

Australian Curriculum, Assessment and Reporting Authority. (2018c). Cross-curriculum priorities. Retrieved from www.australiancurriculum.edu.au/f-10-curriculum/cross-curriculum-priorities/.

Australian Curriculum, Assessment and Reporting Authority. (2018d). Intercultural understanding. Retrieved from www.australiancurriculum.edu.au/f-10-curriculum/general-capabilities/intercultural-understanding/

Australian Curriculum, Assessment and Reporting Authority. (2018e). Ethical understanding. Retrieved from www.australiancurriculum.edu.au/f-10-curriculum/general-capabilities/ethical-understanding/.

Australian Curriculum, Assessment and Reporting Authority. (2018f). Literacy. Retrieved from www.australiancurriculum.edu.au/f-10-curriculum/general-capabilities/literacy/.

Australian Curriculum, Assessment and Reporting Authority. (2018g). Students for whom EAL/D. Retrieved from www.australiancurriculum.edu.au/resources/student-diversity/students-forwhom-eald/.

Bateson, G. (1972). *Steps to an ecology of mind.* Northvale, NJ: Jason Aronson Inc.

Cox, S. & Robinson-Pant, A. (2011). Children as researchers: A question of risk? In S. Cox, C. Dyer, A Robinson-Pant, & M. Schweisfurth (eds.). *Children as decision makers in education: Sharing experiences across cultures.* Pp. 143–152. London: Continuum.

Dewey, J. (1902/1968). *The child and the curriculum.* London: Phoenix Books.

Dooley, K., Exley, B., & Comber, B. (2013). Leading literacies: Literacy teacher education for inclusion and social justice. In C. Kosnik, J. Rowsell, P. Williamson, R. Simon, & C. Beck (eds.). *Literacy teacher educators: Preparing teachers for a changing world.* Pp. 65–78. Boston, MA: Sense Publishers.

Exley, B. (2007). Meanings emerging in practice for linguistically and culturally diverse students: An early years multiliteracies project. *International Journal of Pedagogies and Learning,* 3, 3, 101–113.

Exley, B. & Cottrell, A. (2012). Reading in the Australian curriculum English: Describing the effects of structure and organisation on multimodal text. *English in Australia,* 47, 2, 91–98.

Exley, B. & Richard-Bossez, A. (2013). The ABCs of teaching alphabet knowledge: Challenges and affordances of weaving visible and invisible pedagogies. *Contemporary Issues in Early Childhood,* 14, 4, 345–356.

Exley, B., & Willis, L.-D. (2016). Children's pedagogic rights in the web 2.0 era: A case study of a child's open access interactive travel blog. *Global Studies of Childhood,* 6, 4, 400–413.

Hamston, J. & Murdoch, J. (1996). *Integrating socially: Planning integrated units of work for social education.* Portsmouth, NH: Heinemann.

Hoyte, F., Torr, J., & Degotardi, S. (2014). The language of friendship: Genre in the conversations of preschool children. *Journal of Early Childhood Research,* 12, 1, 20–34.

Janks, H. (2010). *Literacy and power.* London: Routledge.

Kalantzis, M., & Cope, B. (2012). *Literacies.* Port Melbourne, Vic: Cambridge University Press.

Lytle, S. (2013). The critical literacies of teaching. In C. Kosnik, J. Rowsell, P. Williamson, R. Simon, & C. Beck (eds.). *Literacy teacher educators: Preparing teachers for a changing world.* Pp. xv–xix. Boston, MA: Sense Publishers.

Marsh, J. (2010). Countering chaos in Club Penguin: Children's literacy practices in a virtual world. In G. Merchant, J. Gillen, J. Marsh, & J. Davies (eds.). *Virtual literacies: Interactive spaces for children and young people.* Pp. 75–88. London: Routledge.

McInerney, P., Smyth, J. & Down, B. (2011). 'Coming to a place near you?' The politics and possibilities of a critical pedagogy of place-based education. *Asia-Pacific Journal of Teacher Education,* 39, 1, 3–16.

Mills, K. & Exley, B. (2014). Narrative and multimodality in English language arts curricula: A tale of two nations. *Language Arts,* 92, 2, 136–143.

New London Group. (2000). A pedagogy of multiliteracies designing social futures. In B. Cope & M. Kalantzis (eds.). *Multiliteracies: Literacy learning and the design of social futures.* Pp.9–38. London: Continuum.

Ridgewell, J. & Exley, B. (2010). The potential of student initiated netspeak in a middle primary science-inspired multiliteracies project. *Research in Science Education,* 41, 5, 635–649.

Scribner, S. & Cole, M. (1981). *The psychology of literacy.* Cambridge, MA: Harvard University Press.

Smith, S. C. (2015). *Against race and class-based pedagogy in early childhood education.* New York: Palgrave MacMillan.

Teacher Education Ministerial Advisory Group. (2014) Action now: Classroom ready teachers. Retrieved from www.childrenfirst.gov.au/teacher-education-ministerial-advisory-group.

Tierney, V. & Willis, L-D. (2015). Enacting active and informed citizenship in an early years context. *The Social Educator*, 33, 3, 4–16.

Willis, L-D. (2019). Planning for inquiry learning: a Queensland perspective on teaching HASS in initial teacher education. In R. Reynolds (ed.). *Teaching humanities and social sciences in the Primary School 4th ed.* Pp. 94–99. Docklands, Victoria: Oxford University Press.

Willis, L-D. & Exley, B. (2016). Language variation and change in the Australian curriculum English: Integrating sub-strands through a pedagogy of metalogue. *English in Australia*, 51, 2, 74–84.

Willis, L.-D., & Exley, B. (2018). Using an online social media space to engage parents in child learning in the early-years: Enablers and impediments. *Digital Education Review*, 33, 87–104.

Willis, L-D., Grimmett, H., & Heck, D. (2018). Exploring cogenerativity in initial teacher education school–university partnerships using the methodology of metalogue. In J. Kriewaldt, A. Ambrosetti, D. Rorrison, & R. Capeness (eds.). *Educating future teachers: innovative perspectives in professional experience.* Pp. 49–69. Singapore: Springer Nature.

Chapter 4

A Bridge over Troubled Waters

Safe Cross-Cultural Passages with Global Children's Literature

Sherron Killingsworth Roberts and Patricia A. Crawford

Summary of Chapter

The major goals of this chapter include the following:

- to elevate the role of children's literature with global perspectives as a means to bridge cultures;
- to offer teachers key resources for discovering high quality children's books with global perspectives; and
- to provide recommendations and models for the use of multi-genre text sets to enhance readers' global perspectives.

Vignette

Colleen's heart lurched, as she sat in her teacher education methods course, listening to Yangsook Choi's (2003) picturebook, *The Name Jar*. Just last week she had received feedback from her field placement supervisor who had scrawled, "Learn your students' names!!!" on her observation form. At the time, Colleen thought, "Really?! How am I supposed to do that? I don't even know how to pronounce these weird names!" Now, as her professor read aloud, her nervous stomach started to feel the significance of her supervisor's words and the accompanying exclamation points. With each turn of the page, she felt the painful, emotional dilemma experienced by the protagonist, Unhei, as she must decide how to respond when her new classmates seem unable to pronounce her beautiful Korean name. Colleen thought, "I wonder if the children in my class feel the same way as Unhei? What can I do to help?"

Like Colleen, many prospective and practicing teachers find themselves at a complicated tangle of crossroads where varying countries, cultures, perspectives, and belief systems meet. On one hand, it seems that people around the world have never been closer to one another. In daily life, increased opportunities for international travel and shifting migration patterns are factors that bring people together from many different parts of the globe. Even those who are not physically on the move have opportunities to see the world vicariously through the 24-hour news cycle and an increased international media presence. Likewise, many have opportunities to connect virtually with people from around the world through the click of a button on the Internet. Despite of these connections, the world also seems remarkably divided; fraught with misunderstandings, conflicts, and even wars. While schools serve as sites of possibility in which greater understanding and appreciation for diverse cultures and perspectives can be forged, there remain substantive challenges in moving towards this goal. Fortunately, diverse, high quality children's literature can serve as a great help in this regard. The purpose of this chapter is to highlight the ways in which children's literature with global perspectives can serve as a bridge that spans the worlds of children and their cultures.

Historical, Cultural, and Political Context

As Nikolajeva (2011) asserts, "[c]hildren's literature is an international phenomenon" (p. 4). Yet, in spite of the near omnipresence of children's stories around the world, the study of global literature and the way in which it is shared with children remain complex areas of exploration. By its very nature, the definition of global literature is complicated, often impacted by the lens through which one is viewing it. For example, Hadaway and McKenna (2007) suggest that global literature is "... comprehensive and inclusive ... representing literature that honors and celebrates diversity, both within and outside the United States ... (It) includes both multicultural and international literature (p. 5)." Botelho and Sowell (2016) take a similar perspective, but also include a political note: "Global children's literature recognizes the United States as a diaspora, a home to many global cultures with different historical and sociopolitical circumstances" (n.p.). Short (2016) broadens this perspective beyond domestic borders, noting, "Global literature refers to any book set in a global context outside the reader's own location ..." (p. 47) and posits that what constitutes global literature is impacted by the way in which readers interpret their own primary cultural affiliation. Meanwhile, in their work with children who have immigrated to Scotland, Arizpe, Bagelman, Devlin, Farrell, and McAdam (2014a) describe the importance of using globally oriented children's books as multimodal tools to "highlight intercultural encounters between the characters" (p. 9).

Though definitions and perspectives of global literature vary in terms of scope and emphases, it can be agreed that this body of work is one that offers readers perspectives that cut across international borders; providing viewpoints of how different countries and cultures might intersect or compare with one's own culture, either within their home country or abroad. Global literature provides a springboard from which readers can develop a growing awareness of the broader world around them and a better sense of intercultural competence (Hall, 2011; Short 2007; Short, 2016).

The presence and power of global children's literature is certainly not new. Children (and adults) have always been impacted by traditional literature from around the globe (Hadaway, Young, & Ward, 2011). Taking the form of folk and fairy tales, fables, myths, legends, religious texts, and more, these stories, originally passed down orally and only later presented in written texts, helped to both preserve and convey aspects of cultural heritage, probed values, conveyed life lessons, and offered illumination about similarities, as well as differences in cultures around the world. Traditional literature, the oldest form of literature we know, has been explored as a powerful tool for spanning borders of time, place, identity, and ideology in and across many cultures (Englehart, 2011; Lee, 2011; Stephens & McCallum, 1998).

In terms of modern children's literature, strong advocacy for global children's literature can be traced back to the post World War II era. During this time, Jella Lepman, a German Jew who fled during the Holocaust, returned to her native home and found a seemingly endless array of destruction and desolation. Determined to take action to help prevent this type of horror from reoccurring, she put her hope in the power of international children's literature; believing that these books could change hearts and create bridges of understanding (Lepman, 1969/2002). After soliciting text donations from across Europe, she created a traveling exhibit of books, designed to offer hope to children who lived in lands ravaged by war and hatred. This exhibit eventually served as the foundation for the International Youth Library. The central mission of the library continues to be the promotion of "global children's and youth literature of high aesthetic and literary caliber and of significance for cultural literacy" (International Youth Library, 2009, Mission, n.p.). Now housed in Munich's historic Blutenburg Castle, the International Youth Library continues to deliver creative cross-cultural programming to both children and scholars of children's literature from around the world. Beyond her work in establishing the International Youth Library, Lepman also founded the International Board on Books for Young People (IBBY, 2019), an alliance of like-minded others who believed books could indeed be bridges for global understanding (Lepman, 1969/2002; Short, 2009).

Now, many years removed from Lepman's powerful and inspiring post-War initiatives, we still live in a world sorely in need of bridges. Politics continue to divide, battles continue to rage, and children continue to need tangible support to navigate the challenges that surround them. Thus, continued ongoing efforts are needed to ensure that children have access to authentic and inspiring literature that can assist them in understanding global perspectives and developing intercultural competence (Hall, 2011; Short, 2009, 2016). In troubled times, literature offers an avenue for not only sense-making and finding solace, but can also serve as a call to action and praxis (Arizpe, Colomer, & Martinez-Roldan, 2014b; Crawford & Roberts, 2018; Hope, 2008; Roberts & Crawford, 2008). As Lacina and Griffith (2014) note, "There is more need than ever before to prepare children for cross-cultural, global friendships" (p. 30). Literature offers an important and effective means to meet this need.

Theory and Research Base

Global children's literature offers young readers opportunities to consider significant issues within a contextually-rich framework and by way of a developmentally appropriate format (Johnson, Mathis, & Short, 2017; Monobe & Son, 2014; Parsons, 2016). Through these texts, complex concepts with social, cultural and international relevance take form within a cohesive storyline, offering readers an opportunity to make meaning through life-text connections. This type of reading requires a critical lens; one through which children can read both the word and the world (Freire, 1970/2000; Short, 2009).

The research base related to global children's literature focuses on two broad areas: (1) research about the texts, and (2) research about readings of these texts. Text-based research includes literary and content analyses which probe questions not only about the storyline, but also about issues of representation, power, and voice: *What stories are told? How are they told? Who is (and is not) represented? Who has power to act? Who is acted upon?* (Botelho & Rudman, 2009; Johnson, Mathis, & Short, 2017; Leland, Lewison, & Harste, 2013; Stephens, 2015). Research about readers of global literature includes studies of reader responses to the texts: *What do children learn from their readings? What feelings and aesthetic responses accompany these readings? How are children's responses expressed through related talk, writing, and other multimodal work?* (Arizpe, Colomer, & Martinez-Roldan, 2014b; Pantaleo, 2013; Rosenblatt, 1978/1994). Both of these research foci, the texts and their accompanied readings, are important to the work of classroom teachers, since the findings have implications for the choices that teachers make about text selections, pedagogical strategies as well as the ways in which readers' responses are acknowledged, supported, and extended (Johnson, Mathis, & Short, 2017; Leland, Lewison, & Harste, 2013; Parsons, 2016).

Implications for Future Research

There is a constant need for new and evolving research related to global children's literature. As society becomes more diverse and increasingly mobile, there is an ongoing need to make sure that readers of every new generation are able to find themselves in the pages of both classic and new global literature. The core critical issues of representation, power, and response continue to be relevant and important for both researchers and practitioners. As time goes on, it is imperative that researchers continue to explore the ways that individuals and groups are depicted, the ways in which different aspects of culture intersect in texts, and the ways in which children utilize and respond to this literature.

Recommendations for Globally Minded Literacy Teachers

Globally minded literacy teachers can play a significant role in helping their students to develop similar dispositions, by providing access to global literature and sharing it with students in meaningful, contextually rich ways. In this section, resources are first offered for identifying high quality children's literature with global perspectives and conclude with suggestions for using text sets and related response activities to help students engage with this literature.

Identifying Children's Literature with Global Perspectives

Given the myriad of technological linkages, the many inhabitants of the world seem closer than at any other time in history, yet the diverse and often polarized tribes of even one nation reaffirms the need to offer children's literature with global perspectives to mend and bridge toward understanding. Fortunately, there are a growing number of resources for identifying and obtaining this type of high quality literature. The following outlets have vetted the quality and appropriateness of many children's books, often give annotations of quality books, and include recommendations for books to bridge cultural understandings. The following helpful resources can serve as bridges across the sometimes troubled waters of cultural and global interactions, and rightly celebrate books with global perspectives.

WOW: World of Words

World of Words (https://wowlit.org), created by Dr. Kathy Short and hosted at the University of Arizona, states this powerful mission on their website: "WoW builds bridges across global cultures through children's and adolescent literature." This mission is accompanied by three charges to: *Open a book, Open a mind, Change the world.* This research-based website, which includes multiple resources, podcasts, and links to databases, began with the simple, but powerful mission to change the world through children's books. Most notably, this organization develops and shares wonderful lists of global children's fiction and nonfiction books; also included are the Lexiles and measures of complexities as well as suggested grade level bands for teachers and parents.

WoW (World of Words, 2019) also has three online journals. The first, *WOW Stories*, promulgates intentional, research-based strategies for practitioners. The resources within the pages of this website include comprehensive lists of children's books aligned with the United States Common Core State Standards intended to expand our students' perspectives (https://wowlit.org/links/globalizing-common-core-reading-list/). For example, in response to the CCSS recommendation to use *The Black Stallion* (Farley, 1941/1947), Wowlit.org thoughtfully provides an annotated table of high quality children's books set in diverse global contexts to pair with CCSS books, such as *Tua and the Elephant* (Harris, 2012) set in Thailand. Worlds of Words (World of Words, 2019) also publishes online, peer-reviewed reviews of children's and adolescent literature written in English, *WOW Review*, and another for featuring books written in Spanish, entitled *WOW Libros*. No doubt, the rich resources available here will continue to grow and gain notoriety as classroom teachers find effective tools and accompanying strategies to bridge cultures through books with global perspectives.

Mildred Batchelder Award

A unique resource that elevates important and rich cross-cultural insights and perspectives can be found in the Mildred Batchelder Award (www.ala. org/alsc/awardsgrants/bookmedia/batchelderaward). This award (Batchelder, 2019) honors outstanding books originally published in a country other than the United States, in order to provide an American publishing firm with incentives to bring the best books from other countries, often written in another language, to be widely distributed in English in the United States. In this way, the award broadens the influence of the best books from countries around the globe, making them more accessible to English speaking countries. Established in 1966, the Batchelder Award honors Mildred L. Batchelder, former executive director of the Association of Library

Services for Children (ALSC), an influential division of the American Library Association. Batchelder strongly believed in the power of translating the best books for children from around the world to enrich lives and "to eliminate barriers to understanding between people of different cultures, races, nations, and languages" (www.ala.org/alsc/awardsgrants/bookmedia/batcheldera ward/batchelderabout). Therefore, as English becomes a growing, common language around the world, more children and families can be exposed to books of superior quality that offer glimpses of differing cultural perspectives as well as common elements of humanity.

Pictures and brief synopses of award winners and honor books, which include many genres and formats, are available for teachers and parents to use as an entree into another's cultural point of view. Batchelder (1972) noted that this award and the resulting cadre of books develops the "interchange of children's books between countries, through translation, influences communication between the peoples of those countries …" (pp. 307–315). For example, the Batchelder Award and Honor books (Batchelder, 2019) awarded in 2018 hailed from Sweden, France, and Brazil, while awardees in 2017 were translated from Danish, Japanese, Spanish, and Norwegian. This award can be quite impactful not only for authors, illustrators, and larger publishers, but especially for smaller independent publishing companies, such as Chronicle Books, which won for *Over the Ocean* (Gomi, 2017). This book invites consideration of intercultural understanding, as it focuses on the questions of a young child who gazes over the ocean and wonders about someone, who not so different from herself, might be gazing back in her direction.

Notable Books for a Global Society

In 1979, the Children's Literature and Reading Special Interest Group (CL/ R SIG) was established through the International Literacy Association (formerly the International Reading Association). These annual awards (Notable Books for a Global Society, 2019) promote the most comprehensive list of high-quality children's books aligned with their mission to promote "the educational use of children's books by focusing on recently published children's literature, supportive professional books, issues relative to children's literature, and current research findings" (n. p. www.clrsig.org/). To further fulfill this mission, this dedicated SIG also publishes *The Dragon Lode*, a semi-annual journal that disseminates research related to children's literature (www.clrsig.org/dragonlode.html).

Annually, the CL/R SIG selects the top 25 outstanding books for children, ages 5 to 18, including fiction, nonfiction, and poetry, that "reflect a pluralistic view of world society." The first list was published in 1995 with the intention of addressing our global village (www.clrsig.org/nbgs-lists.html). Their website posits the assumptions behind the creation of this important top 25 list:

... today's society is rife with tension, conflict and ignorance of others different from us. If we hope to meet the many challenges that face us in the 21st century, we must recognize the similarities and celebrate the differences among all races, cultures, religions, and sexual orientations, and appreciate that people can hold a wide range of equally legitimate values.

(n.p.)

No doubt, this statement remains true now, with these vetted books continuing to provide important bridges across today's "troubled waters" as they did in 1995. For example, the 2018 awardee list selected 25 titles that featured many powerful books engendering empathy and respect for all children, especially those with themes regarding indigenous peoples, refugees, and immigrants, such as *Her Right Foot* (Eggers, 2017), *Refugee* (Gratz, 2017), *Stolen Words* (Florence, 2017), and *Lucky Broken Girl* (Behur, 2018).

USBBY

The last two resources, USBBY and IBBY, are often surprisingly overlooked by some classroom teachers accustomed to relying solely on the American Library Association's Newbery and Caldecott Awards. Yet, the United States Board of Books for Young People (USBBY, 2019, www. usbby.org) is an organization that recommends a wealth of books that pinpoint global connections and promote international understanding. USBBY (USBBY, 2019) also works hard to ensure that the inherent rights of children to read books in their native tongue that relate to their own cultures. In addition, USBBY also hosts a biannual children's literature conference and publishes the *Bridges to Understanding* book series, which recommend annotated bibliographies of high quality, international literature for young people. Therefore, USBBY (2019) is the United States counterpart and subsection of the International Board on Books for Young People (IBBY, 2019), and as such, forwards the book selection from the United States to the larger IBBY biennial awards.

IBBY

IBBY (IBBY, 2019), or the International Board of Books for Young People, is a global organization that comprises over 45 countries, each submitting recommendations for the world's best offerings in children's literature to create a biennial award. This biennial award honors the author, the illustrator, and the translator. This list captures the best books in children's literature across the world for a particular country published over the last two years. This outlet is dedicated to ensuring that children all over the world are given access to the best books in languages other than English. The honor list books are listed quite simply in tables on the IBBY website showing the country of origin, the language of text, the author's name, and the specific title (all without annotation, pictures, or links to information about the books). Further, the actual books are housed in several locations around the world including Munich, Zurich, St. Petersburg, Bratislava, Tokyo, Kuala Lumpur, and Tucson. Thus, teachers can consult the website (www.ibby.org/awards-activities/awards/ibby-honour-list/for) for the biennial list to start finding books that bridge our understandings of each other's cultures. Overall, this amazing organization has links to the participating nations, promotes April 2 as International Children's Book Day, promulgates important intersections of high needs students, and provides many best book lists, such as books regarding about students with disabilities, from around the world and in languages other than English.

For example, the website also highlights an important IBBY project entitled Silent Books. Responding to the large influx of African and Middle Eastern refugees arriving in Lampedusa, an island in the province of Sicily, Italy, IBBY worked tirelessly to create the first library for children on Lampedusa. Given the range of languages, a collection of hundreds of wordless picture books was assembled to promote understandings across languages and peoples, without the dependence on any one language. These books were later exhibited all over the world. Additionally, IBBY (IBBY, 2019) publishes *Bookbird: A Journal of International Children's Literature* (www.ibby.org/bookbird/), a refereed, quarterly journal, whose mission is to "communicate new ideas to the community of readers interested in children's books" (n.p.). This journal also regularly includes informative articles highlighting awards for children's literature from other countries around the world.

Sharing Global Perspectives Through Text Sets

Teachers who are intent on honoring their students' backgrounds and heritages as well as expanding their students' global perspectives might consider using text sets as a means of developing critical thinking and empathy as well as reinforcing close reading skills across many genres of books (Nichols, 2009, 2014; Zwiers & Crawford, 2011). As outlined by Leland and Harste (1994), text sets are groups of books assembled around a common topic with preference given to curiosity and inquiry from various, even discrepant, points of view. Text sets, therefore, should include multiple genres and reading levels, which makes the topic accessible to a wide range of student interests and literacy levels. These multi-genre text sets, which likely include realistic fiction, historical fiction, biography, informational books, websites, and poetry, insist on a multiplicity of lens. Therefore, they can address the complexity inherent within the kind of global perspectives honored in this book. This text set strategy also marries well with social studies content (Crawford & Roberts, 2016; Koralek, 2015; Leland, Lewison, & Harste, 2013) because it allows students to explore various perspectives, dispositions, and values in regard to a particular topic (Nichols, 2009, 2014). As teachers plan for students to read, discuss, and analyze books from multiple genres, one can see how global perspectives highlight "their places and their particular experiences as part of the universal whole of humanity" (Lehman, Freeman, & Scharer, 2010, p. 19).

To illustrate, the topic of immigration for a text set provides readers bridges to intercultural connections that can expand our insulated worlds. This topic also has timely and timeless qualities. The pervasive history of immigration in the United States is now punctuated by current statistics on the portion of immigrants who are also refugees (UNHCR, 2015). "A staggering 1 in 10 of the world's children – or more than 230 million – currently live in countries and areas affected by armed conflicts" (UNICEF, 2015). Today's students need historical information, powerful stories, and related resources to build bridges to understanding. Many outstanding books from multiple genres can provide students needed historical information, powerful perspectives and stories, and related resources to help build these bridges. Therefore, historical fiction chapter books such as Gratz's (2017) *Refugee*, which includes three different, but related stories of children refugees fleeing genocide and injustice: a 1930s Jewish refugee, a 1994 Cuban refugee, and a Syrian refugee in 2015, all coming to America. Students need quality literature and assistance to navigate the complicated issues and impacts of immigration. A powerful example of a recent IBBY (IBBY, 2019) winner is *Marwan's Journey* (de Arias, 2018), a picturebook translated from Spanish to English, which shows a young boy's courageous journey into the unknown, step-by-brave-step. To add the aesthetic texture of poetry, students of all ages and abilities will benefit from a beautiful book, *Somos Como las nubes/We are Like the Clouds* (Argueta, 2016). Argueta captures the daunting shifts that must be navigated in leaving home and adjusting to new places, often because of the complex questions surrounding identity that come with cross-cultural passages: *Where is my home? Who am I? Who was I? Where do I really belong?* Mirroring these changing roles, one of Argueta's poems (2016) entitled "We Introduce Ourselves to the Border Patrol" echoes a child's worries about identity as he remembers his name amidst the stars marking the vastness of the desert and the length of the journey.

An additional illustrated book rounds out the text set by providing important information to learners. With great subheadings, engaging insights, and intriguing visuals, *Refugees and Migrants* (Roberts, 2017) is a powerful nonfiction companion text that can serve alongside the fictional offerings for classrooms intent on boosting critical thinking and empathy around this topic. Woodson's (2018) realistic fiction novel, *Harbor Me*, provides additional viewpoints to issues of deportation and immigration within its lyrical pages as well. Supplemental, yet integral to the topic are the delightful and poignant picturebooks that include children in cross-cultural relationships due to immigration, such as *One Green Apple* (Bunting, 2006), *I'm New Here* (O'Brien, 2015), *Yoon and the Jade Bracelet* (Recorvits, 2008), *My Two Blankets* (Kobald, 2015), *Big Red Lollipop* (Khan, 2010), and the aforementioned *The Name Jar* (Choi, 2001). An example of an innovative book recognized by NBGS is *Drawn Together* (Le, 2018), which artfully elevates cross-cultural understandings across cross-generational language barriers through a mutual love of drawing. Each of these books advances helpful scenarios showing native and immigrant children at home and at school as fodder for discussion and comparison.

Surely, immigration brings many struggles regarding identity, as carefully retold in another Argueta (2007) book entitled *Alfredito Flies Home*, in which young Alfredito returns to his El Salvador homeland, after fleeing four years earlier. Alfredito's complex emotions including the excitement of finally going home, the joy of reuniting with loved ones, the comfort of familiarity, and the unsettling dissonance experienced upon leaving to return to the United States are artfully crafted in this thoughtful picturebook. All of these award-winning books bring important global perspectives to complex topics related to immigration, refugees, and border crossings and were harvested from the resources cited above.

Concluding Remarks

The world in which we live is a complex one that necessitates the development of global awareness and a sense of connection among global citizens. Children's literature with global perspectives can serve as an ideal medium for assisting children in making connections as they glimpse the breadth, depth, and complexity of the people and world around them through authentic, high quality literature. Just as Jella Lepman (1969/2002) envisioned a literary bridge that would heal and inspire children impacted by World War II, educators today can work towards a similar vision. Together, educators can identify and thoughtfully share literature that helps readers to better understand themselves and others. Offering multiple genres of authentic literature and meaningful engagement can bridge the cross-cultural complexities and help children develop an informed perspective, an empathetic outlook, and a vision for being a global citizen.

Discussion Questions and Applications

Q1: How can teachers model thoughtful responses to global literature?

Application: Read alouds provide a wonderful opportunity for teachers to model thoughtful responses to literature. Teachers can use well-chosen literature selections as springboards to make their thought processes and affective responses visible to students. Although many types of literature will work, picturebooks are very effective tools in this process, because they invite responses to both words and visual texts, usually include content that is accessible for a variety of developmental levels, and can be shared in a compact amount of time. As teachers share the book, they can articulate their thoughts and questions (e.g. *"Hmmmm … . I'm looking at the cover and wondering what this book is about." "I wonder why [the character] did that. What do you think?" "This story takes place in [country]. I'd like to know where that is." "How do you think [the character] feels? Why do you think this? Have you ever felt that way?"*). Students can then be encouraged to use similar strategies when they read (or listen to) literature.

Q2: How can teachers help students to have authentic conversations about global literature?

Application: Literature circles propose requirements regarding the space, time, and purpose for engaging students in meaningful, authentic conversations (Daniels, 2002; Peterson & Eeds, 2007). Ideally, these small group discussions will offer opportunities for students to choose their own texts related to the goals or unit of study, set their agenda for discussing the text, and ask meaningful questions.

Q3: How can teachers help students to make text-life connections?

Application: Books with global perspectives certainly furnish students opportunities to learn about particular places and situated events. However, they also afford readers with the chance to tap into the affective realm and think and feel along with the characters in the storyline. Teachers can encourage students to find connections between their own life experiences and those that characters encounter. One powerful way to prompt these types of text-life connections across borders with books is by giving students a *Life Connections & Conversations* bookmark (see Figure 4.1). These bookmarks include prompts that support readers in important scenes to connect their own life experiences with them (Included with permission from Kaczmarczyk, Allee-Herndon, & Roberts, 2019).

Q4: How can teachers help students to gain empathy by reading global literature?

Application: Global literature offers readers an opportunity to see circumstances, history, politics, and daily events from a different perspective. Readers gain a new perspective and a sense of empathy as they "walk in the shoes" of particular characters or see life through the eyes of that character. Teachers can nurture this sense of empathy within global contexts by exposing students to a breadth of information through the use of text sets and facilitating rich discussions via literature circles (both described above). Teachers can also ask

**LIFE CONNECTIONS
& CONVERSATIONS**
What are you reminded of in
your own life?

◆ **AN EMOTIONAL SCENE
from the book** that reminds
you of your own life
  ▲ I loved the part...
  ▲ I thought about a time...
  ▲ I remember...

◆ **A FUNNY SCENE from the
book** that reminds you of
your own life
  ▲ That ___ reminded me of...
  ▲ I could just picture... b/c...
  ▲ I laughed at...

◆ **A 'FIRST' IN YOUR OWN
LIFE from the book** that
reminded you of your own life
  ▲ When I read about...
  ▲ I remembered...
  ▲ The first time I...
    reminded me of...

◆ **A LESSON LEARNED in the
book** that parallels a lesson
in your own life
  ▲ I learned...
  ▲ My family is learning...
  ▲ I loved the way ___
    learned...

**LIFE CONNECTIONS
& CONVERSATIONS**
What are you reminded of in
your own life?

◆ **AN EMOTIONAL SCENE
from the book** that reminds
you of your own life
  ▲ I loved the part...
  ▲ I thought about a time...
  ▲ I remember...

◆ **A FUNNY SCENE from the
book** that reminds you of
your own life
  ▲ That ___ reminded me of...
  ▲ I could just picture... b/c...
  ▲ I laughed at...

◆ **A 'FIRST' IN YOUR OWN
LIFE from the book** that
reminded you of your own life
  ▲ When I read about....
  ▲ I remembered...
  ▲ The first time I...
    reminded me of...

◆ **A LESSON LEARNED in the
book** that parallels a lesson
in your own life
  ▲ I learned...
  ▲ My family is learning...
  ▲ I loved the way ___
    learned...

**LIFE CONNECTIONS
& CONVERSATIONS**
What are you reminded of in
your own life?

◆ **AN EMOTIONAL SCENE
from the book** that reminds
you of your own life
  ▲ I loved the part...
  ▲ I thought about a time...
  ▲ I remember...

◆ **A FUNNY SCENE from the
book** that reminds you of
your own life
  ▲ That ___ reminded me of...
  ▲ I could just picture... b/c...
  ▲ I laughed at...

◆ **A 'FIRST' IN YOUR OWN
LIFE from the book** that
reminded you of your own life
  ▲ When I read about....
  ▲ I remembered...
  ▲ The first time I...
    reminded me of...

◆ **A LESSON LEARNED in the
book** that parallels a lesson
in your own life
  ▲ I learned...
  ▲ My family is learning...
  ▲ I loved the way ___
    learned...

Figure 4.1 Life connections and conversation bookmark

students to "think and feel" with particular characters, by constructing journal entries, letters, postcards, self-portraits, or even mock social media profiles, all constructed from the viewpoint of the focus character.

References

Arizpe, E., Bagelman, C., Devlin, A. M., Farrell, M., & McAdam, J. E. (2014a). Visualizing intercultural literacy: Engaging critically with diversity and migration in the classroom through an image-based approach. *Language and Intercultural Communication, 14*(3), 304–321.

Arizpe, E., Colomer, T., & Martinez-Roldan, C. (2014b). *Visual journeys through wordless narratives. An international inquiry with immigrant children and The Arrival.* London: Bloomsbury.

Batchelder, M. L. (Autumn, 1972). Translations of children's books. *Minnesota Libraries,* 307–315.

Botelho, M. J., & Rudman, M. K. (2009). *Critical multicultural analysis of children's literature: Mirrors, windows, and doors.* New York, NY: Routledge.

Botelho, M. J., & Sowell, N. (2016). Teaching global children's literature: What to read and how to read. *Education Week.* August 9. (n.p.) Retrieved from https:// blogs.edweek.org/edweek/global_learning/2016/08/teaching_global_childrens_li terature_what_to_read_and_how_to_read.html

Crawford, P. A., & Roberts, S. K. (2016). Connecting words to the world: Literature connections for social studies through text sets. *Childhood Education, 92*(3), 250–253.

Crawford, P. A., & Roberts, S. K. (2018). Wandering from wars: Children's picturebooks portraying refugees and providing hope. *Dragon Lode: Children's Literature Journal, 36*(2), 14–19.

Daniels, H. (2002). *Literature circles: Voice and choice in book clubs and reading groups.* Portland, ME: Stenhouse.

Englehart, D. S. (2011). A story to tell: The culture of storytelling and folklore in Ireland. *Childhood Education, 87,* 409–414.

Freire, P. (1970/2000). *Pedagogy of the Oppressed, Thirtieth Anniversary Edition.* London, UK: Continuum.

Hadaway, N. L., & McKenna, M. J. (Eds.). (2007). *Breaking boundaries with global literature: Celebrating diversity in K-12 classrooms.* Newark, DE: International Reading Association.

Hadaway, N. L., Young, T. A., & Ward, B. (2011). Passing on and preserving our stories: Universal experiences in children's literature around the world. *Childhood Education, 87,* 381–386.

Hall, V. (2011). Global perspectives in Caldecott award books: An analysis of books from the 1970s and 2000s. *Childhood Education, 87,* 430–436.

Hope, J. (2008). "One day we had to run": The development of the refugee identity in children's literature and its function in education. *Children's Literature in Education, 39,* 295–304.

IBBY. (2019). The International Board of Books for Young People. Retrieved from www.ibby.org/awards-activities/awards/ibby-honour-list/

International Youth Library. (2019). *Mission statement for the International Youth Library* (n.p.). Munich, Germany: IYL. Retrieved from https://www.ijb.de/en/about-us/mission.html

Johnson, H., Mathis, J., & Short, K. G. (Eds.). (2017). *Critical content analysis of children's and young adult literature: Reframing perspective.* New York, NY: Routledge.

Kaczmarczyk, A., Allee-Herndon, K., & Roberts, S. K. (2019). Using literacy approaches to begin the conversation on racial illiteracy. *Teaching Tips in the Reading Teacher, 72*(4), 523–528. DOI: 10.1002/trtr.1757

Koralek, D. (2015). Social studies: From a sense of self to a sense of the world. *Young Children, 70*(3), 6–7.

Lacina, J., & Griffith, R. (2014). Making new friends: Using literature to inspire cross-cultural friendships. *Reading Today*, Nov/ Dec, n. p. Retrieved from https://robinrgriffith.files.wordpress.com/2016/02/making-new-friends-using-literature-to-inspire-cross-cultural-friendship.pdf

Lee, G. (2011). Teaching traditional values through folk literature in Korea. *Childhood Education, 87,* 402–408.

Lehman, B., Freeman, E., & Scharer, P. (2010). *Reading globally, K-8: Connecting students to the world through literature.* Thousand Oaks, CA: Corwin.

Leland, C., & Harste, J. (1994). Multiple ways of knowing: Curriculum in a new key. *Language Arts, 71*(5), 337–345.

Leland, C., Lewison, M., & Harste, J. (2013). *Teaching children's literature: It's critical!* New York: Routledge.

Lepman, J. (1969/2002). *A bridge of children's books.* Dublin, Ireland: O'Brien Press.

Mildred Batchelder Award. (2019). Retrieved from www.ala.org/alsc/awardsgrants/bookmedia/batchelderaward

Monobe, G., & Son E. H.(2014). Using children's literature and drama to explore children's lives in the context of global conflicts. *The Social Studies, 105* (2), 69-74, doi: 10.1080/00377996.2013.820164

Nichols, M. (2009). *Expanding comprehension with multigenre text sets.* New York, NY: Scholastic.

Nichols, M. (2014). *Talking about text: Guiding students to increase comprehension through purposeful talk.* Huntington Beach, CA: Shell Education.

Nikolajeva, M. (2011). Translation and crosscultural reception. In S. A. Wolf, K. Coats, P. Encisco, & C. A. Jenkins (eds.). *Handbook of research on children's and young adult literature* (pp. 404–416). New York, NY: Routledge.

Notable Books for a Global Society. (2019). Retrieved from www.clrsig.org/

Pantaleo, S. (2013). Revisiting Rosenblatt's aesthetic response through *The Arrival. Australian Journal of Language and Literacy, 36*(3), 125–134.

Parsons, L. T. (2016). Storytelling in global children's literature: Its role in the lives of displaced child characters. *Journal of Children's Literature, 42*(2), 19–27.

Peterson, R., & Eeds, M. (2007). *Grand conversations: Literature groups in action.* New York, NY: Scholastic.

Roberts, S. K., & Crawford, P. A. (2008). Real life calls for real books: Literature to help children cope with family stressors. *Young Children, 63*(5), 12–17.

Rosenblatt, L. (1978/1994). *The reader, the text, the poem: The transactional theory of the literary work.* Carbondale, IL: Southern Illinois University Press.

Short, K. G. (2007, Spring). Children between worlds: Creating intercultural connections through literature. *Arizona Reading Journal*, *33*(2), 12–17.

Short, K. G. (2009). Critically reading the word and the world: Building intercultural understanding through children's literature. *Bookbird*, *47*(2), 1–10.

Short, K. G. (2016). Reading outside the comfort zone: The dangers and possibilities of reading globally. *The Dragon Lode*, *35*(2), 46–50.

Stephens, J. (2015). Editorial: Critical content analysis and literary criticism. *International Research in Children's Literature*, *8*(1), vi–viii.

Stephens, J., & McCallum, R. (1998). *Retelling stories, framing culture*. New York, NY: Routledge.

UNICEF. (2015). *UNICEF: More than 1 in 10 children living in countries and areas affected by armed conflict*. Retrieved from www.unicefusa.org/press/realeases/unicef-more-1-10-children-living-countries-an

United Nations High Commissioner for Refugees. UNHCR. (2015). The number of people displaced by war has reached a staggering high. Retrieved from www.unhcr.org/news/latest/2015/6/558193896/worldwide-displacement-hits-all-time-high-war-persecution-increase.html

USBBY. (2019). United States Board of Books for Young People. Retrieved from www.usbby.org

World of Words. (2019). Retrieved from https://wowlit.org

Zwiers, J., & Crawford, M. (2011). *Academic conversations: Classroom talk that fosters critical thinking and content understandings*. Portland, ME: Stenhouse.

Children's Literature Cited

Argueta, J. (2007). *Alfredito flies home*. Toronto, ON: Groundwood Books. Illustrated by L. Garay.

Argueta, J. (2016). *Somos como las nubes/We are like the clouds*. Berkeley, CA: Groundwood Books/House of Anansi Press. Illustrated by A. Ruano.

Behur, R. (2018). *Lucky broken girl*. New York, NY: Puffin Books.

Bunting, E. (2006). *One green apple*. New York, NY: Clarion Books. Illustrated by Ted Lewin.

Choi, Y. (2003). *The name jar*. Decorah, IA: Dragonfly Books.

de Arias, P. (2018). *Marwan's journey*. Salzburg, Austria: Michael Neugebauer Publishing. Illustrated by L. Borras.

Eggers, D. (2017). *Her right foot*. San Francisco, CA: Chronicle Books. Illustrated by S. Harris.

Farley, W. (1941/1947). *The black stallion*. New York, NY: Yearling Books.

Florence, M. (2017). *Stolen words*. Toronto, ON: Second Story Press. Illustrated by G. Grimard.

Gomi, T. (2017). *Over the ocean*. San Francisco, CA: Chronicle Books.

Gratz, A. (2017). *Refugee*. New York, NY: Scholastic.

Harris, R. P. (2012). *Tua and the elephant*. San Francisco, CA: Chronicle Books. Illustrated by T, Yoo.

Khan, R. (2010). *Big red lollipop*. New York, NY: Viking/Penguin. Illustrated by S. Blackall.

Kobald, I. (2015). *My two blankets*. New York, NY: HMH Books for Young Readers. Illustrated by F. Blackwood.

Le, M. (2018). *Drawn together*. New York, NY: Disney/Hyperion. Illustrated by D. Santat.

O'Brien, A. S. (2015). *I'm new here*. Watertown, MA: Charlesbridge Publishing.

Recorvits, H. (2008). *Yoon and the jade bracelet*. Toronto, CA: Douglas & McIntyre. Illustrated by G. Swiatkowska.

Roberts, C. (2017). *Refugees and migrants (children in our world)*. Hauppauge, NY: Barron's Educational Series. Illustrated by H. Kai.

Woodson, J. (2018). *Harbor me*. New York, NY: Nancy Paulsen Books.

Chapter 5

Digital Literacies in the UK
Creating, Navigating, and Curating Content

Natalia Kucirkova and John Potter

Summary of Chapter

- Literacy is wider than print literacy in the digital age and incorporates the many ways with which we make and share meanings. Our classrooms need to reflect those wider engagements with media artefacts and texts and the skills and dispositions towards them which younger learners exhibit.
- Digital curation is a new literacy practice that accommodates children's agency and which has the potential to enhance learning. We have shared some examples from classrooms that support the development of curatorship with digital media.
- Globally minded teachers are also 'new literacy' aware teachers who understand the influence of digital practices and texts across linguistic and other domains of difference.

Introduction

Traditional models of children's books are based on the assumption that there is a space, or a gap, between the adult author and the child reader. The traditional model of games, videos, learning materials and other activities designed for young children follows a similar logic: there is a distance between consumers and producers. However, with the advent of digital media, the space between authors and readers (and adults and children) has the potential to be less hierarchical, to become a 'third space' in effect, in which the expertise is shared and porous between them (Potter & McDougall, 2017). This is because digital media offer possibilities for accessing and authoring new content, as well as for sharing and amending it with others. It is also because new media offer new possibilities for customisation of screen design and appearance, so that anyone can adjust the layout of a digital text or apply filters to their pictures.

Today's children with access to digital devices and spaces can make their own multimedia content on Wiis, Leapsters, Kindles, iPads or smartphones.

They can simultaneously take pictures, add their own voiceovers to videos, share them with friends and comment on their friends' uploads. In this chapter, we will discuss the process through which children assemble various pieces of content to communicate their 'self' with others. This process involves many generative choices that children make when communicating with the world around them and signalling their belonging to others. Their transient affiliations, preferences and intertextual references can all be part of the process of communication and representation which, in other writing has been labelled as a kind of *curation process* in digital media.

In this chapter, we will situate the curation process in light of contemporary theories and studies with young children. We have selected examples that inspired our own projects of children's literacy activity with digital texts and artefacts. We will locate the work in the contemporary context of children's lives in the UK, including their digital learning lives. We will explore how the connections can be made to wider themes in contemporary literacy practices in the world.

Vignette

In the Robin School Year 1 classroom (5–6-year-olds), the morning lesson starts with a little dance. The teacher plays a popular song on the interactive whiteboard and the children enthusiastically move to the rhythm. After this warm up, the children sit down around small tables, in groups of six. Each table has laptop computers available for individual children's use. The children are coding with the Purple Mash coding software today. Everyone can choose different coding exercises, such as programming different objects or animals to move in different directions or at a different speed. The children enthusiastically share their creations with the friends sitting next to them. I hear children say: 'My cars are racing at speed 10 now!' or 'My fish moved to the right, how do I get it up?' The teacher supports children's choices and helps them navigate to the relevant links as and when necessary.

Theory and Research Base

Our theoretical base pulls together concepts that have emerged from curriculum studies located in English, New Literacies, media and cultural studies. We present these in the context of practical examples in a range of settings. We must state right at the outset that our view is not based on instrumentalist designs for 'digital literacies', which are focused primarily on skillsets. Rather, we are interested in the series of negotiations between lived experiences and practices around the digital.

The so-called '3Cs' – the context, content and the child – are a helpful way of framing wider topics and approaching the discussion of children and technology (Guernsey, 2012). In our case, in this chapter, our 3Cs are: the *context* the school learning environment and children's use of digital media in the classroom; the *content* of literacy and digital literacy activities; the *children* are British pre- and primary-schoolers, aged between three to 11 years. We use several terms in this chapter that our readers will be familiar with but to which they might attach different meanings. We will, go on in the next section to present our overarching conception of literacy.

New Literacies

The 3Cs are closely related to work that spoke of 'strata', the 'operational, cultural and critical' layers of meaning-making which run in parallel with considerations of 'language, meaning and power' (Green, 2002). These are ways to operationalise and organise learning within the umbrella of children's New Literacies. As James Paul Gee has pointed out (2015), 'New Literacies' is an umbrella term that is derived from the work of many writers working in the last two or three decades across interconnected disciplines, ranging from anthropology, through to semiotics and cultural studies, taking in education and linguistics (e.g. Cope & Kalantzis, 2000; Kress & Van Leeuwen, 2001; Pahl & Rowsell, 2012; Street, 2003). Their shared view about literacy concerns its situated and ideological nature in practices, the ways in which literacy is contingent upon context and the ways in which meanings are always made in negotiation between people, artefacts and texts. Importantly for us, 'New Literacies' seek ways to account for the digital and the mediated nature of meaning-making in the context of new technologies.

Historical and Cultural Context

The cultural context that we are most familiar with is that of English-speaking Western countries where literacy curriculum is subject to high levels of governmental scrutiny and teachers' accountability. In England, individual assessment and public accountability hold sway as children are obliged to sit the phonics screening check aged six and a standardised assessment test at the end of their primary education. We recognise and accept the claim that literacy is associated with important, essential skills of speaking and listening, reading and writing print – and this is fully set out in the official documentation for the education system in the UK (DFE, 2013). However, in this chapter, we are concerned with moving beyond this definition of literacy, and believe that literacy is not only about the importance of children's reading and writing skills with print but also about their ability to participate actively in a lifelong process of learning about the world and the self. This means working from the basis of the 'New Literacies', that of a negotiation with the digital and its impact on all forms of meaning-making. According to this perspective, literacy is a complex array of skills and dispositions towards the present moment, existing in a dynamic relation to both the digital and the ways in which learning is organised (Potter & McDougall, 2017). Such a conceptualisation recognises that every day, children are encountering media and swimming in visual culture. In a broader definition of literacy as a dynamic force, formal aspects of reading and writing are still regarded as an important, but not the only, part of literacy instruction. However, not all teachers and indeed not all literacy researchers, would agree on this broader definition of literacy, nor on the ways of operationalising it.

As Snow and Dickinson (1991) helpfully outline, there are two approaches to literacy, which are often disconnected in practice but intertwined conceptually. First, there is the cognitive and psycholinguistic tradition that characterises literacy as a skill that can be tested and incrementally improved through performance indicators. The second tradition, as in the case of 'New Literacies', focuses on literacy as embedded in socio-cultural values. Children bring their 'funds of knowledge' (González, Moll, & Amanti, 2006) to the classroom and their literacy experiences correspond to what the society values and valorises. The former approach is dominant in many Western schools, where there is great emphasis placed on students' ability to identify letters, phonemes and words. The latter approach is the one we foreground in this chapter and that, as has been outlined above in the context of 'New Literacies' is a view that connects literacy to the power embedded in diverse socio-cultural and geo-political contexts. It follows that literacy is neither value- nor context-free and what counts as desirable literacy in one society does not automatically translate to another society. Similarly, while alphabetical writing has been a constant in literacy teaching, the communication of meaning via digital media is changing at a breath-taking speed and scale. Given these changes, the so-called 'New Literacies' provide important understanding of the contemporary frames of learning. We now move onto a discussion of how 'New Literacies' connect to digital media.

Digital Media

It is hard to think of any contemporary activity that would not involve some type of digital media: our everyday relationships, conversations and learning are constructed with and within diverse digital media. This does not mean that non-digital learning or play are non-existent or lower in status. Quite the contrary, an optimal combination of digital and non-digital media should be the goal of all our meaning-making efforts. Marsh (2017) listed several connections that can be made as children learn and play with a range of media, including: physical/virtual; non-digital/digital; online/offline; material/immaterial; public/private; local/ global. Children themselves encounter the online and offline worlds of play and digital media across multiple contexts, including in their everyday play with one another (Burn & Richards, 2014) and in school settings in which they move seamlessly between material and (im)material contexts (Burnett & Merchant, 2014). There are many nuances in studying cross-cultural interaction and dealing with the social consequences of meaning-making in the digital age, including the ethics, privacy or security of communication with digital media (Coiro, Knobel, Lankshear, & Leu, 2010).

However, all too often, diverse digital media are merged into one big box labelled 'technology' that divides opinions on whether they are worth the investment of children's and teacher's time. Technology as represented by the larger ed-tech companies can quickly age and become outdated, as they continuously push out new devices and new software programs. Whether you prefer old or new media, you are likely to be using some educational technologies in your school, for example to document and evaluate children's progress with classroom management systems or for projecting the content of your lesson on the interactive whiteboard. You might be using digital media to support your teaching or to enhance an activity with additional resources (for example by using a weather app to enrich a Science lesson).

In this chapter we foreground digital media that are ubiquitous in our personal lives: smartphones and tablets. These touchscreens are not always integrated into classroom life, for many complex political and social reasons, not to mention, at times, practical considerations.

With their small screen, portability and user-friendly interface, smartphones and tablets are designed for individual use or very small group use. They are thus best suited for one-to-one interactions and personalised learning, which is not the norm in public schools. Touchscreens are content-free but users can populate them with their own photos, videos, voice-overs, documents and apps. Many of these apps come with algorithms that are capable of measuring students' engagement with particular activity and tailor subsequent learning topics based on the students' performance. We are both excited by and concerned by aspects of these capabilities and we recognise this tension in our own work and in the ways in which teachers feel about these activities. Our concern relates to the low quality and commercial nature of many apps offered for young children as well as the low levels of understanding of how information is collected and processed about users in the context of Artificial Intelligence and 'Datafication' (Bradbury & Roberts-Holmes, 2017). An uncritical use of data-based software programs can easily slip into reducing children's activities to numbers and quantifiable targets that are controlled by commercial companies. Our excitement and interest, however, arises from the possibilities for engagement and connection with outside culture which are afforded by the use of digital media, in particular as it is connected to children's agency as learners.

Children's Agency

'Agency', like 'identity', has many definitions, each one derived by adherents of particular positions on the social world (Buckingham, 2017). So, for example, where some see the agency in relation to the social structures which shape or constrain humans in some way, others view agency as the potential for individual action on the world, through choice and action as a result of particular affordances. For us, 'agency' is critical in forming a child's identity and refining a sense of who they are in terms of volition and children's own choices. From a psychosocial perspective, agency is one of the 12 motivation-related constructs widely studied in psychology research: attitudes, expectancy, extrinsic motivation, goals, interest, intrinsic motivation, reading motivation, self-belief, self-concept, self-efficacy and value (Conradi, Jang, & McKenna, 2014). When studied in schools, agency is often translated into students' agentic engagement in the classroom, though we recognise its complexity and appreciate the efforts of others to introduce understanding based on relations between children, teachers and material artefacts (Burnett & Bailey, 2014; Dezuanni, 2017).

Reeve and Tseng (2011) described agentic engagement as students' attempt to constructively contribute to the learning session. Agentic engagement occurs when students

> enrich the learning activity (look for an opportunity to make the task more enjoyable), modify it (make a suggestion, change the level of difficulty), personalize what is to be learned (communicate likes and dislikes, generate options), afford themselves greater autonomy (express a preference, offer input), and gain greater access to the means needed for better understanding (solicit resources, request assistance).
>
> (p. 258)

These facets inform our research when we document children's agency in engaging with digital media. They are helpful for gauging children's autonomy and creativity with specific digital spaces, such as, for example, children using the TikTok platform for sharing short videos that they made.

Children's Agency with Digital Media

Over the years, we have been fortunate to work with teachers whose interest in 'New Literacies' translated into their pedagogical practice. Our UK colleagues, Professors Guy Merchant and Cathy Burnett, have tirelessly worked on collaborative projects with teachers who were able to combine stringent curriculum demands with creative projects (Burnett & Merchant, 2014). However, it is worth pointing out that many teachers in the UK find such activities challenging, even though they may share the philosophical underpinning of 'New Literacies'. The UK operates a high stakes, high accountability system focused on narrowly defined criteria of success. It follows that most teachers have very little time for dedicating their lessons to children's agentic engagement with media and for tailoring the content to the children's own choices. Even though digital media might enable a creative renewal of classroom practice, they are often perceived as a tool to transform instruction through disrupting existing practices. In our work, the alignment of technologies with established pedagogic practice was seen as a key strength for building on teachers' existing creativity and established professional expertise.

For digital media to work well in classrooms, it is essential to acknowledge the complexity of every classroom. Burnett (2014) describes a study with primary-school teachers who were interested in the implications of media for literacy. Based on her interviews and observations of children's interactions around digital texts, Burnett concludes that the boundaries of classrooms are shifting, both because of the portability of technologies as well as the ideas and perspectives that children bring to the classroom. Classrooms are distinct, fluid spaces but also porous in terms of children's engagement with digital media outside the school. In her review of current practices with digital media in the UK, she argues that recognising the complexity of 'classroom-ness' is a sine qua non for successfully integrating digital media into schools (Burnett, 2016).

In a similar vein, Selwyn (2010) writes about the narrow conceptualisation of the usefulness of digital media in classrooms. Selwyn has conducted several studies in schools where the use of digital media got reduced to the function of information-retrieval or for documenting children's engagement in other activities. Yet, the potential of digital technologies is much wider. Children's engagement with digital games or e-books adds new dimensions to their play and reading: digital media teach them about the organisation of texts and pictures, about the layout of multimedia on screen and its navigation. Engagement with digital media also encourages children to apply artistic and creative thoughts to new artefacts and recognise the craft that goes into making authentic content. One could argue that children's use of digital media is about children making a statement about who they are and how they understand others. Through making short films or posting their selfies, children develop an awareness of their own identity. These are vital process: awareness of self activates the process of self-reflection and ultimately, belonging to others. A wider understanding of digital media and 'New Literacies' implies that their use in schools needs to be broader than a training in technical competency. We are interested in the opportunities for children's active and active engagement with digital media. We frame this agentic engagement in the wider principles of curatorship and creation of content.

Curatorship: A New Literacy Practice

You can think of curatorship as a skill-set that follows on 'curation'. Curatorship subsumes other processes such as collecting, cataloguing, arranging and assembling materials for sharing with others (Potter & McDougall, 2017). These processes unite crucial learning processes such as intrinsic motivation, empowerment and curiosity. Potter's (2012) theory of curatorship describes the literacy practice through which children assemble digital resources to negotiate identities and selves: 'This active curatorship becomes, perhaps, a useful metaphor to describe an emergent literacy practice in new media production' (p. xv).

Others are an engagement with provisionality and collection. The idea that a person can retrieve, collect and share material alongside self-produced work into an intertextual whole is an important one. Sometimes, for children, this involves creative activity, such as collecting a digital scrapbook, editing a short film, making music but it could equally well involve signalling particular provisional likes of particular media and popular culture. The latter is about children's building on their transient affiliations or their funds of knowledge (Merchant, 2005; Parry, 2013). One component of curation is also media production theorised as a craft skill (Cannon, 2018), that brings into play many creative, agentive actions on the world. In sum, curation matters because

> it goes to the heart of how meaning is made between people, between communities, using the many modes of communication in the digital age. It touches on issues of identity and community (because communities also make meaning through curation) as well as safety (because people may not always know the meaning of their curated assemblages or even that they are making them in front of hostile audiences or in unsafe spaces). It involves open, personal, and tacit knowledge about the world and our relationship to it and to one another.
>
> (Potter, 2017, p. 190)

Creation

One first step in the curation process is creation. When children produce their own content, they become the content owners and assume control of their own products. When thinking about children's volitional creation of digital content, it is helpful to consider the so-called '5As of personalisation' – authorship, autonomy, attachment, authenticity and aesthetics – which relate to a set of five agency indices: control, intention, volition, ownership and singularity (Kucirkova, 2017). These agency indices guide children's actions, experiences and learning. The 5As can come from the child and be agentic or they can come from the technology provider/publisher and minimise children's agency. To illustrate this difference, let us consider the case of personalised books.

Personalised books are a fast-growing area of children's publishing, with publishers of personalised books reporting record revenues in the past few years. For example, in the UK the publisher Wonderbly sold 132k copies of their personalised book titled *Lost My Name* in the year of its launch and more than three million copies worldwide between 2014 and 2017. Printed and digital books contain different levels, forms and types of personalisation. An analysis of personalisation features in a hundred most popular children's digital books in 2016 revealed that current titles focus on personalisation in three ways: story characteristics, narrative and appearance (Kucirkova, 2018). These three key personalisation possibilities are not fundamentally different from personalisation in children's printed books. Story characteristics (such as the main character's name, story location) can be personalised in several printed titles. For example, with Snowflake Stories, users can, according to the publisher, 'personalize the entire story' with 'Child's name and age written into the story'; and 'Names and roles of cast members integrated into the story'; 'The child's photo for the dedication and a fully personalized cover' www.snowflakestories.com/.

Once parents/guardians personalise the digital template, the final book is a book individualised for their child. The book contains a child's photos, name or favourite toys and thus looks as if it was created by the parent or the child. The adult clicks on 'buy' and the bespoke gift is delivered to their home. The final book is about the child but the child's involvement in its creation was non-existent. We would say that the child's agency in this personalisation process was minimal and that the many learning opportunities associated with the creation process were lost.

This is different with personalised books designed for children's own creation or co-creation of content. For instance, with the Mr Glue Stories app, children can seamlessly and simultaneously change the name of the main story character as they read the story, and this name then automatically appears on all book pages. As for personalising story narrative, we can think of parallels with the Choose Your Own Adventure printed books by R. A. Montgomery, which offer children a choice of various story endings. While in the printed book children are guided to different page numbers depending on which ending they choose for their adventure, in the digital book (e.g. *Little Red Riding Hood* by Nosy Crow), they can simply tap on different hotspots.

With printed books, children can add their own drawings, scribbles and writings; they can tear or curl individual pages or even pierce holes into the books. With digital books, such external changes wouldn't be possible without breaking the device but there are other possibilities, such as adding children's own digital drawings, their own pictures, music sounds and e-stickers

Table 5.1 The creation process and some suggested questions for ensuring children's agency, adapted from Kucirkova, 2017

Elements of personalisation	Agency attributes	Questions
Authorship	Volition = capability of conscious choice and decision	To what extent is the content based on children's own imagination?
Autonomy	Control = power to direct or determine	To what extent was the creation of the final product the child's independent work?
Attachment	Ownership = the state of belonging and possessing	Who owns the final product?
Authenticity	Singularity = the quality of being individual, one of a kind	To what extent is children's content genuine and responsive to the child's own situation?
Aesthetics	Intention = an aim that guides action	To what extent does the final product reflect the child's own taste and preference?

to a digital book, which all contribute to the child's sense of agency in communicating the meaning they want. Moreover, children's creative twists add new ideas to the way content is organised, which could involve the layout on the page/screen or activities with it.

Teachers interested in supporting children's agency in making their own content, might find the following questions helpful. Table 5.1 lists the 5As with psychology theories on identity and some suggested questions for interrogating the extent of children's agency in a creation process.

Inspirational Practice

In this section, we provide some examples that illustrate the ways in which teachers can open up dialogue with the children in their classroom and orchestrate creation and curation of new content. It has often been said teachers need to successfully 'orchestrate' the use of digital media in their classrooms – the analogy being that they need to bring particular resources and content into play at key moments in their lessons, or over a sequence of lessons, much like a conductor of an orchestra needs to bring particular instruments into play when the orchestra are performing a piece. This process, which entails emphasising and focusing children's attention on key material, concepts and ideas at particular points, can be facilitated by the ease of use and responsiveness of smartphones and tablets.

Figure 5.1 Drafting Our Story app, step 1

In one of our studies, the 'Remembrance Project' (Kucirkova & Littleton, 2017), we worked with a lower primary school in the south of England. The children who took part in the study were aged between five and nine years and they used iPads in the context of a ten-month long story-writing project on the theme of Remembrance and World War II. The project was undertaken in partnership with the local community group and a technology company called AirWatch Ltd. Our analyses were based upon classroom observations and interviews undertaken by two researchers from The Open University who followed the work of two teachers and their classes of Year 4 children over this period.

The project involved the children, working in groups of four, to devise and conduct audio-recorded interviews with members of the local community who visited the school to share their wartime reminiscences and stories. The children then collaboratively planned, wrote and edited stories based on these accounts and other relevant research and artefacts. The children used an iPad app, called Our Story, to support the collective creation, reviewing, editing and revision of digital multimodal stories on the theme of Remembrance. Each story was shared, discussed and reviewed with other children and class members. TeacherTools, a piece of software developed by the company AirWatch, facilitated secure and efficient storage and transfer of personal digital story content. It also enabled the teachers to plan and pace the processes of sharing and reviewing digital stories.

Figure 5.2 Drafting Our Story app, step 2

One of the key strengths noted by the teachers was the capacity to 'lock' the classes into the approved app, shared content and salient URLs. The teachers recognised that it is vital that children are explicitly taught the skills they need to seek out appropriate, and evaluate the quality of, on-line resources. They also noted that as teachers of young children they had a duty of care and that the 'locking' of content gave them peace of mind, knowing that no inappropriate or sexually explicit content could be accessed in the course of their ongoing classroom activity which involved significant periods of groupwork, as well as whole-class teaching. A number of the children commented that they liked the fact that they didn't have to worry about accessing anything 'nasty'.

The potential to seed resources according to interest and need was seen as being integral to ensuring that the needs of all students, including those with particular needs, are met. Specific apps, such as for example the Our Story app, offered particularly powerful options for children to exercise their agency. The Our Story app was developed at The Open University and is freely available from the App Store. The app can be used for creating multimedia stories of any content or length with texts, images, audio or short videos. In making their

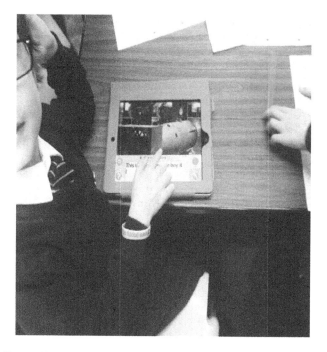

Figure 5.3 Sharing the Our Story app

stories, the children proceeded through the following stages: planning the story, audio-recorded interviews with World War II survivors, drafting and editing the stories with the Our Story app digitally, printing final stories in full colour, sharing the final stories with the interviewee and parents at a school assembly. The pictures in Figures 5.1 to 5.3 capture this process.

Elsewhere projects have considered the nature of children's engagement with digital video, animation and games. While in this project, children's multi-media stories were static, there are other forms of digital media that support children's use of dynamic, playful and productive literacies (Cannon, Potter, & Burn, 2018). In a different kind of iPad project, the children built on their experience of using iPads outside school and made short films (Potter & Bryer, 2016). In this instance, all the craft skills of filmmaking were conflated into the single onscreen space: planning, shooting, editing and exhibiting.

Implications for Future Research

Why is this research important for teachers, and to the children they teach? We believe that this research is important because learners and teachers are working together in a shared space that is itself part of a wider media ecosystem. The world beyond the classroom is media-rich and the skills and dispositions that children exhibit in those spaces will become important facets of their lives through time (Gilje & Groeng, 2015; Potter, 2011). But there are important drivers within the school system which have been a part of our argument in this chapter. We are aware of the performative forces that act on teachers who try to innovate and introduce more digital media into their curriculum offer. However, we also believe that there are important gains to be made from connecting the curriculum to wider, lived experience, to bringing into the world of the classroom some of the practices and texts with which learners are familiar and negotiating with the changing ways in which meaning is made.

Recommendations for Globally Minded Literacy Teachers

What do teachers need to keep in mind as they teach children from diverse world cultures, languages and backgrounds? For the globally minded teacher there is much to offer from an inclusive digital practice. In areas where teachers are working with a diverse range of learners from many cultures, it behoves them to discover more about the rich media lives of their students. If we are being inclusive in our definition of literacy practices then we must also be aware of the diverse global media available to children and families who are able to connect to them. It is easy to assume that the media-world is a homogenous space in which the global north and vast corporations predominate. However, there are vast numbers of resources on many platforms in many languages available to support learning in home languages and construct transmedia texts across different linguistic forms. The examples we shared in this chapter show that touchscreens can be usefully employed for connecting classroom and home lives, adults' and children's perspectives, past and contemporary experiences.

At the same time, teachers may come into contact with children who do not have access to story apps or filmmaking, for whom media is only accessible in the spaces of the classroom, and then only subject to the availability within media-rich schools where teachers are employing an inclusive definition of literacy. Not all children have come from backgrounds in which such resources are commonplace and a globally minded educator can make no assumptions about access, in either direction: media-rich or media-poor. The globally minded literacy teacher will use time and resource to explore these areas further with the children and families with whom they work.

Discussion Questions and Application

We offer four discussion questions for facilitating teachers' reflection on the issues we described in this chapter. We use the example of the Our Story app that children used in the Remembrance Project to illustrate how these questions might inform classroom practice.

1. To what extent is the adult–child relationship in digital media use equitable?

    The Our Story app invites a shared use by adults and children: the user interface is simple and iconic so that even pre-schoolers can use the app on their own. However, to share their stories and to make their stories richer in content, children are invited to collaborate with adults. Often, children's skills in using digital media are more advanced than those of adults and, conversely, adults' traditional literacy skills are mostly more advanced than those of young children. The use of a joint platform, such as a story-making app, can bring the

2. How much is children's meaning-making part of a simple information transaction or a meaningful negotiation between people, artefacts and texts?

    When children make their own multimedia stories with the Our Story app, they are free to choose the content. There are no templates for them to fill out, no digital worksheets to complete. Of course, children make their stories for others to see and their audience awareness guides their aesthetic and content-related choices. They are thus negotiating the meaning in their head and the meaning received by others. They need to make sure that the text or audio they share is comprehensible by others but also that they bring something original and authentic to the story to engage others. This amalgam of literacy events and expectations is part of the 'New Literacies' approach.

3. Are children's choices and volition respected and acted upon in the classroom?

    The Our Story app allows for a flexible combination of text, audio and visual content but that doesn't mean that children's agency is automatically present when using the app. If teachers direct children's story-making with a fixed idea of what the final story should look like, children's agency can be easily marginalised. The process of agentic engagement thus requires an understanding on the part of the teachers of the processes that shape children's motivation and self-concept. Globally minded teachers need to negotiate the difficult balance between preparing children for tests mandated by the curriculum and for long-term goals outside the classroom.

References

Bradbury, A., & Roberts-Holmes, G. (2017). *The Datafication of Primary and Early Years Education.* London: Routledge.

Buckingham, D. (2017). Media Theory 101: Agency. *The Journal of Media Literacy,* 64 (1 & 2), 12–15.

Burn, A., & Richards, C. (Eds). (2014). *Children's Games in the New Media Age: Childlore, Media and the Playground.* Farnham: Ashgate.

Burnett, C. (2014). Investigating pupils' interactions around digital texts: A spatial perspective on the 'classroom-ness' of digital literacy practices in schools. *Educational Review*, 66(2), 192–209.

Burnett, C. (2016). *The Digital Age and Its Implications for Learning and Teaching in the Primary School*. York, UK: The Cambridge Primary Review Trust.

Burnett, C., & Bailey, C. (2014). Concpetualising collaboration in hyrbid sites: Playing Minecraft together and apart in a primary classroom. In C. Burnett, J. Davies, G. Merchant, & J. Rowsell (Eds), *New Literacies Arond the Globe: Policy and Pedagogy* (pp. 50–71). Abingdon, Oxon: Routledge.

Burnett, C., & Merchant, G. (2014). Points of view: Reconceptualising literacies through an exploration of adult and child interactions in a virtual world. *Journal of Research in Reading*, 37(1), 36–50. doi:10.1111/jrir.12006

Cannon, M. (2018). *Digital Media in Education: Teaching, Learning and Literacy Practices with Young Learners*. London: Palgrave.

Cannon, M., Potter, J., & Burn, A. (2018). Dynamic, Playful and Productive Literacies. *Changing English*, 25(2), 180–197. doi:10.1080/1358684X.2018.1452146

Coiro, J., Knobel, M., Lankshear, C., & Leu, D. J. (2010). *The Handbook of Research on New Literacies*. New York: Lawrence Erlbaum Associates.

Conradi, K., Jang, B. G., & McKenna, M. C. (2014). Motivation terminology in reading research: A conceptual review. *Educational Psychology Review*, 26(1), 127–164.

Cope, B., & Kalantzis, M. (Eds.). (2000). *Multiliteracies: Literacy Learning and the Design of Social Futures*. New York: Routledge.

Dezuanni, M. (2017). Agentive realism and media literacy. *The Journal of Media Literacy*, 64(1 & 2), 16–19.

DFE. (2013). *The Primary National Curriculum*. London: HMSO.

Gee, J. P. (2015). The new literacy studies. In J. Rowsell & K. Pahl (Eds), *The Routledge Handbook of Literacy Studies* (pp. 35–48). London: Routledge.

Gilje, Ø., & Groeng, L. M. (2015). The making of a filmmaker: Curating learning identities in early careers. *E-Learning and Digital Media*, 12(2), 212–225. doi:10.1177/2042753014568177

González, N., Moll, L. C., & Amanti, C. (2006). *Funds of Knowledge: Theorizing Practices in Households, Communities, and Classrooms*. London: Routledge.

Green, B. (2002). A literacy project of our own? *English in Australia*, 134, 25–32.

Guernsey, L. (2012). *Screen Time: How Electronic Media from Baby Videos to Educational Software Affects Your Young Child*. New York: Hachette (formerly Basic Books).

Kress, G., & Van Leeuwen, T. (2001). *Multimodal Discourse: The Modes and Media of Contemporary Communication*. London: Arnold.

Kucirkova, N. (2017). How can digital personal (ized) books enrich the language arts curriculum? *The Reading Teacher*, 71(3), 275–284.

Kucirkova, N. (2018). A taxonomy and research framework for personalization in children's literacy apps. *Educational Media International*, 55(3), 255–272.

Kucirkova, N., & Littleton, K. (2017). Developing personalised education for personal mobile technologies with the pluralisation agenda. *Oxford Review of Education*, 43 (3), 276–288.

Marsh, J. (2017). The internet of toys: A posthuman and multimodal analysis of connected play. *Teachers College Record*, 119, 120305.

Merchant, G. (2005). Electric involvement: Identity performance in children's informal digital writing. *Discourse: Studies in the Cultural Politics of Education*, 26(3), 301–314.

Pahl, K., & Rowsell, J. (2012). *Literacy and Education: Understanding the New Literacy Studies in the Classroom* (2nd Edition). London: Sage.

Parry, B. (2013). *Children, Film and Literacy*. London: Palgrave MacMillan.

Potter, J. (2011). New literacies, new practices and learner research: Across the semi-permeable membrane between home and school. *Lifelong Learning in Europe*, XVI(3), 22–35.

Potter, J. (2012). *Digital Media and Learner Identity: The New Curatorship*. New York: Palgrave MacMillan.

Potter, J. (2017). Curation. In K. Peppler (Ed.), *The SAGE Encyclopedia of Out-of-School Learning* (pp. 189–191). Thousand Oaks, CA: Sage.

Potter, J., & Bryer, T. (2016). 'Finger flowment' and moving image language: Learning filmmaking with tablet devices. In B. Parry, C. Burnett, & G. Merchant (Eds.), *Literacy, Media, Technology: Past, Present and Future* (pp. 111–128). London: Bloomsbury.

Potter, J., & McDougall, J. (2017). *Digital Media, Culture and Education: Theorising Third Space Literacies*. London: Palgrave Macmillan.

Reeve, J., & Tseng, C.-M. (2011). Agency as a fourth aspect of students' engagement during learning activities. *Contemporary Educational Psychology*, 36(4), 257–267.

Selwyn, N. (2010). *Schools and Schooling in the Digital Age: A Critical Analysis*. London: Routledge.

Snow, C. E., & Dickinson, D. K. (1991). Skills that aren't basic in a new conception of literacy. In E. M. Jennings & A.C. Purves (Eds.) *Literate Systems and Individual Lives. Perspectives on Literacy and Schooling* (pp. 179–191). Albany, NY: State University of New York Press.

Street, B. (2003). What's 'new' in new literacy studies? Critical approaches to literacy in theory and practice. *Current Issues in Comparative Education*, 5(2), 77–91.

Chapter 6

Improving Early Grade Literacy
Implementation of Mother Tongue Instruction Policy in Kenya

Evelyn Jepkemei

Summary of Chapter

- The language of instruction in an education system by and large affects the coherence of the curriculum and determines the quality of education.
- The evolution of language of instruction policy in Kenya has had a tumultuous journey, and it is virtually impossible to discuss the language and instruction without situating it in history.
- The language of instruction in early grades in Kenya is an issue that evokes passionate debate but remains unresolved.
- Policy makers and research should focus on how to resolving issues and operationalize policies relating to language of instruction.

Vignette

Mumbua was in school to coach a teacher who is teaching English to first graders. Since it was the beginning of the year, the first graders have been in school for less than two months. Although the national policy guidelines provide for teaching mother tongue, the same policy states that English must be taught in English. In class, some of the children were experiencing schooling for the first time having skipped pre-school. The teacher starts her class with teaching sounds, gives the children instruction and asks a few questions. The children are silent and their eyes reflect confusion and anxiety. The coach notices the confusion and asks the teacher quietly if all the children understand English, The teacher states that some understand very little English and the majority do not. The coach asks the teacher to teach the children in mother tongue. Suddenly the class is lively, children are raising hands and are competing to answer questions. The coach helps the teacher to help explain simple instructions in English using mother tongue. The teacher says to the children, "stand up". The children stare at her and at the coach. Next, the teacher says *"ukilai"* and all the children stand up. Then she says *"ukilai"* is the mother tongue word for stand up in English. The repeats "stand up" and all the children rise to their feet.

Historical, Cultural, and Political Context

Like in most African communities, communication in traditional Kenyan ethnic groups was typically transacted in narrative form (song, stories, proverbs, etc.) where informal education; often known as indigenous education, was the mode of transferring values and skills to the next generation (Reitmaier, Bidwell & Mardsen, 1990). Through songs, proverbs and other forms of narratives children learned about their family, clan community and leadership and acquired skills necessary to be functional in society.

The coming of missionaries in Kenya disrupted the long tradition of informal education through oral narrative but also introduced language policies that governed formal education. Missionaries introduced formal education, written language and language policy (Mbiti, 1990). Bishop Steere, Reverend Krapf and Father Sacleux were among the first missionaries to introduce colonial education. The issue of language in education became an item of discussion in the United Missionary Conference in Kenya in 1909 where the decision was taken to use of tribal languages (mother tongue) in the first three grades in primary school, and Kiswahili which was used more pervasively than the tribal languages in grades four and five. English was to be used in the rest of the classes up to the university (Gorman, 1974). Mother tongue is community languages spoken by groups of people depending on their ethnic extraction. They are considered markers of identity. There are languages used by larger groups such as Kikuyu, Luhyia, Luo and Kamba and Kalenjin. Examples of minority languages include Ilchamus, Ogiek, Endorois, Njemps, Burji and Gabra. Kiswahili is a Bantu language that borrowed heavily from Arabic and Portuguese from trade interactions along the coast. Kiswahili is more acceptable across different tribal groups because of its ubiquity.

The colonial administration became involved in education and by 1910, 35 schools had been established and run by missions but with support from the government based on a segregationist approach. This segregation led to development of separate educational systems for Europeans, Asians and Africans. According to Corfield (1960), early years' instruction was provided in mother tongue and the main aim was to develop literacy skills for the "natives." Missionaries contributed in developing orthographies for indigenous languages. Kiswahili was appointed the "lingua franca" of the colony. The colony reorganized the education system, which saw the segmenting of education system into primary, intermediate and secondary segments. The goal of the new education system was to ensure African learners were literate after four years of primary education course. Education commission reports that included Beecher's Commission of 1949, Binn's Commission of 1952, and the Drogheda Commission of 1952 recommended teaching of English in lower primary alongside the mother tongue, and called for the dropping of Kiswahili in the curriculum, except in areas where it was spoken as first language. The implementation of this policy took effect in 1953–1955 (Gorman, 1974).

Before Kenya attained independence in 1963, the British colonial power governed Kenya as colony that part of the British Empire. The colonial language policy is defined in two distinct periods: before World War II and after World War II. Before World War II development of language policy included stakeholders that included the colonial government administrators who were particularly focused on controlled teaching of English to the natives to fill low labor positions and the Christian missionaries who whose interest was to spread the gospel using local languages. British settlers did not favor the idea of Europeanization of Africans through teaching of English, for fear that they would reject low cadre wage if they were extensively exposed.

The end of World War II introduced a paradigm shift in colonial language policy. This was the time of active struggle for independence and the colonial government felt the need to develop a westernized segment of the population who would take up the reins of government. This was an important strategy for the British colonial government in ensuring continued protection of its stakes in the seemingly imminent independent Kenya. Language policy in education during this period then elevated English. Local languages, especially Kiswahili, were seen to be instrumental in uniting Kenyans in the violent struggle for independence and it became necessary to discourage their use especially in education. The exclusive use of English was encouraged to create a rift between locals and slow down the rise of nationalist freedom fighter groups.

When Kenya eventually attained independence from colonial rule in 1963, the new government embarked on ensuring the growth and success of the new republic. Several sectors were central to the success of the new government, especially in its effort at Africanization of the economy, and education was relied on to provide the human resource. The Ominde Commission of 1964 was tasked to look into education policy, and language in education was one of the questions addressed by the commission. Kenya is linguistically heterogeneous and in consideration of this fact the commission strongly advocated for the use of English as a language of instruction across the entire education system in spite of Kenyan's desire for a trilingual approach to education. Although the Ominde Commission recommendations contradict the previous systems in de-emphasizing local languages, it was upheld by the new government and the aim was to create an integrated system of education for all Kenyans and abolish racial based education that had been in place formerly. Within three years of independence half of the grade one pupils in Kenya were receiving instruction in English (Ministry of Education, 1966). This was the beginning of the yo-yoing of language policy in education in independent Kenya.

In literate, economically developed societies, the dialect spoken by the members with the most formal education and the highest socioeconomic status tends to achieve the greatest social status. Typically, that dialect becomes the standard for that particular culture, used in writing and in education. Standard dialects also offer a tool through which speakers with different linguistic and social backgrounds can communicate. While there seems to be a general consensus in the role of language in cultural, political and economic advancement, most African countries are unable to select a unique language through which formal business can be conducted. This in part is due to the copiousness of dialects even within one language group. This is abundantly evident in Kenya, a ubiquitously multilingual country. Over the years the debate about language in Kenya has not yielded any favorable development for local languages and instead, Kiswahili which is spoken in East Africa and parts of Central Africa has been advocated for as the compromise language. Article 7 of the Constitution of Kenya (Republic of Kenya, 2010) stipulates that Kiswahili and English are co-official languages. Kiswahili, also, enjoys the status of the national language. Under the same article, the state is required to promote and protect the diversity of language of the people of Kenya and to promote the development and use of indigenous languages, Kenyan Sign Language, braille and other communication formats and technologies accessible to persons with disabilities.

One would expect that the implementation of these constitutional provisions would be smooth and simple. Ogechi (2002) observed that Kenyan speaks at least three languages based on different ethnolinguistic groups. It is estimated that there are between 41 and 61 languages spoken in Kenya (Muaka, 2011). In urban areas, English and Kiswahili are mostly spoken, and in addition there is a complex informal urban slang variety commonly spoken by urban youths called Sheng, with a grammar that is proximate to Kiswahili. From an independent point of view, the actual array of languages spoken in Kenya remains to be established with any degree of accuracy due to the lack of in-depth and systematic studies on languages and their dialects. Education is the first opportunity for language promotion and there have been different policy proposals regarding language in education in Kenya since colonial time.

The Gachathi Commission of 1976 was appointed to review education policy and among its recommendations was emphasis on mother tongue instruction, effectively requiring that the different local languages recognized as mother tongue be used as the language of instruction in lower grades. The commission introduced the concept of the language of the "catchment area" recognizing that Kenyans did not necessarily live in their ancestral land where their mother tongue would be spoken. In such cosmopolitan areas, Kiswahili was recommended for use in place of mother tongue. In a few affluent areas in urban centers, English was recognized as the language of the catchment area and used as the basic language of communication. A blanket mother tongue approach would therefore be defined by using terms such as language of catchment area. This argument by the Gachathi Commission was made from a cultural preservation perspective, the main idea being that to preserve the Kenyan culture local languages must be propagated. Later in 2005, the government through the Sessional Paper no. 1 of 2005 reinforced the aspiration to preserve culture by stating that one of the goals of education in Kenya is to promote respect for and development of Kenya's rich and varied cultures (Republic of Kenya, 2005). This perspective of language in education completely precludes any consideration of the role and practice of language in pedagogy.

Language as a Cultural and Political Medium

Language plays a critical role in facilitating communication and society values language as a medium of cultural expression and group identity. The Africa Union (AU) Agenda 2063 places culture at the heart of the continent's development schema (Africa Union, 2014). The AU Agenda 2063 envisions a continent that is united "where culture will flourish. National languages would be the basis for administration, and there would be a strong work ethic based on merit. Traditional African values of family, community and social cohesion would be firmly entrenched" (p. 19). Adesanmi (2002) observed that growth and development of macro and micro-economics, of cutting-edge technology and industry should be more germane to the continent's linguistic and cultural advancement. Similar sentiments have been expressed by variously, and not least by Lumumba (2018) who argues that "the reason Africa cannot sit at the table of nations as an equal can be attributed to the fact that the linguistic map of Africa is defined by terms such as Anglophone, Francophone …" (p. 8), adding that the identification of Africa by foreign linguistic dominance continues the subjugation of the continent.

The argument that that trifle attention is given to the teaching of African history, cultures and languages in the educational system of many African countries is perhaps as old as the struggle for political independence. In very specific cases, outright hostile treatment of local languages has been documented. For example, Ngugi Wa Thiong'o (1986) painfully narrates an experience he had in primary school:

> … thus one of the most humiliating experiences was to be caught speaking Gikuyu in the vicinity of the school. The culprit was given corporal punishment – three to five strokes of the cane on bare buttocks – or was made to carry a metal plate around the neck with inscriptions such as "I am stupid" or "I am a donkey." Sometimes the culprits were fined money that they could hardly afford.
>
> (p. 11)

Unfortunately Wa Thiong'o's experience is not an isolated case. Paradoxically, local languages is still prohibited in most schools in Kenya today.

The symbiotic relationship between language and education is recognized universally, although in Kenya policy makers and scholars are divided about the teaching of local languages in schools. There are strong sentiments favoring sciences on the one hand and languages are liberal arts on the other. The seesaw of arguments between practical skills and liberal education has had an impact on education policy. Zakaria (2015) in defending a balanced approach to education discusses the value of nonscientific disciplines such as language and anthropology. Educators perceive the argument for purely practical market skills that include technology and engineering as a false dichotomy where a hierarchy is created between science, technology, engineering and math (STEM) on the one hand and arts and culture on the other. Creating, managing and solving underdevelopment is a human cultural concern, and language naturally comes to the fore as it fuels imagination, thereby creating more intellectual creativity, encouraging broader reflection on the future of society. Nowhere has the friction between the need to preserve culture and the value for practical skills been felt more than in language policy in education. Some scholars believe that cultural and linguistic identity is the premise for any form of human development. For example, Lumumba (2018) strongly argues that for Africa to have a coherent cultural agenda that could power her innovation, development, science and technology for the next 50 years, there has to be a radical encouragement of the leadership to pay more attention to the teaching of African languages in the school systems of their respective countries. This sentiment envisages holistic development that involves cultural and economic transformation. This is perhaps the reason language in education will continue to dominate public policy discussions for a long time.

While some scholars and social activists openly denounce English hegemony as a legacy of colonial domination, sections of society have reconciled themselves to the identity of English as the language associated with progressive social status and therefore do not find value in the argument for local languages in education. Others have highlighted technical and logistical challenges militating against building the capacity of local languages in a country that is extensively multilingual. For example, in many language groups there is always a contest between the standard language (or what dialect would be selected for standardization), local dialects and several slangs. Ngugi Wa Thiong'o, who is well known for his influential literary works in English, has opted for Kikuyu, his mother tongue. He avows that by writing in his mother tongue, he is engaging in the struggle to decolonize the mind; and is encouraged by the reception of his novel *Caitani Mutharabaini* (Devil on the Cross) within the Gikuyu community, revitalizing a reading culture that was dying out.

The rise of Sheng (derivative of abbreviations of Swahili and English) slang, which is mainly used by the urban youth is an interesting phenomenon that scholars believe is a reaction to linguistic hegemony and formality (Ogechi, 2005). Sheng sources its lexicon mainly from English and Kiswahili, but also from other Kenyan languages including Kikuyu, Dholuo, Kamba, Kisii or Luhya. Sheng is often seen as an impugnation against the formalization of English and Kiswahili. It flouts the structure and rules of these languages and flourishes on what is regarded as informal and temporary lexicon and structure. These developments have compounded policy formulation pertinent to language and education.

Language in Education: Conflicting Policy Positions and Subsequent Controversy

Where the language discourse has intersected with education, the result is often a blend of international treatises adopted and modified at best, and fought at worst. The discourse and practice of language in education in Kenya have turned language policy into a highly contested process. Local scholars are often on one side of the gamut, local policy makers on the other, and school teachers and students are left in the middle of the debate with the complicated task of making sense of and implementing the policy. In such a scenario, it has been observed that often teachers do what is convenient to them. For example, in Kenya the Ministry of Education has directed that mother tongue be used as language of instruction grades 1 through 3. The Ministry of Education in Sessional Paper No. 1 of 2005 the critical role of the language of instruction especially at the levels when learners acquire basic literacy skills in the broader agenda of providing quality education. Several studies support the use of mother tongue in lower classes (Bunyi, 2012; Gacheche, 2010; Kazima, 2008). Fontem and Oyetade (2005) argue that language of instruction significantly determines not only the quality of content but also level of efficiency during instruction. Thus standards of language proficiency and subsequently overall learning outcomes depend fundamentally on the selection of language of instruction.

The fervent debate about the language of instruction focuses on the policy that official language of instruction in lower grades is mother tongue or the language of the catchment area. In linguistically dissimilar areas, the policy maintains that Kiswahili or the language of "the catchment area" be used as language of instruction. The same policy also designates that English is used as language of instruction in class four upwards. However, there is no clarity on transition strategies nor do teachers and other stakeholders consider language transferability and its benefits to learning. The design of the national syllabus is linear in its approach and although Kiswahili is also taught as a subject, the approaches in teaching both English and Kiswahili are not linked in pedagogy, and the syllabuses encourage teaching the languages completely independent of each other. This practice makes it difficult for policy makers, without backing of robust evidence to convince parents and teachers of the benefits of teaching mother tongue to their children, especially in an environment of extremely competitive and high stakes examinations conducted in English. Despite the immersion approach to teaching of English, literacy outcomes have remained low for a long time in Kenya. Schools have resorted to extra tuition outside designated teaching time, yet it is still possible to find nonreaders in upper grades of primary school. Parents and teachers feel that teaching mother tongue consumes time that should be used to empower learners for exams at the end of eight years. Other stakeholders feel that teaching mother tongue in school confines children to their "tribe" and denies them the "exposure to the world" that comes with speaking English.

The language of instruction policy in Kenya is supported and opposed in equal measure by various stakeholders. From a political point of view, teaching Kiswahili and English provides a platform to unite the country. Scholars, on the other hand, fight for teaching mother tongue, citing evidence that children can learn multiple languages simultaneously, that literacy skills developed in mother tongue are transferable to a second and third language and that there are distinct advantages in teaching children in a language they are proficient in. Arguments for and against mother tongue instruction are made for cultural, political and pedagogical reasons.

Rationale for Mother Tongue as Language of Instruction

The Dakar Framework for Action (UNESCO, 2000) recognizes the need to make education contextually located and locally accessible by adapting primary education to reach ethnic minorities. Learners who are proficient in the language of instruction are more likely to engage meaningfully with content and learn more effectively (Abadzi, 2011). This argument is premised on the observation that people naturally learn best when they are taught in a language they already are proficient in and often this language is mother tongue.

Mother tongue is the language in which children first learn to express their thoughts and establish relationship with their immediate social environment; the learner's language competency in mother tongue will continue to develop even after they have acquired a second and third language. Evidently, the culture of a people is expressed in mother tongue; hence the argument that mother tongue propagates respect for cultural heritage. Abadzi (2011) also strongly argued that mother tongue provides children with a sense of belonging and self-confidence and motivates them to participate in all school activities thereby providing a smooth transition from home to school. Deciding on language of instruction is a critical decision for multilingual countries such as Kenya, and there is evidence that policy formulation often ignores the pragmatic side of implementing language related policies. In rolling out policy its implications for teacher training and deployment should be carefully considered. Frequently, inclusion of mother tongue in education is treated as a political issue and a complex obstacle in education space where "more important problems" need solutions, and as such, mother tongue is overlooked as a facilitative tool for learning (Trudell, 2012). Proponents of use of mother tongue in education present compelling arguments, yet few countries in Africa use local languages in education. Tanzania has managed to use Kiswahili since independence but Zanzibar, the sister island, introduced English as language of instruction in 2015. New research, however, endorses the use of trans-lingual and multilingual approaches for teaching and learning inside the classroom (Lewis, Jones & Baker, 2012). Creese and Blackledge (2010) build on Cummins (2000) "two solitudes" hypothesis to argue for utilization of bilingual instructional strategies where multiple languages are employed side by side. This approach advocates for a consideration of language ecology where language skills develop in an interdependent fashion. This concurrence has already been explored for leverage in improving literacy outcomes (Garcia & Wei, 2014).

In Kenya, by the time a child starts school most are already able to meaningfully communicate in the language they have acquired from primary caregivers in their environment. In rural Kenya, the first language would be mother tongue (tribal language) and Kiswahili in some areas. Piper and Miksic (2011), like other scholars established that Kenya the official language-in-education policy is not implemented in schools. They reported that teachers used mother tongue in some instances, combined with code switching. While the policy directs that mother tongue is used in lower classes, it also recommends whole language approach in upper classes. The whole language approach is considered a child-centered reading instruction that focuses on the constant interaction and frequent exposure to real, vocabulary-rich literature as opposed to phonics approach. The phonics approach is the systematic and explicit instruction of letter-sound correspondence in the effort to help children develop reading competence. Using the phonics approach teachers develop a plan of instruction that includes a carefully selected set of letter-sound relationships that are organized into a logic sequence (Armbruster, Lehr, Osborn, O'Rourke, Beck, Carnine & Simmons, 2001). The whole language approach, on the other hand, requires that teachers carefully organize time and space to allow students to independently and collectively engage in vocabulary and text, at their own speed and often in the own ways (Church, 1996). The whole language approach is based on a separate underlying proficiency model rather than the more efficient common underlying proficiency model. Under the latter model, when two languages are taught simultaneously, efforts are made to ensure that both languages benefit from each other and ensure that a child moves from a more familiar language to one that is less familiar. Most importantly, it recognizes that a speaker's broad linguistic resource and that languages are not insulated opaque entities with distinct margins.

Language of Instruction Policy and Early Grade Literacy in Kenya

Kenya is one of the countries that spends a large portion of its GDP on education. For a long time, there have been concerns about learning outcomes that are evidently incommensurate to the investment made (Glennerster, Kremer, Mbiti & Takavarasha, 2011). Several studies report worrying trends in literacy and numeracy outcomes, particularly in lower grades (Mugo, Kaburu, Limboro & Kimutai, 2011; Piper & Mugenda 2012; Wasanga, Mukhtar & Wambua, 2010). The Primary Math and Reading initiative was developed as a partnership between USAID, Department of International Development (DFID), Government of Kenya and RTI International to mitigate the poor learning outcomes in literacy and numeracy. It was designed as a randomized control trial implemented in 547 schools, inclusive of 299 schools in Nairobi's slum areas. The main components of the Primary Reading and Math initiative were pupils' books for grades 1 and 2 pupils at a 1:1 ratio in both Kiswahili and English, scripted teachers' guides, in-service training for teachers on innovative approaches of teaching reading and instructional support (coaching) from government Curriculum Support Officers (CSOs) or coaches employed by the project. Primary Reading and Math initiative – Rural Expansion was implemented in two rural counties, Machakos and Bungoma, a move that made it possible to include mother tongue instruction as one of the components of the project in addition to four initially tested in Primary Reading and Math initiative. With carefully designed books, and instructional approach, Piper, Zuilkowski and Ong'ele (2016) reported positive impact of Primary Reading and Math initiative on literacy. On mother tongue instruction, they noted,

> … One of the zonal TAC tutors, tasked with training and supporting teachers in mother tongue, was not a native Lubukusu speaker. She had a basic receptive vocabulary but was unable to speak the language. She supported teachers in Kiswahili rather than in Lubukusu but encouraged the teaching of mother tongue lessons. After two visits to a school in the zone led by this TAC tutor, the program staff found that none of the teachers had used the mother tongue materials because of fears that the non-Lubukusu speaking children would not be able to decode the language and that the school lacked mother tongue-speaking teachers. With some encouragement, however, lessons began to be taught in mother tongue. Two other zones resisted teaching in mother tongue, primarily because the subject would not be examined, and Kenya is an exam-driven education system.
>
> (p. 797)

Piper and colleagues (2016) concluded that children's learning outcomes were improved in all the languages taught. Interestingly, the Primary

Reading and Math initiative approach emphasized letters, letter sounds, and decoding. Piper and colleagues found that students who were taught to decode in English or Kiswahili could also decode in mother tongue. They also observed significant variances between the Primary Reading and Math initiative without mother tongue and the Primary Reading and Math initiative with mother tongue in oral reading fluency and reading comprehension. The children in the non-mother tongue Primary Reading and Math initiative performed nominally better in oral reading fluency and reading comprehension skills in the local mother tongue, indicating that regardless of the language taught, children need exposure to explicit instruction in vocabulary.

Piper, Zuilkowski, Kwayumba and Oyanga (2018) emphasized the need for the government to remove ambiguity around mother tongue instruction especially with current focus on improving literacy outcomes. Given the irregular implementation of policy arising out of conflicting policies, resistance from teachers and parents, the Ministry needs to make concrete decisions for language policy in early grades as the foundation of learning.

Teacher preparation featured prominently in the Primary Reading and Math initiative intervention. Through in-service training of teachers, it was possible to empower teachers, even those who are not native speakers of the language to teach mother tongue. Begi (2014) highlights lack of training on mother tongue pedagogy, adding that it is not enough for a teacher to be able to speak the language.

Within the context of the Kenyan linguistic complexity, it is imperative for the policy makers to engage with disparate linguistic groups to explore practicality of implementation of mother tongue instruction in education, and whether mother tongue should be taught as a subject or as a language of instruction. If the choice is made to teach mother tongue as a subject, then more complex and expansive political and cultural engangements are required. It is imperative to provide technical support language groups to create a teaching structure. This will include languages with limted lexicon or no orthography currently developed. Although the Primary Reading and Math initiative is only one medium-scale study carried out in real world settings on mother tongue in Kenya, it is apparent from a literacy instruction point of view as well that designed pupils' books, teacher training and teacher coaching drive learning outcomes in literacy.

The scale-up of the Primary Reading and Math initiative dubbed Tusome (Let's Read) was rolled out in early 2015, and it is only implemented in English and Kiswahili in all public and selected low cost primary schools in Kenya. Results of the external evaluation of Tusome at midline shows significant improvements of literacy in early grades in Kenya. The report shows large effect sizes from baseline to midline ranging from 0.40 to 1.07 for Class 1 and 0.41 to 2.57 for Class 2 (MSI, 2017). If the Ministry of

Education makes a decision to enforce the language of instruction policy as currently formulated, it will need to modify Tusome to include mother tongue materials and training for teachers.

In 2018, Kenya introduced a new curriculum that was piloted in 470 schools. Despite the existing policy in mother tongue instruction in lower grades, mother tongue curriculum was not part of the piloted curriculum. The fact that Mother tongue was ignored in a larger curriculum reform effort points to the paradox of using mother tongue in education. As such there is a dearth of evidence on interactions between mother tongue instruction policy and curriculum content. This curriculum pilot has been scaled up in 2019, and teacher induction programs have excluded mother tongue instruction.

The Complexity of Language, Teacher Preparation and Curriculum

Communities in urban centers and outskirts of urban centers value Kiswahili as a medium of informal communication, and according to Kim and Piper (2018) it is favored instructionally compared with other local languages. While Kiswahili is not the official language of instruction, it is taught as a compulsory subject across the primary and secondary school curriculum. In an environment of high stakes testing, Kiswahili has gained some influence nationally, being the second language after English, and examined as a compulsory subject at the end of both primary and secondary levels of education. Culturally and politically, Kiswahili is often perceived as a language of unity and the second language for children in rural areas. For a large percentage of children in urban and peri-urban areas, Kiswahili and mother tongue are acquired concurrently. Still, it is not surprising to find that a child encounters Kiswahili and English for the first time in school especially those who grow up in relatively monolingual areas.

The terms "mother tongue" and "first language" are sometimes used interchangeably to mean the first language a child acquires. For example, Kiswahili is mother tongue to children born of Swahili parents' lineage and can be traced to any of the Kiswahili dialects along the East African coast and parts of Democratic Republic of Congo. However, many children acquire Kiswahili as their first language, especially in urban areas even though it is not their ancestral language. The child's first language, whether it is the mother tongue or not, is the most important to consider for purposes of learning. Githinji (2014) surveyed schools in Nyeri area of Central Kenya and found that most schools preferred English as the language of instruction, citing that in some cases, code switching and code mixing was used in class where learners were not adequately proficient for exclusive english instruction. In a surprise finding, Kiswahili and Kikuyu were the least preferred. Also Khejeri (2014) revealed that in Hamisi in

Western Kenya, English and Kiswahili were used for instruction but mother tongue was least preferred for instruction. Mose (2016) found similar results in Nyanza region. These studies reveal a chasm between policy directing schools to teach mother tongue and use it as the Language of Instruction and practice at school level where teachers ignore the policy.

Although the Ministry of Education policy on language of instruction states that mother tongue be used in grades one to three, research shows that this policy is not implemented (Begi 2014; Mbaabu 1996; Mose 2016). Where mother tongue is taught, often it is taught as a language and not as the Language of Instruction. This in part results from lack of materials. All educational materials are written in English, save for Kiswahili. It is hard to imagine how teachers would be expected to use English materials to conduct instruction in mother tongue.

Some scholars have expressed reservations about the lexical capacity of indigenous languages to address the demands of modern science and technology and cover the spectrum of classroom instruction. Critics also observe that local languages' limited geographical coverage, absence of standardized formats and orthography of most of them and the existence of dialects impede efforts to use local languages in education (Batibo 2009). Most of the Kenyan languages do not have any written material, leaving KICD to publish any mother tongue books as the publisher of the last resort, an arrangement that has failed to popularize mother tongue due to inadequate materials.

Some languages do not have a standardized format and have no orthography. They also have a limited number of speakers, and are less used in the media or in literature writing. Standardization, intended to make a suitable language of instruction, requires codifying of a language group to minimize variations to enable the standardized format to be adapted to a wide range of formal functions. Historically, language used in education has been standardized. Formal Kiswahili, for example, is derived from a Zanzibari dialect, Kiunguja (Polomé, 1983). This dialect was the basis for standardization of Kiswahili and catalyzed utilization of Kiswahili as a formal language and its use in literature, education and government surged.

It is important that language is accepted by users and perceived as worth the effort to acquire it and ought to be teachable to on obligatory standard with sufficient resources for its dissemination. In Kenya currently Kiswahili and English (L1 and second language) meet these criteria better than any mother tongue (Gacheche 2010). Conversely, it can also be argued that use of language (such as making Kiswahili the national language) transposes it to a position to satisfy the laid down criteria, thus enhancing its capacity in terms of literary works and breadth of use.

In considering Kenya's linguistic heterogeneity even in areas where one language group is dominant, it quickly becomes apparent how large language configurations mask significant variances within and between dialects in one language group. Besides, there are children in schools in areas outside their ancestral homes where their language is spoken. Implementing the language policy for lower grades in Kenya runs the risk of excluding such children. When missionaries selected the Nandi dialect for bible translation, it didn't take long before differences arose that forced a hybrid of language that catered for most dialects in the Kalenjin group (Gacheche 2010). Such dynamics are sure to be experienced in the quest to use mother tongue in instruction. For example, a language group such as Kalenjin has more than seven distinct dialects with dissimilar vocabulary and sometimes varying orthographies.

Further complicating matters, the approaches to teacher deployment by the Teachers Service Commission are inconsistent with language policies. Recently, the commission has emphasized "delocalization" of teachers, where teachers are deployed to teach in schools away from their home areas. Although Piper, Zuilkowski, Kwayumba and Oyanga (2018) noted that it is sometimes possible to teach mother tongue even in areas where teachers are not native speakers of the language, such a decision definitely increases the likelihood of teachers' inability to speak the catchment area of their school and thus inability or unwillingness to teach mother tongue.

Pre-service training is an important aspect of shaping teachers' approaches to pedagogy. The current teacher training curriculum does not include mother tongue as part of a systematic preparation for teaching mother tongue. Current pre-service teacher training in Kenya provides teachers content knowledge of the curriculum excluding mother tongue (Bunyi, 2005) but does not prepare them to work in a culturally and linguistically diverse classroom. Student teachers are equipped to teach in English and in Kiswahili, therefore enhancing their confidence when handling these languages in the classroom. Contrariwise, without support books and lack of preparation through training, it is difficult to see how teachers can be incentivized to teach mother tongue. Moreover, teachers' in-service training system is currently unsystematic and unregulated. It is a positive that the in-service training participation rate among school professionals has increased with introduction of Tusome early grade reading program. However, government driven in-service training to cover mother tongue is uncertain and fragmented. A further issue is the implementation of the knowledge and competence acquired through in-service training. The incentive of Kenyan teachers to adopt the most current educational research is relatively low. Curriculum Support Officers are expected to support teachers, but evidence shows that CSOs lack basic skills and facilities to access schools and support teachers.

Any successful instruction must have enough materials to support curriculum delivery. In 2002 when the curriculum was revised, the syllabuses were written in English and virtually all the documentation needed by the ministry from the teachers would be exclusively in English. The Kenya Publishers Association produces the bulk of school books but does not find books on mother tongue profitable. Although the Kenya Institute of Curriculum Development can make materials in mother tongue, schools have low demand for them because of the focus on examination classes from grades 6–8. The list of approved books to schools supplied by the government also does not have any titles in mother tongue and therefore schools cannot use the Free Primary Education Funds to purchase any available titles in mother tongue. Teachers have argued that there aren't sufficient incentives to teach mother tongue as a subject or use it as a Language of Instruction since there are insufficient materials. Moreover, most parents and teachers have negative attitudes towards teaching mother tongue in schools. According to Khejeri (2014), teachers and parents saw more disadvantages than advantages in teaching mother tongue in schools. Also, Manyonyi, Mbori and Okwako (2016), in a study in schools in Bungoma South Sub County, indicated that teachers believed that mother tongue added no value to the academic performance of learners.

Implications for Research

Although copious research is cited in discussion relating to language in education, unfortunately most of the research has not taken into consideration all the factors relevant in operationalizing language policy in education in Kenya. In applying results of rigorous studies, to other educational contexts, even within the same country there is need to consider contextual factors. Questions that may be necessary for further research might include benefits of mother tongue language instruction; the impact of settings for language instruction for a population; areas of emphasis for promoting language for culture and development of proficiency in literacy.

Discussion Questions and Application

For language in education policies to achieve the desired results in multilingual/multi-ethnic communities such as Kenya, they should be based on sound theoretical constructs that take the sociolinguistic realities of such communities into account and see multi-ethnic/multilingual societies that are diverse. Teachers who have ethnically different backgrounds from the areas in which they teach may not be able to speak the dominant mother tongue at school, unless the primary language is English or Kiswahili. Teachers and students might establish different approaches to communicate with their friends from different linguistic or ethnic groups. In such a situation, teachers might want to consider some questions for innovative thinking. These questions might include

1. Which specific mother tongues can be taught in multilingual contexts, where multiple languages are spoken?
2. What forms of support are in place to ensure that mother tongue instruction is effective and instruction is balanced with instruction in English or Kiswahili?
3. How do parents view the use of the mother tongue languages selected for instruction? Do they support learning of their children in the mother tongue and English of Kiswahili?
4. What level of proficiency should teachers achieve in the languages to be taught, and how can teachers' language proficiency be developed and supported?
5. How can ICT innovations be utilized teach language in multilingual environments where children are learning multiple languages simultaneously?

Conclusion

There is generally consensus on the potential benefits of a mother tongue-based instruction in improving learning outcomes, and on the need for an L1-based system that provides a link to development of literacy in multiple languages. Language in education policy in Kenya has shifted back and forth on the issue of mother tongue since colonial times. The case of mother tongue instruction seems to be lost in politically and culturally directed discourse. Often, the educational role of mother tongue is completely ignored. Without doubt, Primary Reading and Math initiative provided evidence on how mother tongue affects learning outcomes. It is also clear that there is inadequate research in appraising benefits of mother tongue especially in the linguistically complex environment such as Kenya. While the results from Primary Reading and Math initiative are enlightening there is need for more research to boost language policy positions enacted by government. Evidenced based results provide a better platform for policy engagement and a shift from politically or culturally driven conversation. The role of local languages in propagating culture and nationhood cannot be overstated. In discussing learning outcomes in literacy, the science of language learning is important engagement about how language is used in education. Considering the potential cost of implementing mother tongue, it is significant for policy makers to be convinced of the importance of making mother tongue the Language of Instruction in early grades in Kenya.

The challenges discussed related to teacher preparation, instructional materials and policy conflicts threaten any potential benefits of implementing the mother tongue policy in Kenya. Other challenges include selection, standardization and building the capacity of languages to address education demands. Considering Kenya's linguistic complexity, the Ministry of

Education will need to weigh the cost of effectively implementing a mother tongue instruction policy. Moreover, engaging with other actors such as county governments, representatives of language speakers is necessary in building consensus among parents, teachers and community leaders.

References

Abadzi, H. (2011). *Reading fluency measurements in EFA FTI partner countries: Outcomes and improvement prospects*. Washington, DC: World Bank.

Adesanmi, P. (2002). Europhonism, universities and other stories: How to speak for the future of African literatures. In Toyin Falola and Barbara Harlow (Eds.). *Palavers of African literature: Essays in honor of Bernth Lindfors* (Vol. 1, pp. 105–136). Trenton, NJ: Africa World Press.

Africa Union. (2014). *Agenda 2063: The Africa we want*. Addis Ababa: AU.

Armbruster, B. B., Lehr, F., Osborn, J., O'Rourke, R., Beck, I., Carnine, D., & Simmons, D. (2001). *Put reading first*. Washington, DC: National Institute for Literacy.

Batibo, H. (2009). The inter-cultural dimension in the use of language of wider communication by minority language speakers. *Journal of Multicultural Discourses*, 4(2), 89–102.

Begi, N. (2014). Use of mother tongue as a language of instruction in early years of school to preserve the Kenyan culture. *Journal of Education Practice*, 5(3), 37–49.

Bunyi, G. (2005). Language classroom practices in Kenya. *Decolonisation, Globalisation: Language-in-education Policy and Practice*, 131–152.

Bunyi, G. (2012). *Real options for literacy policy and practice in Kenya*. Paris: UNESCO.

Church, S. (1996). *The future of whole language: reconstruction or self-destruction?* Portsmouth, NH: Heinemann.

Corfield, F. D. (1960). *Historical survey of origins and growth of Mau Mau*. London: Her Majesty's Stationery Office.

Creese, A., & Blackledge, A. (2010). Translanguaging in the bilingual classroom: A pedagogy for learning and teaching? *The Modern Language Journal*, 94(1), 103–115.

Cummins, J. (2000). *Language, power and pedagogy: Bilingual children in crossfire* (Vol. 23). C. Baker, & N. Hornberger (Eds.). New York: Cromwell Press.

Fontem, A. N., & Oyetade, S. O. (2005). Declining Anglophone English language proficiency in Cameroon: What factors should be considered. In E. M. Chia, I. Kashim, H. Tala, & K. Jick (Eds.). *Globalization and the African Experience: Implications for language literature and education* (pp. 64–87). Accra: ANUCAM.

Gacheche, K. (2010). Challenges in implementing a mother tongue based language in education policy: Policy and practice in Kenya. *POLIS Journal*, 4 (Winter), 1–45.

Garcia, O., & Wei, L. (2014). Translanguaging and education. In O. Garcia, & L. Wei (Eds.), *Translanguaging: Language, bilingualism and education* (pp. 63–77) London: Palgrave Macmillan.

Githinji, W. (2014). A situational analysis of language of instruction in lower primary school in Nyeri County, Kenya. Nairobi: Unpublished PhD Thesis Kenyatta University.

Glennerster, R., Kremer, M., Mbiti, I., & Takavarasha, K. (2011). Access and quality in the Kenyan education system: A review of the progress, challenges and potential. *EJISDC, 526*, 397–446.

Gorman, T. P. (1974). The development of language policy in Kenya with particular reference to education system. In W. H. Whiteley (Ed.). *Language in Kenya* (pp. 397–446). Nairobi: Oxford University Press.

Kazima, M. (2008). Mother tongue policies and mathematical terminology in the teaching of mathematics. *Pythagoras, 67*, 56–63.

Khejeri, M. (2014). Teachers' attitudes towards the use of mother tongue as a language of instruction in lower primary schools in Hamisi District, Kenya. *International Journal of Humanities and Social Sciences, 4*(1), 75–85.

Kim, Y. G., & Piper, B. (2018). Cross-language transfer of reading skills: An empirical investigation of bidirectionality and the influence of instructional environments. *Reading and Writing*, 1–33. 10.1007/s11145-018-9889-7

Lewis, G., Jones, B., & Baker, C. (2012). Translanguaging: Developing its conceptualization and contextualization. *Education Research and Evaluation, 18*(7), 655–670. 10.1080/13803611.2012.718490

Lumumba, P. (2018, 08). The vision of our founding fathers. *Keynote speech given in Africa conference on religious liberty*. Kigali, Rwanda: All Africa Religious Liberty Congress.

Management Systems International. (2017). *TUSOME external evaluation – Midline report*. Nairobi: Management Systems International.

Manyonyi, J., Mbori, B., & Okwako, E. (2016). Attitude of teachers towards use of mother tongue as medium of instruction in lower primary. *International Journal of Education and Research, 4*(8), 315–334.

Mbaabu, I. (1996). *Language policy in East Africa: A dependency theory perspective*. Nairobi: Education Research and Publications.

Mbiti, J. S. (1990). *African religions and philosophy*. Nairobi: Heinemann.

Ministry of Education. (1966). *Triennial survey report*. Nairobi: Her Majesty's Stationery.

Mose, P. N. (2016). Bilingualizing linguistically homogeneous classrooms in Kenya: Implications on policy, second language learning, and literacy. *International Journal of Bilingual Education and Bilingualism*, 1–14. 10.1080/13670050.2016.1268567

Muaka, L. (2011). Language perceptions and identity among Kenyan speakers. In *Selected proceeding of the 40th Annual Conference on African Linguistics* (pp. 217–230). Somerville, MA: Proceedings Project.

Mugo, J., Kaburu, A., Limboro, C., & Kimutai, A. (2011). *Are our children learning? Annual learning assessment report*. Nairobi: UWEZO. Retrieved from www.uwezo.net/wpcontent/uploads/2012/08/KE_2011_AnnualAssessmentReport.pdf

Ogechi, N. O. (2005). On lexicalization in Shen. *Nordic Journal of African Studies, 14*(3), 334–355. Retrieved from https://njas.fi/njas/article/view/258/243

Ogechi, N. O., & Bosire-Ogechi, E. (2002). Educational publishing in African languages, with a focus on Swahili in Kenya. *Nordic Journal of African Studies, 11*(2), 168–184. Retrieved from https://njas.fi/njas/article/view/353

Piper, B., & Miksic, E. (2011). Mother tongue and reading: Using early grade reading assessments to investigate language-of-instruction policy in East Africa. In A. Gove, & A. Wetterberg (Eds.), *Early grade reading assessment: Application and intervention to improve basic literacy* (pp. 139–182). Research Triangle Park, NC: RTI Press. Retrieved from www.rti.org/pubs/bk-0007-1109- wetterberg.pdf

Piper, B., & Mugenda, A. (2012). *The primary math and reading (Primary reading and math initiative) Initiative: Baseline report. Prepared for USAID/Kenya under the education data for decision making (EdData II) project, task order no. AID-623-M-11-00001 (RTI Task 13).* Research Triangle Park, NC: RTI International. Retrieved from http://pdf.usaid.gov/pdf_docs/pa00hx75.pdf

Piper, B., Zuilkowski, S. S., Kwayumba, D., & Oyanga, A. (2018). Examining the secondary effects of mother-tongue literacy instruction in Kenya: Impacts on student learning in English, Kiswahili, and mathematics. *International Journal of Education Development, 59,* 110–127.

Piper, B., Zuilkowski, S. S., & Ong'ele, S. (2016). Implementing mother tongue instruction in the real world. *Comparative Education Review, 60*(4), 776–807. 10.1086/688493

Polomé, E. C. (1983). Standardization of Swahili and modernization of Swahili vocabulary. *Language Reform: History and Future, 3,* 53–57.

Reitmaier, T., Bidwell, N. J., & Mardsen, G. (1990). Situating digital storytelling within African communities. *International Journal of Human-Computer Studies, 6*(10), 658–668.

Republic of Kenya. (2005). *A policy framework for education, training and research.* Nairobi: Government Printer.

Republic of Kenya. (2010). *The constitution.* Nairobi: Government Printer.

Trudell, B. (2012). Of gateways and gatekeepers: Language, education and mobility in francophone Africa. *International Journal of Education Development, 32*(3), 368–375.

UNESCO. (2000). Dakar framework for action – education for ALL: Meeting our collective commitments. In *World Education Forum* (pp. 26–28). Paris: UNESCO.

Wa Thiongo, N. (1986). *Decolonising the mind.* Nairobi: Heinemann.

Wasanga, P., Mukhtar, A. O., & Wambua, R. (2010). *Report on monitoring of learner achievement for class 3 in literacy and numeracy.* Nairobi: KNEC.

Zakaria, F. (2015). *In defense of a liberal education.* New York: WW Norton & Company.

Part II

Intermediate to Adolescent Literacy

Chapter 7

Critical Literacy in South Africa
Tracking the Chameleon

Ana Ferreira

Summary of Chapter

- The development of the field of critical literacy in South Africa has been shaped both by the changing political terrain as well as by a series of curriculum changes.
- Critical literacy teaching materials for the classroom can be valuable not only as a teaching resource but as a scaffold for assisting in-service teachers to develop the requisite critical orientation to texts; and in assisting pre-service teachers to develop critical literacy practices through materials design.
- Using a critical literacy orientation to curriculum design, it is possible to use the discursively constructed classroom space for productive, if unpredictable, work across difference.

Vignette

Kelsey: But you're not necessarily streetwise just because of the place that you live in. I mean I live in like – I mean most of us live in South Africa and most of the girls that come to [school name] come from very good families and they kind of live in their own bubble. I mean, um –

Multiple spontaneous comments [unclear], challenging Kelsey.

Kate: But Kelsey, don't you think – don't you think –
Kelsey: You live in a protected area –
Teacher: But you're always aware, aren't you?
Kelsey: … you're not exposed to half of the bad things that are … *[Ongoing buzz of responses.]* Not to the same extent …

Sonia: Ja, [speaking loudly over the buzz] we don't have any reason to be as scared as a person living in Soweto and like …

Student: But you're not living in Soweto.

Kate: I just prefer to be aware, like streetwise, than live in a kind of like safe community and be completely ignorant.

[…]

Bontle: … what Kate said about people in Soweto being more in danger or whatever. I feel like – I only started living in the suburbs like last year, okay, so my whole life I grew up in Tembisa. So all I'm saying is that I felt more at home in – … Oh, I feel that it's so much more homely than, um than Sandton [with dismissive hand gesture]. Because I think that the only reason you guys might feel that you are in danger is because you don't know these people. Um, it's how the people in Salem were to like the natives, like – [Lesego: Salem?] … Ja, that whole witch hunt that happened. Ja, I think that's just fear of the unknown that makes you think that you are in danger. Like all those people in the township,[1] like I might not know them but when I like walk there I'm like 'hi', you know. It's like they're family, that's how it is.

A conversation in an English/Language Arts classroom, Grade 11.

Historical, Cultural and Political Context

Historical Context and Philosophical Underpinnings

Critical literacy is a chameleon literacy. Its appearance shifts and shimmies in response to the changing sociopolitical terrain in which it is operating. If language is a social practice, rather than an autonomous set of portable skills, then the very shape of language, its contours, meanings and actions, is embedded in society. But it goes further than that. The late Ursula Le Guin, science fiction author extraordinaire, wrote a novel entitled *The Dispossessed* (1974). It was set on an earth-like planet whose local language had no possessives. And whose society had no concept of ownership. As a younger reader, this blew my mind. What I took from it was a growing realisation of how language *actively constructs* meaning. Without possessive forms in their language (e.g. my, yours, to own), the people in Le Guin's fictional society were unable to entertain ideas of ownership or possession.

Without sliding into the murky waters of linguistic determinism, what might this mean for the languages we use, the ways in which we use them and the possibilities they hold for constructing – or ruling out – particular ways of seeing the world, ourselves and others?

Brazilian educator Paolo Freire spoke of how reading the word was a form of reading the world (Freire & Macedo 1987). He believed that for poor communities, becoming literate was a form of empowerment not only because illiteracy exacerbated their marginalisation, but because literacy enabled them to begin challenging literacy forms and practices that contributed to their oppression (Freire 1970). His ideas were foundational to the critical pedagogy movement, which views teaching as an inherently political act, and prioritises the use of education for social justice. Taking a more formal linguistic approach, the work of Norman Fairclough uses critical discourse analysis to investigate how societal power relations are established and reinforced through language use (Fairclough 1989, 1995). These influential thinkers were themselves influenced by the ideas of philosophers such as Marx, Gramsci, Althusser, Fanon and Foucault, and their own work has been taken up in various ways in different contexts. So, critical literacy itself is an 'evolving discourse in its dynamic relations with other discourses and practices' (Morgan 1997, p. 6). Janks maintains that

> [c]ritical literacy resists definition because power manifests itself differently in different contexts and at different historical moments; it is affected by changing technologies and different conditions of possibility. What remains constant, however, is its social justice agenda and its commitment to social action, however small it be, that makes a difference.
>
> (2010, p. 40)

In South Africa, the work done under the banner of critical literacy education has largely drawn on both the emancipatory and the linguistic orientations to language and power, and a strong focus has been on the critical analysis of texts. Gunther Kress's (Kress & Van Leeuwen 1996, 2001) work on multimodality, and the New London Group's (1996; Cope & Kalantzis 2000) framework for a multiliteracies pedagogy have been influential in expanding the notion of what counts as 'text' and 'language' and thus shifting the analysis of power beyond the linguistic mode to consider other semiotic modes of meaning making.

So, what of this chameleon literacy in the South African context?

South Africa emerged from centuries of racial and ethnic oppression – first colonialism and then apartheid – into full democracy in 1994, a mere 25 years ago. It is therefore unsurprising that earliest critical literacy work in South Africa, emerging in the late 1980s under the repressive apartheid regime, is tied to emancipatory education. The provision of schooling was racially segregated and highly unequal, not only in terms of the quality of the respective curricula but also in terms of material resources. The battle lines between the oppressor and the oppressed were thus so starkly drawn that the mandate for social justice educators was clear. But initially this was tricky work.

The state's official position was that education was ideologically neutral, and that there should be no engagement with political or social issues in the classroom – 'no sex, politics or religion' (Janks 1990). The literature curriculum for white students, for example, was underpinned by a depoliticised, cultural aesthetic form of reading and analysis which highlighted character and universal themes; while for black students the prescribed literature was required to 'in no way relate to the political and social interests of aspirations of the students' (Janks 1990, p. 247). People's English in the late 1980s called for the politicisation of the English syllabus by defining language competence as, among other things, the ability to: 'hear what is said and what is hidden'; 'to explore relationships, personal, structural and political'; and 'to understand the relationship between language and power' (Janks 1992, pp. 64–65). And thus, in 1992, when outlining the work she was undertaking with regard to the development of critical language awareness (CLA) teaching materials for the classroom, Janks stated that 'the choice of CLA in South Africa is a political commitment to education for democracy' (p. 69). At the time, the only spaces for experimenting with alternative (read: counter-hegemonic) teaching materials were in the independent education sector and it was in these spaces that Janks trialled what she saw as teaching materials that would be available for use under the new political dispensation.

It is well nigh impossible to overstate Janks's contribution to the field of critical literacy in South Africa. Her work with the development of critical literacy teaching materials for the classroom demonstrates her ability to make complex theory accessible to students; and a great deal of her writing theorises classroom practice for critical literacy education. Her synthesis model for critical literacy (Janks 2000) has been widely taken up, locally and internationally. Tracking the subject matter of her publications over the years provides a sense of precisely the shifting sociopolitical terrain with which a critical social literacy should engage, and hints at the workings of a chameleon literacy, analysing discourses that deal with such issues as the status of domestic workers in democratic South Africa, the relevance of the TRC's findings for the teaching of critical literacy, xenophobia and constructions of foreign African nationals as other, and, more recently, engaging with aspects of the #FeesMustFall movement.

Shortly after independence and the move to democracy in 1994, curriculum reform began. Critical literacy was made visible and explicit in the new outcomes based education curriculum (OBE), known as Curriculum 2005, in the second of seven outcomes for languages, reading: 'Learners show critical awareness of language usage' (DoE 1997). This curriculum was seen as making a significant break with the past and providing meaningful opportunities for the transformation of language education (Prinsloo & Janks 2002). It was at this point that critical literacy became a distinct feature of teacher education since it was not enough simply to insert the phrase into the curriculum – teachers needed to develop knowledge and skills in the area of critical literacy. In particular, work was done around how to move pre-service teachers beyond basic text decoding questions or 'comprehensions' to the kinds of questions that interrogated the text, taking it apart in order to understand its construction and purpose, and the way in which it was positioning the reader – in short, how language was used to maintain or reinforce particular power relations (Granville 1996, 2001). Even at this early stage of critical literacy education work, it was recognised that identity investments were often at stake when tackling the kinds of thorny issues that needed critical deconstruction. Threats to identity in the form of resistance therefore needed to be confronted both at the level of the school learner (Janks 2001b; McKinney 2004), as well as at the level of the trainee teacher (Granville 1997).

In the decade or so after the demise of apartheid, a thought-provoking debate arose about what critical literacy might – or should – look like in South Africa now that there was a democratically-elected government in power and a new, state-of-the-art constitution (Constitution of the Republic of South Africa, 1996) in place in which the rights of all were enshrined in various ways. To what extent was a critical orientation to language and literacy – and thus inevitably the social – desirable in the context of a nascent democracy where nation building and social cohesion seemed to be the more important priorities? McKinney (2004), for example, maintained that her university undergraduate students felt 'stranded in critique' when required to engage with the recent apartheid past through their literary setworks. She argued, drawing on Kress (2000), that during this relatively unstable period of post-apartheid transition, a forward-looking, solutions-orientated approach might be more productive, suggesting that the emphasis of critical literacy work should shift 'from critique to that of design' (2004, p. 65). Janks (1996), however, conceded that while the need for critical literacy might be less obvious in a post-apartheid South Africa, that it was a country with its values in transition; not only were there multiple discourses in circulation, but many of these demonstrated a continuity with apartheid ways of thinking and required ongoing challenging. The different perspectives are thought-provoking but ultimately all parties (Janks 1996, 2012; Kress 2000; McKinney 2004) argue for the importance of the interrelationship of critique and (re)design – since redesign was inevitably preceded and informed by critique – and thus it seems to come down to a matter of emphasis and nuance in relation to the priorities at hand.

It was during this phase that Janks developed her synthesis model of critical literacy, bringing together four different orientations to critical literacy – power, access, diversity and design – and foregrounding their need to operate inter-dependently in order to ensure that the aims of both deconstruction and reconstruction are met (2000). This model emerged in response to the need for a more complex, multi-dimensional vision of social justice than that needed under apartheid. And it is also relevant that Janks began to talk about power as being more than merely 'a negative force which constructed and maintained relations of domination by protecting the interests of a small white minority' (2000, p. 175), and thus also potentially available to be used for transformative purposes.

The growing awareness of the relationship between language and power in society at large was further reinforced by the official report produced by South Africa's Truth and Reconciliation Commission (TRC) (1998). The TRC documents demonstrated a sophisticated understanding of language and power, in particular the power of language to produce certain effects, such as construct identities, and produce social action (Janks 2000). This was seen as evidence of its awareness, for example in its awareness of the discur-sive power of language: 'Language as discourse and rhetoric does things: it constructs social categories, it gives orders, it persuades us … It moves people against other people' (TRC 7: 124, 294).

Conversely, while Curriculum 2005 raised the profile of 'critical language awareness', it nevertheless demonstrated a superficial understanding of lan-guage and power, limiting it to features of persuasion and manipulation rather than seeing language as inherently ideological (Janks 2001a). How-ever, instead of strengthening the presence of critical literacy, the second wave of curriculum change further diluted it. Initially it took an educator trained in critical literacy to understand and enact what was meant by CLA. In the new (R)NCS curriculum, rolled out in 2002, it now took a canny educator with a trained gaze to spot and exploit the spaces or 'hooks' in the curriculum on which critical literacy work could be hung. Certainly, Govender's (2011) work on the analysis of curriculum-compliant school textbooks endorsed by the education department shows that not only do these textbooks demonstrate virtually no significant engagement with CLA but they also demonstrate an insensitivity to diversity, and engage in stereo-typing and other problematic forms of representation.

In the most recent – and most prescriptive – iteration of the curriculum, unleashed in 2012 and known as the CAPS curriculum (from Curriculum Assessment Policy Statements), the emphasis on broad coverage and rapid pace of content delivery is so extreme that even the most competent of teachers are hard-pressed to tackle anything in depth.[2] Chetty (2015, p. 1) describes this curriculum as a throwback to past curricula where knowledge transmission and reproduction reigned and which ran 'counter to the eman-cipatory imperatives' of the early post-apartheid curriculum.

It needs to be said, however, that despite the fact that South African schooling now has one curriculum for all its learners, an essential break with the racially segregated curricula under apartheid, the inequalities in the provision of material and human resources within the schooling system remain entrenched. Even those who argue for the importance of critical literacy in the curriculum emphasise that too many poor and marginalised schoolchildren struggle to access adequate schooling and thus 'have no expectations of receiving a critical education' (Chetty 2012, p. 23). This is echoed in the findings of some of the more recent literacy research done in historically under-resourced township schools (Lloyd 2016, p. 1), which shows that the 'orientations to reading that were offered were characterized by a focus on the surface meaning of the texts and by an absence of critical engagement'.

This relatively broad overview of the schooling context suggests that critical literacy has become increasingly sidelined in the curriculum, and thus is less visible in the classroom. Nevertheless, research work into critical literacy education continues, much of it in teacher education in the higher education sector. And, this work has become interestingly diversified. There is work being done in early literacy, some in relation embodiment and spatiality (Dixon 2010; Dixon & Janks 2019, in press); some of the work being done in teacher education pertains to raising student-teachers' critical consciousness through literary texts (Pillay 2015; Pillay & Wasserman 2017); there is work on expanded forms of literacy, such as critical visual literacy and multimodal textual analysis (Archer 2013; Ferreira & Newfield 2014; Milani & Shaikjee 2013); digital spaces are being explored in relation to critical literacy (Kajee & Balfour 2011; Mnyanda & Mbelani 2018; Reid 2011); pedagogies of discomfort are being applied to transformation agendas (Gachago, Ivala, Condy, & Chigona 2013; Kajee 2018); literary texts that feature people with disabilities are being analysed in relation to their discourses and positioning strategies (Walton 2012); and the relationship between criticality and imagination is being harnessed for the purposes of creating a critical writing pedagogy (Mendelowitz 2017).

In addition, while the broad identity categories of race, gender and socio-economic class remain central to the critical analyses of discourses, categories of identity (or subjectivity) are becoming more nuanced, and difference and its attendant power relations are themselves increasingly diversified. For example, the work being done by Govender (2017) on heteronormativity and sexual identities, particularly in relation to what he has called 'a pedagogy of coming out' (2017); issues of xenophobia and the textual representation of immigrants (Janks & Adegoke 2011; Janks 2014b); and even the notion of critical diversity literacy, which is being applied both in higher education as well as in the workplace (Kiguwa 2017; Steyn, Burnett, & Ndzwayiba 2018).

Language Learning

One of the strands of critical literacy work that has taken hold in South Africa is closely aligned with critical sociolinguistics, or critical applied linguistics (Makoni & Pennycook 2006; Canagarajah 1999). It concerns the politics of language at a macro level, looking at language varieties and power. Questions such as, what languages are chosen to be spoken where, by whom and why? How do differences among languages (or language varieties) become hierarchically organised, and come to constitute different forms of linguistic capital, with some being consistently accorded value, while others are consistently sidelined? And, who benefits from these practices? And so on. In South Africa, work falling into this area is centrally concerned with deconstructing the historically entrenched hegemonic power of the English language, a colonial and now global language, contesting the practices that continue to undergird this hegemony, and empowering indigenous African languages. While it is not within the scope of this chapter to unpack the complexities that constitute this work, it is important to briefly delineate the contours of the multilingual terrain in South Africa.

The Constitution of the new South Africa (1996) stipulates that there are 11 official languages in the country: nine indigenous African languages, English and Afrikaans (and now Sign Language), and it enshrines the right of every child to receive their schooling in whichever of these languages is the language of the home. However, for various complex structural, ideological and other reasons, the manner in which the policy of additive multilingualism has been taken up by schools has resulted in the continuing devaluation of indigenous African languages and the ongoing strengthening of English as the language of knowledge, education and social mobility. In her seminal work in this area, McKinney (2016) has coined the term 'Anglonormativity' to refer to

> the expectation that people will be and should be proficient in English, and are deficient, even deviant, if they are not ...[and it] is further linked to the valuing of a narrow range of linguistic resources associated with racialised, prestige varieties of English.
>
> (2014, p. 106)

The aims of such work are to dislodge the logic of coloniality that still pervades the schooling system and to work towards ensuring that learners full linguistic repertoires are acknowledged as valued resources for language and literacy learning.

And finally, it needs to be said that while in principle a critical literacy orientation to texts and society can be applied to any language, in South Africa almost no work of this kind exists outside English. The only exception is an article published by Ngwenya (2006) where he advocates for the need for CLA to be applied to the teaching of reading and viewing in isiZulu, particularly in light of the norms of gendered politeness and patriarchy that manifest themselves in language usage and need to be challenged. Unfortunately, however, this call does not appear to have been taken up, or at least not in a way that has been visible to a non–isiZulu speaker/reader such as the author. There would thus appear to be considerable scope for critical literacy work in the area of indigenous African languages.

Theory and Research Base

The term 'best practice' is problematic from a critical literacy perspective because of its normative overtones. It tends to suggest a universalisation of what counts as effective critical literacy work, whereas in fact it is the particularities of contexts that generate the possibilities and needs for particular kinds of critical literacy work. Nevertheless, it is always useful to be exposed to examples of practice and to consider how these might be adapted or revised for one's own context. Three examples of such work follow.

1. Materials Production: South African Critical Literacy Materials Go Global

In 1993, Janks edited a series of six Critical Language Awareness (CLA) workbooks, writing two herself (1993a, 1993b) and having colleagues write another four (Granville 1993; Newfield 1993; Orlek 1993; Rule 1993). While the series was generally well received, it was criticised (Young 1993, in Janks 1996) for being simply about countering apartheid discourses and thus having no traction in the new dispensation. But history tells a different tale. In 2014, after extensive circulation and school classrooms, especially in the 1990s, these materials were revised and extended into a glossy, full-colour book entitled *Doing Critical Literacy: Texts and Activities for Students and Teachers* (Janks, Dixon, Ferreira, Newfield, & Granville 2014), published by Routledge.

The early workbooks were written and published in the final years of apartheid where they functioned as the alternative classroom materials discussed earlier. They were 24-page, newsprint, soft-cover booklets in A4 format, designed to encourage a 'new way of looking at language' (Janks 1993a, p. ii). While each workbook had a different focus denoted by its title – e.g. *Language, Advertising and Power* (Granville 1993); *Language and the News* (Rule 1993); or *Languages in South Africa* (Orlek 1993) – they all began with the same one-page explanation of what constituted CLA (see Figure 7.1). This is a breakdown of the highly sophisticated theories of power that inform Janks's approach to CLA and is, remarkably, written in the kind of plain-speak that makes it accessible to the average high school English student. Figure 7.2 is an example of a page *from Language, Identity and Power* (Janks 1993b). A characteristic feature of all the workbooks was the manner in which various forms of speech bubble were used to ask a range of questions: either issue-based questions on a broad, macro level (e.g. questions 1 and 2, Figure 7.2), or to focus attention on close analysis of linguistic features at a micro level (e.g. questions 7 and 8, Figure 7.2). The 2014

CRITICAL LANGUAGE AWARENESS (CLA)

This workbook is part of a series called *Critical Language Awareness*. All the workbooks in the series deal with the relationship between language and power. This relationship is not obvious and so the materials attempt to raise awareness of the way in which language can be used and is used to maintain and to challenge existing forms of power. There can be little doubt that power matters, both to people who have it and to those who do not. This series will try to show that because there are connections between language and power, language also matters.

In any unequal relation of power there are top dogs and underdogs. How people get to be on top in a society has to do with what that society values. It may be age or maleness or class or cleverness or a white skin. It is easier for those who have power to maintain it if they can persuade everyone in the society that there is nothing unnatural about these arrangements, that things are this way because that is the way they are meant to be.

If people consent to being powerless then the people in power need to use less force (armies, police, punishments) to maintain their power. Convincing and persuading people to consent to society's rules is often the job of families, religions, schools and the media. All these social institutions use language and it is largely in and through language that meaning is mobilised to defend the status quo.

But language is also used to challenge the status quo. By refusing to consent and by working together people can bring about change. What makes CLA 'critical' is its concern with the politics of meaning: the ways in which dominant meanings are maintained, challenged and changed.

When people use language to speak or write, they have to make many choices. They have to decide what words to use, whether to include adjectives and adverbs, whether to use the present, the past or the future, whether to use sexist or non-sexist pronouns, whether to join sentences or to leave them separate, how to sequence information, whether to be definite or tentative, approving or disapproving. What all these choices mean is that written and spoken texts are constructed from a range of possible language options.

However, not all the options are linguistic -- many texts are a combination of verbal and non-verbal elements. Students are asked to think about the non-verbal choices such as photographs, pictures, gestures, graphs, which affect the meaning of texts.

Many of the choices are social choices. Every society has conventions which govern people's behaviour, including their language behaviour. There are social rules controlling who should speak, for how long, when and where, and in which language. There are social norms for polite and impolite forms of speech; there are taboo words and topics. These unwritten rules of use govern what a speech community considers appropriate language behaviour.

These social norms are a good indication of power relations as many of them reflect the values of the people or groups in society who have power. This is particularly true when different groups do not have equal language rights. Here is an obvious example. Where teachers have more power than their students, they can call their students what they like. They can use first names or surnames only, or even insulting names that they have made up. Students, however, have to call teachers by their surnames and a title such as Mr or Ms; some students even have to call their teachers 'Sir' or 'Mistress'.

We forget that these rules of use are social conventions – they start to look natural and to seem like common sense. We forget that they are human constructions. It is easier to remember this when we compare the rules of different speech communities. Some groups think that it is rude to look a person in the eye when you speak to them. Other groups believe the opposite. Neither is more natural than the other. Both are conventions.

Critical Language Awareness emphasises the fact that texts are constructed. Anything that has been constructed can be de-constructed. This unmaking or unpicking of the text increases our awareness of the choices that the writer or speaker has made. Every choice foregrounds what was selected and hides, silences or backgrounds what was not selected. Awareness of this prepares the way to ask critical questions: Why did the writer or speaker make these choices? Whose interests do they serve? Who is empowered or disempowered by the language used? We hope that students will also ask these critical questions about the workbooks in the series.

What the series hopes to do is to teach students how to become critical readers. Critical readers resist the power of print and do not believe everything they read. They start from a position of strategic doubt and weigh texts against their own ideas and values as well as those of others. This is not opposition for opposition's sake. If CLA enables people to use their awareness to contest the practices which disempower them, and to use language so as not to disempower others, then it can contribute to the struggle for human emancipation.

Hilary Janks

Figure 7.1 Critical language awareness

Reproduced here with the kind permission of Hilary Janks (1993a, p. iii)

LEAVING A GROUP

Read the passage first, then answer the questions.

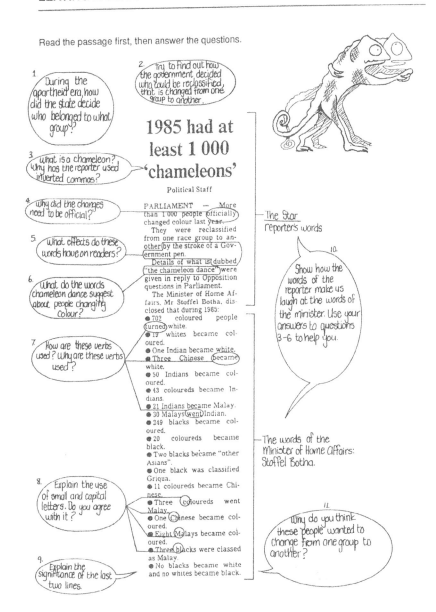

1. During the apartheid era, how did the state decide who belonged to what group?

2. Try to find out how the government decided who could be reclassified, that is changed from one group to another.

3. What is a chameleon? Why has the reporter used inverted commas?

4. Why did the changes need to be official?

5. What effects do these words have on readers?

6. What do the words chameleon dance suggest about people changing colour?

7. How are these verbs used? Why are these verbs used?

8. Explain the use of small and capital letters. Do you agree with it?

9. Explain the significance of the last two lines.

1985 had at least 1 000 'chameleons'

Political Staff

PARLIAMENT — More than 1 000 people officially changed colour last year.

They were reclassified from one race group to another by the stroke of a Government pen.

Details of what is dubbed "the chameleon dance" were given in reply to Opposition questions in Parliament.

The Minister of Home Affairs, Mr Stoffel Botha, disclosed that during 1985:

● 702 coloured people turned white.
● 19 whites became coloured.
● One Indian became white.
● Three Chinese became white.
● 50 Indians became coloured.
● 43 coloureds became Indians.
● 21 Indians became Malay.
● 30 Malays went Indian.
● 249 blacks became coloured.
● 20 coloureds became black.
● Two blacks became "other Asians".
● One black was classified Griqua.
● 11 coloureds became Chinese.
● Three coloureds went Malay.
● One Chinese became coloured.
● Eight Malays became coloured.
● Three blacks were classed as Malay.
● No blacks became white and no whites became black.

The Star reporter's words

10. Show how the words of the reporter make us laugh at the words of the minister. Use your answers to questions 3-6 to help you.

The words of the Minister of Home Affairs: Stoffel Botha.

11. Why do you think these people wanted to change from one group to another?

Figure 7.2 Pages from the *Language, Identity, and Power* workbook

Reproduced here with the kind permission of Hilary Janks (1993b, p. 9)

book runs to 161 pages and has nine chapters, some reflecting the foci of the earlier workbooks, others bringing in areas of interest that have emerged since the workbooks were published, most notably the chapter on 'Time, space and bodies' by Dixon (2014), and a chapter by Janks on 'Redesign – from critical awareness to social action', which has a green section on the environment (literally green).

The materials are directed at the student, providing texts and activities to engage with. These materials are important, however, not only as teaching resources but as a means of supporting or scaffolding new teachers – or teachers new to critical literacy – to begin to experiment with critical literacy and incorporate it into their classroom practice. I believe that the two most important ways in which they operate are their implied principles of text selection, and their modelling of a critical literacy orientation towards texts through question and activity design.

Text Selection

The majority of the texts gathered for discussion and analysis in these materials are authentic texts often reproduced in their original format; they are multimodal and represent multiple genres, consisting of both words and images spatially arranged in various genre-specific ways.

For example, Figure 7.2 contains an actual article from a newspaper of the time, with the text in the recognisable newspaper-column format of the genre. Similarly, the activity in Figure 7.3 is set on an actual advert printed in a South African newspaper in 2002, although the format has been dismantled for the purposes of making visible the anchoring or positioning role play by the accompanying verbal text. The significance of this is that it is in these 'everyday' texts by which we are surrounded that issues of power and representation play themselves out, and this makes their critical analysis not only worthwhile but necessary. Janks talks of 'little p politics and big P politics' – the micropolitics of everyday life versus the type of politics associated with politicians, and the state – and maintains that they are both equally important terrain for the analysis of power.

Orientations to Text

While the judicious selection of texts is helpful for critical literacy analysis, what makes an activity critical is the orientation taken towards the text. Is the reader expected to adopt an appreciative, compliant or even reverential attitude towards the text? Clearly not. A critically literate reader would approach the text with the understanding that there is no such thing as a neutral text, that all texts are positioned and positioning, and would have the intention of deconstructing the text in order to expose the ways in which language, and other semiotic modes, may be reproducing unequal

WORDS ANCHOR PICTURES

What do you see in the photograph below? How would you describe it? If you had to provide a caption for it, what would you say?

FIGURE 5.5

Anchorage

Photographs that do not have any text to guide the reader's interpretation can mean almost anything. Roland Barthes, a famous French scholar, used the term *anchorage* to refer to the way the surrounding words fix or 'anchor' the meaning of a picture.

> The photograph was used in an advert for *Matrix*, a tracking system that can be fitted into a car to assist recovery if it is stolen. The words below are part of the advert. Read the text and answer the questions.

With NoGo Zones from Matrix. If you're not supposed to be there, we'll know about it.

For a second, imagine that you are hijacked and kidnapped with your car. Imagine that you are tied up and have no way of reaching a panic button. Frightening isn't it? Now imagine that you are with Matrix. With our flagship MX3, Matrix introduces NoGo Zones, pre-programmed areas that we have identified as dangerous or unlikely for you to go to. When your car is taken into one of these areas, the Matrix unit sends a signal to our National Control Centre and we immediately send out the cavalry—without you having to lift a finger! Because Matrix's MX3 is constantly comparing the location of your vehicle against its database of known NoGo Zones, this is the ideal safety system for you and your family. So call 0800 77 99 88 and allow us to sell you peace of mind.

IT'S YOUR LIFE. IT'S YOUR CHOICE. CALL MATRIX 0800 77 99 88 FOR NOGO ZONES. WWW.MATRIX.CO.ZA

FIGURE 5.6 The verbal text that goes with the image in Figure 5.5

1. How is the verbal text (Figure 5.6) *positioning* you to interpret the photograph (Figure 5.5) in a particular way?

2. If your home was one of the ones shown in the photograph, would you be more likely to be an *ideal reader* or a *resistant reader* of this text? Explain.

3. Look carefully at the photograph itself. Does it match the idea of a 'NoGo Zone'? Can you notice details of the photograph that help you to 'read against' the verbal text?

4. Design your own advert, for a product or service of your choice, using the same photograph in a completely different way. Explain how your text positions the reader differently from the Matrix advert.

Section 5: Critical visual literacy

Figure 7.3 Critical questions on an advertisement page

(Ferreira & Newfield 2014, p. 87)

relations of power. And the role of question design is central to the ability to design a textual analysis activity that teaches students to critically deconstruct a text. All texts work to position readers. Unless the questions that are used to interrogate the text work *against* the text, they will themselves merely assist in further entrenching the position of the reader as an ideal reader. This is well captured in Newfield's (2011) incisive critical reflection on her materials construction.

Reading against the Text: from Visual Literacy to Critical Visual Literacy

In 1993, Newfield wrote the CLA workbook *Words & Pictures* (1993); and then co-authored the chapter on critical visual literacy in the 2014 book (Ferreira & Newfield 2014). In an astute retrospective analysis of this shift in theoretical orientation (Newfield 2011), Newfield argues that while *Words & Pictures* (Newfield 1993) was well aligned with the aims of visual literacy and media education at the time, using a critical literacy lens it becomes clear to her that the overriding orientation of the materials was towards reading *with* the text, using close reading practices in ways which encouraged textual appreciation of the various texts. She demonstrates this by revisiting an activity on a print advertisement for a high-end chain of bookstores in South Africa (Newfield 1993, pp. 8–9). The worksheet, Newfield states, is insufficiently critical, 'allowing visual literacy students to be manipulated and interpellated by the advertisement's implicit ideology … readers are pulled into the ideal reading position for the advertisement … [and] seduced by the [bookstore] ad' (2011, p. 85). Newfield concludes that a critical reading of this advert would need to surface its Eurocentric and colonial discourses through its question design.

Staying within the same genre of everyday text, Figure 7.3 is an example from the critical visual literacy chapter (Ferreira & Newfield 2014) of an advertisement that is tackled critically. In order to sell its product (a car tracking system), the advert works with old apartheid discourses of *die swart gevaar* (translated directly from Afrikaans as 'the black threat'), constructing poor, black people as a threat to race and class privilege, in the process conflating criminality and poverty. The fact that this is a highly problematic text makes it easier to read against and ripe for critical deconstruction. However, it could have been accompanied by generic advertising questions such as: What type of service is being advertised? Who is the target audience of this advertisement? How does the visual support the wording? Does this advertisement convince you to purchase [the product]?[3] In that case, only readers who are already well versed in critical analysis would be able to provide an oppositional or resistant reading of the advert. It is thus useful to think of the set of questions needed for a critical literacy analysis of a text as a form of counter-text themselves. This is another reason why, as a new teacher to critical literacy, existing teaching materials for critical literacy work offer valuable models for developing one's own classroom practice.

2. Initial Teacher Education: Engaging Controversial Topics through Worksheet Design

Govender's work (2017, 2019) on critical literacy teacher education in the university space has been selected here for two reasons. First, it serves as an example of how to use controversial topics for engaging pre-service teachers with critical literacy work. Second, it demonstrates how the designing of classroom materials for the teaching of critical literacy is a performance of critical literacy and thus an effective way of preparing them for their own classroom practices.

Context of Research

The research (Govender 2017, 2019) centres on a second-year teacher education course designed and taught by Govender in the English language curriculum of a Bachelor of Education (BEd) programme. This was a critical literacy course and the focus was on gender and sexual diversity. To prepare students to deconstruct heteronormativity across a range of available multimodal texts, they were taken through Fairclough's (1989) model for critical discourse analysis, Janks's pedagogies for critical literacy (2010, 2014a), and Kumashiro's (2002) critical antioppressive pedagogy. The assessment task required students to 'design a short set of worksheets that use critical literacy to address an issue related to how gender and sexuality are conflated' (p. 134) and then write a one-pager critically reflecting on the design of their worksheets.

Working with a Controversial Topic

Govender argues for the need to engage pre-service teachers with controversial topics and for the importance of doing so in a mainstream course rather than an elective course which would cater only for those already interested in the topic. Pre-service teachers (or their learners), he states, need to be able to 'step out of their own shoes to analyse and (re)evaluate their subject positions regarding social justice, diversity and power' (2019, p. 125). He recognises that this is a risky endeavour but emphasises the importance of 'confronting real and uncomfortable issues, identities and ideologies' (p. 127). He further emphasises that gender and sexuality is but one example of the multitude of relevant contentious or sensitive issues available for discussion in the critical literacy classroom but argues that given the persistence of homophobia, the instances of '"corrective rape" of predominantly Black lesbian women, and the bullying in schools that serves to regulate hegemonic masculinities' (p. 132), this is an issue deserving of critical confrontation.

Designing Critical Literacy Worksheets

Students either chose authentic texts from those provided for their use, or sourced their own in consultation with their lecturer (e.g. advertisements, news articles, google image collections, etc.). By working closely with these texts, students are being encouraged to develop an awareness of how everyday texts are complicit in problematic forms of representation. As Govender explains, the production of these materials is, in effect, a performance of critical literacy, and thus their materials 'constitute the discursive manifestations of their own transforming understandings' (2019, p. 133) of the terrain – both in relation to the issues of sex, gender and sexual diversity, as well as in relation to the ability to take up a critical literacy orientation to texts in general.

Two Examples of Student-teachers' Performances

As expected, students' performances as critical literacy worksheet designers varied. I have selected two contrasting examples to provide a sense of the range.

Worksheet 1 does not disrupt normative conflations of sex and gender, and merely reproduces conventional male-female binaries in various ways. Examples of questions or instructions are as follows:

- Look at the different sports activities. Choose which sport do males play and which sport females play.
- Choose which colours are mainly used for females and which colours are mainly used for [males].
- You bought presents for your two best friends one is a boy and one is a girl. Decorate the box according to which colours your friends would like.
- Choose whether these activities are suitable for a male or female. (Govender 2019, p. 140).

Worksheet 2, however, deconstructs gender normativity by asking about commonsense and heteronormative assumptions about 'what makes a family?' (2019). See Figure 7.4 below. Govender makes the following points about how the materials work to help learners explore ideas of sex and gender in the context of what counts as a family:

- Activities 1 and 2 work to draw out learners' assumptions about what families look like.
- In Activity 3, the student uses a stick-figure image of a conventional (read: heteronormative), happy family but, using simple questions, manages to draw attention to the 'work' the image is doing in defining normative sex and gender roles in families:
  - ○ Questions 3.1 and 3.2 work with Fairclough's description of text – thereby attempting to make learners aware of the text's construction

Part A: Grade 5

What makes a family?

1. Individual activity

Write a paragraph describing what you see in this picture. Who do you think each person could be in this picture?

2.   Group activity

Get into groups of five and read your paragraph to the group. Share what you thought of the picture. Did the other people in your group have paragraphs that said the same thing you did?

Retrieved 28/09/2013 from http://thinkprogress.org/lgbt/2013 /06/26/2218921/how-the- supreme-court-acknowledged-that- gay-people-and-their-families- exist/

Retrieved 28/09/2013 from http://www.cairns.com.au/article/2013/01/19/2 38544_local-news.html

3. Group activity

3.1 What is this picture of?

3.2 How do you know? Describe what you see.

3.3 What is 'gender' and 'sex'? (Use dictionary to help you)

3.4 Who says that this how moms, dads, boys and girls should dress?

3.5 Do the clothes drawn in this picture show us gender, sex or both? Explain. *How are gender + sex represented?*

3.6 Do you agree that this is what a family should look like? Discuss.

4. Individual activity

4.1 Draw a picture of your own family.
4.2 Write a paragraph describing each person in your picture and who they are in your family.

Homework activity:
Find pictures of families and family members in magazines and bring them to class with you.

Page **1** of **11**

Figure 7.4 Worksheet 2

Reproduced here with the kind permission of Navan Govender (2019, p. 138)

- ○ Questions 3.4, 3.5 and 3.6 encourage learners to consider where ideas about gender and sex come from, how 'natural' these ideas are and thus provide space for such norms to be challenged – in this way they begin to touch on Fairclough's interpretative and explanatory levels of discourse analysis.

- The sequence of the activities is also a factor in 'enabl[ing] learners to make critical moves in practice and understanding' (p. 139), particularly since a later activity (not shown on the image), asks learners to re-visit the first image here and to deconstruct and evaluate it (pp. 138–139).

Thus, as Govender has stated elsewhere in relation to materials design (2018, p. 44), 'design involves negotiation between text, theory and interest'. And a materials design task at the end of a course on critical literacy proves to be a valuable way of inducing this negotiation in emerging critical literacy teachers. So, while Govender also points to the tenacity of gender and sexual hegemonies and the difficulties of disrupting these in a short course, he maintains that the materials design activity is useful in creating the conditions for students to experiment with new ways of thinking about gender and sex.

3. A Critical Literacy Orientation to Curriculum Design

Lastly, I turn to some of my own research in an attempt to demonstrate a particular critical literacy orientation to curriculum design, namely that of using learner diversity as a tool for surfacing and engaging the politics of difference and power in the classroom. I have used poststructuralist discourse analysis to analyse classroom talk in order to identify subject positions students take up and the discourses they draw on. This builds on previous work that uses this kind of discourse analysis for positionality in classroom settings, both internationally (Baxter 2002; Davies 1994) and locally (McKinney 2004, 2011); and on pedagogies that use the classroom as a contact zone for students' diverse funds of knowledge (Ferreira & Janks 2007), or diverse linguistic identities (Ferreira & Mendelowitz 2009).

The data is in the form of transcripts of classroom talk in a racially desegregated English (or Language Arts) Grade 11 classroom at an elite school in Johannesburg. I argue that when learners' diverse knowledges, experiences and ways of being are invited into the classroom space as valued and legitimate resources, two things can occur: firstly, this works against the assimilationist model which is dominant in mainstream South African education and privileges western knowledge and practices; secondly, opportunities are made for students to re-think their own assumptions and preconceptions when they interact across historically constructed differences and gain access to multiple discourses. Space constraints do not allow for presentation of the extended extracts of classroom talk or the detailed moment-by-moment analysis that has been undertaken elsewhere (Ferreira 2013). Instead, in Table 7.1, I provide four short extracts from two different lessons, capturing key moments of the extended discussion, and thereafter I extrapolate some of the more significant findings and draw out the implications for the critical literacy classroom.

Table 7.1 Extracts from classroom talk on crime, place, and privilege

Extract 1 (Lesson 1)

17 Kelsey:	…. Like I understand we're growing up and life might not be like it is in America where you can just walk around and not feel like you're going to get raped or something like that but like in a way it educates you to the point where like you know – you're more streetwise than you would be. … we're so used to living in this kind of environment that it makes you so much more aware of what's going on, because you're not ignorant to what's actually happening in the world and that there is poverty and that there is stealing

[…]

30 Alice:	Um, you know, I think it's quite strange how we look – we think that we so accustomed to the dangers of being a teenager in South Africa or whatever and then we like go overseas and it's good and everything. I mean like we – the girls in this class, we're like the top 2% of South Africans, we're like the highest class, you know. And then we say ja, no it's really terrible you know we can't walk in the streets but I mean imagine living in Diepsloot,[4] you know – [T: Interesting.] – I mean we can't even touch on how dangerous it is in South Africa.

Extract 2 (Lesson 8)

22 Kate:	…. And I mean at least when you're streetwise you have the ability to like prepare yourself for it. If you grow up in a safe society, you come to like for example like South Africa or another like crime-ridden place, I mean and you get completely caught off guard. I mean that could sometimes even cost you your life.
23 Kelsey:	But you're not necessarily streetwise just because of the place that you live in. I mean I live in like – I mean most of us live in South Africa and most of the girls that come to [school name] come from very good families and they kind of live in their own bubble. I mean, um –
24:	*Multiple spontaneous comments [unclear], challenging Kelsey.*
25 Kate:	But Kelsey, don't you think – don't you think –
26 Kelsey:	You live in a protected area –
27 T:	But you're always aware, aren't you?
28 Kelsey:	…you're not exposed to half of the bad things that are… *[Ongoing buzz of responses.]* Not to the same extent…
29 Sonia:	Ja, *[speaking loudly over the buzz]* we don't have any reason to be as scared as a person living in Soweto and like…
30 S:	But you're not living in Soweto.

[…]

Table 7.1 (Cont).

| 41 *Michelle:* | Um, in response to Kate, I don't think that we've become – I don't think that as South Africans, especially our little micro-community – I don't think that we're all streetwise, I think we're just paranoid. And I think that makes a difference, like… *[laughter]* [S: I agree, I agree with Michelle.] I think the only way to get streetwise, like 'streetwise', is like if you really live in Hillbrow … |

Extract 3 (Lesson 8, cont.)

| 52 *Bontle:* | … what Kate said about people in Soweto being more in danger or what-ever. I feel like – I only started living in the suburbs like last year, okay, so my whole life I grew up in Tembisa. So all I'm saying is that I felt more at home in – … Oh, I feel that it's so much more homely than, um than Sandton *[with dismissive hand gesture]*. Because I think that the only reason you guys might feel that you are in danger is because you don't know these people. Um, it's how the people in Salem were to like the natives, like – [Lesego: Salem?] … Ja, that whole witch hunt that happened. Ja, I think that's just fear of the unknown that makes you think that you are in danger. Like all those people in the township, like I might not know them but when I like walk there I'm like 'hi', you know. It's like they're family, that's how it is. Like I feel more like…um… uh… |

[…]

75 *Nguvi:*	I totally agree with Bontle because it's like when I lived in Zim, like – okay, I always grew up – like we lived in a more uptown part of town, but I did have family that lived more in the location parts – and even when I went to visit there and stay over, it was so homely like – you know how every-one's like 'oh my god, you went to that place is-!' – you know how every-one's like 'oh no, Soweto, you've got to be streetwise' – there it actually wasn't. It was exactly the way Bontle described it, where it's actually so homely. But obviously you can't expect to walk around at [T: Ja]…, you know, and come back alive, that kind of thing. [T: Ja]
76:	*Multiple simultaneous voices.*
77 *T:*	I do however believe that Michelle said Hillbrow, which is very different from either Tembisa, Soweto or Bryanston.

Extract 4 (Lesson 8, cont.)

| 82 *Lesego:* | I'm just… ?… what Bontle said about …?… Okay, fine, I moved to Rand-burg when I was 5. And I actually realised something. My parents are really strict, I'm the only child right so they're very protective over me. And I've realised that since I've been living in the suburbs they want to know every single move I make *[murmurs of agreement]* – where am I going? What am |

(Continued)

Table 7.1 (Cont).

	I doing? Who am I with? And if I – if I – if I lived in Soweto all of this time, from when I was [?] till now, I would just like walk out the house and it would be like okay, cool, I'll see you later. Because I actually went to Anele's house and um she's just living the life! *[laughter]* … She just leaves the house and I remember she was like to her parents 'no ok sharp we'll see you at 8' and it was like cool, and we left at like 10 in the morning and we actually came back at half past nine and they were like 'oh, how was your day?' This is like half past nine at night. And she was like 'no it's okay, it's all good' and stuff like that. And she's like 'mom I'm coming back I'm just going to the garage' – and the garage is like down *[wild gesture to indicate far distance, laughter]* and it was like half past nine at night –
85 T:	And your mouth was hanging open!
86 Lesego:	And it was like 'are you serious? Does your mom–?' She's out the door …
87 Alice:	I want to go to Anele's house, guys! *[laughter]*

The classroom talk at hand is centred around the issues of youth, safety, crime, place, privilege and parental leniency. This topic emerges unplanned during an open-ended student discussion that is framed by a broader unit of work that explores what it means to be a teenager in South Africa and the importance of our recent past. As the conversation continues, students shift and reposition themselves as new students enter the discussion introducing new discourses.

Students' Subject Positions Shift as They Are Exposed to New Discourses Introduced by Their Peers

- Kelsey introduces a 'streetwise' discourse (Ext 1, T17) that is countered by Alice who points to the real danger being in the townships (Ext 1, T30).
- Later, it is Kelsey herself who refutes the possibility of being streetwise (Ext 2, T23) and uses the discourse introduced in a previous lesson by Alice to critique her own initial position.
- Later still, Bontle (Ext 3, T52) – one of the only three Black students in the class – introduces a counter-discourse to that of Alice and Kelsey by constructing townships as safe, homely, convivial places. This is reinforced by Lesego's contribution which associates parental leniency and greater teenage freedom with the township (Ext 4, T82 and 91).
- Finally, Alice too shifts her subject position by constructing the township as a desirable place to visit (Ext 4, T87).

Such Shifts in Position Can Index a Shift in the Power Relations and, in This Case, Are Also Indicative of Racialised Asymmetrical Relations of Knowing

After Bontle introduces the counter-discourse of the township (Ext 3, T52), one by one the only other two black girls in the classroom insert themselves into the conversation and take up positions of solidarity with Bontle – Nguvi (Ext 3, T75) and Lesego (Ext 4, T82). In this discursive classroom space, who has and does not have knowledge of the township is racialised. The white students do not have their own direct knowledge of the townships to draw on and therefore operate on hearsay, assumptions, stereotypes and rumours. While none of the black students currently live in a township, they either have memories of living in the township, or remain connected to the township through family and friends and thus they have crossover knowledge of the suburbs and the townships. From this position, they can step in to 'correct' their peers' perceptions. At this point they begin to over-romanticise the townships, making no attempt to engage with the complexity of spatial and emotional geographies of these enduring though shifting apartheid-constructed places. However, because knowledge of the townships is racialised, the white students – without any direct knowledge of their own – are unable to question the authority of the black students. Furthermore, by virtue of the fact that two contrasting discourses on townships co-exist in this classroom space, townships can no longer be viewed as one-dimensional – as would be the case if either of these discourses existed unchallenged.

Shifting power relations between the students and their different knowledges are suggested by the ways in which they are repositioning themselves and one another. Specifically, the black students' participation in the classroom talk appears to have had a discernible effect on the kinds of discourses that emerged. Working together, these three students introduced new discourses powerful enough to reposition some of the students that had been working with contrasting discourses. While alternative discourses do not necessarily dislodge the discourses they are challenging nor do these challenges necessarily effect permanent change, once the taken-for-granted has been questioned, it can no longer be taken-for-granted (Dyson 1997, p. 16). The fact that the contrasting discourses on townships co-exist in this pedagogic space by the end of this interaction can only mean that neither discourse is operating invisibly.

Inserting a New Discourse into the Conversation

Bontle recruits established, mainstream 'school' discourses to assist her in introducing the counter-discourse around townships. She deconstructs her white peers' construction of the townships as crime-ridden and dangerous by suggesting that, like the people of Salem in Arthur Miller's *The Crucible* (a recent literary setwork), they fear the unknown. Through her counter-construction of the township as convivial, she reverses their othering gaze and constructs them as outsiders. In addition, however, it is interesting to note that Bontle recruits high cultural capital, in the form of a classic literary text, to assist her challenge. She thus employs the middle class ways of arguing that are dominant in mainstream schooling, drawing metaphorically on the experiences depicted in a literary text to legitimise her own line of reasoning. This functions as a hybrid moment where this text, which is shared classroom knowledge, is used to introduce new knowledge, namely knowledge of the townships and township life to which Bontle (and the two other students) who is in the minority, has access.

The classroom talk under analysis occurred within a section of work that invited students' own knowledges, experiences and ideas into the classroom, specifically in relation to their positions as young people in post-apartheid South Africa. Such engaged conversations cannot be scripted into the curriculum – they can be risky, uncomfortable, volatile or even elusive. But the curriculum design can attempt to create the conditions of possibility for these kinds of interactions and conversations to emerge. When this happens, learners can benefit by having their own positionality made visisble and thereby having the chance to consciously re-think and deliberately re-position themselves in relation to the available discourses in and beyond the classroom space.

Implications for Future Research

So where to next for the chameleon literacy? The reverberations of the #FeesMustFall movement are still being felt throughout the higher education sector and beyond, and they have the potential to both challenge and reinvigorate the field. At the time of writing this chapter, the education department is preparing to release revised curriculum documentation for the schooling sector, and it is rumoured that this revision is responding to the calls for the curriculum to be decolonised. Critical literacy is, I believe, well placed to contribute to this move providing that (1) the curriculum does not hamstring critical literacy through a superficial understanding of language, discourse and power; and (2) that the field itself – as well as its practitioners – is prepared to be 'unsettled' and undergo rigorous self-examination, particularly with regard to its past, present and future relationships to (de)colonisation. Decolonial scholars Tuck and Yang (2012), for example, would be likely to refer to much of what passes as critical literacy work as 'settler moves to innocence', which they describe as the 'attempt to reconcile settler guilt and complicity, and rescue settler futurity' (p. 1). Indeed, it is interesting to note that a disproportionate number of those involved in critical literacy education work in South Africa are white women (including the author). It may well be fruitful, as well as uncomfortable, to ask why that may be so, and why there are so few voices of people of colour doing this work?

Discussion Questions and Application

1. To what extent does your current language or literacy curriculum support the teaching of critical literacy, either explicitly or implicitly? Might your curriculum's orientation to literacy be in any way influenced by the current sociopolitical climate?
2. What everyday texts exist in your immediate physical and digital environments that you and your students might be able to subject to critical analysis? Consider how these texts use language, as well as other semiotic modes, to construct particular versions of the world. Who benefits from this way of thinking, or of seeing the world? How could you and your students generate counter-texts that would challenge them?
3. What contentious issues are alive in your community that might benefit from being critically discussed, researched and acted upon in your community? Ask your learners for suggestions.
4. If the topic is a sensitive one that could provoke discomfort in your learners, do you feel confident enough and strongly enough about it to tackle it? If so, how would you generate the kind of 'safe space' in your classroom that would make this discomfort productive rather than threatening?
5. Use the internet to find out what critical literacy classroom projects are being done in other parts of the world that you might be able to link up with and contribute to.

Acknowledgements

I would like to thank my colleagues Kerryn Dixon and Grant Andrews for their insightful comments on this paper.

Notes

1   In a South African context, a township was a racially segregated residential area designated for 'non-white' people under apartheid, associated with poverty and overcrowding and contrasting starkly with the whites only suburbs in relation to infrastructure and socioeconomic status. The fact that 25 years into democracy continue to reflect racialised demographics points to the difficulty in eradicating spatial forms of apartheid.
2   I am grateful to my colleague Bronwen Wilson-Thomson for sharing her insights on the impact of curriculum change on the literacy curriculum.
3   Regrettably, these questions were copied, virtually verbatim, from the matriculation or school-leaving examination papers for English in 2017 and 2018.
4   Diepsloot is a sprawling township on the northern edges of Johannesburg. It is a densely populated area comprising a mix of shacks and low-cost housing,

lacking in basic services and infrastructure and associated with high levels of unemployment, crime, and drug and alcohol abuse. It is not far from the affluent areas where many of these students live.

References

Archer, A. (2013). Power, social justice and multimodal pedagogies. In C. Jewitt (ed.), *The Routledge handbook of multimodal analysis*, pp. 189–197. London: Routledge.

Baxter, J. (2002). Competing discourses in the classroom: A post-structuralist discourse analysis of girls' and boys' speech in public contexts. *Discourse & Society*, 13(6), 827–842.

Canagarajah, S. (1999). *Resisting linguistic imperialism in English teaching*. Oxford: OUP.

Chetty, R. (2012). Critical literacy for poor learners: An engagement with power and marginalization. *International Proceedings of Economics Development and Research*, 47(5), 21–26. doi:10.7763/IPEDR

Chetty, R. (2015). Freirean principles and critical literacy to counter retrograde impulses in the curriculum and assessment policy Statement. *Reading & Writing*, 6(1), 1–7.

Cope, B. & Kalantzis, M. (eds.) (2000). *Multiliteracies: Literacy learning and the design of social futures*. London: Routledge.

Davies, B. (1994). *Poststructuralist theory and classroom practice*. Victoria, Australia: Deakin Press.

Department of Education (DoE). (1997). *Senior Phase (Grades 7–9). Policy document*. Pretoria: Department of Education.

Dixon, K. (2010). *Literacy, power, and the schooled body: Learning in time and space*. New York: Routledge.

Dixon, K. (2014). Time, space and bodies. In H. Janks, K. Dixon, A. Ferreira, S. Granville & D. Newfield (eds.), *Doing critical literacy: Texts and activities for students and teachers*. London & New York: Routledge.

Dixon, K. & Janks, H. (2019). Researching a child's embodied textual play. In N. Kucirkova, J. Rowsell & G. Falloon (eds.), *The Routledge international handbook of learning with technology in early childhood*, pp. 88–106. New York: Routledge.

Dixon, K. & Janks, H. (in press). Becoming critical: Young children engaging with texts and the world. In A. Woods & B. Exley (eds.), *Literacies in early childhood: Foundations for equity and quality*. Melbourne: OUP.

Dyson, A.H. (1997). Rewriting for, and by, the children: The social and ideological fate of a media miss in an urban classroom. *Written Communication*, 14(3), 275–312.

Fairclough, N. (1989). *Language and power*. London: Longman.

Fairclough, N. (1995). *Critical dicourse analysis*. London: Longman.

Ferreira, A. (2013). *Subjectivity and pedagogy in a context of social change*. PhD diss., University of the Witwatersrand.

Ferreira, A. & Janks, H. (2007). Reconciliation pedagogy, identity and community funds of knowledge: Borderwork in South African classrooms. *English Academy Review*, 24(2), 71–84.

Ferreira, A. & Mendelowitz, B. (2009). Opening up the contact zone: An undergraduate English course as multilingual pedagogic space. *English Teaching Practice and Critique*, 8(2), 54–79.

Ferreira, A. & Newfield, D. (2014). Critical visual literacy. In H. Janks, K. Dixon, A. Ferreira, S. Granville & D. Newfield (eds.), *Doing critical literacy: Texts and activities for students and teachers*, pp. 83–100. London & New York: Routledge.

Freire, P. (1970). *Pedagogy of the oppressed*. London: Penguin.

Freire, P. & Macedo, D. (1987). *Literacy: Reading the word and the world*. South Hadley, MA: Bergin & Garvey.

Gachago, D., Ivala, E., Condy, J. & Chigona, A. (2013). Journeys across difference: Pre-service teacher education students' perceptions of a pedagogy of discomfort in a digital storytelling project in South Africa. *Critical Studies in Teaching and Learning*, 1(1), 22–52.

Govender, N. N. (2011). Critical literacy: Do textbooks practise what they preach? *English Quarterly Canada (Online)*, 42(3/4), 57.

Govender, N. N. (2017). The pedagogy of 'coming out': Teacher identity in a critical literacy course. *South African Review of Sociology*, 48(1), 19–41.

Govender, N. (2018). Deconstructing heteronormativity and hegemonic gender orders through critical literacy and materials design. In E. Walton & R. Osman (eds.), *Teacher education for diversity*, pp. 36–52. London and New York: Routledge and Taylor & Francis.

Govender, N. N. (2019). Negotiating gender and sexual diversity in English language teaching: 'Critical'-oriented educational materials designed by pre-service English teachers at a South African University. In Mario E. Lopez-Gopar (ed.), *International perspectives on critical pedagogies in ELT*, pp. 125–149. Cham: Palgrave Macmillan.

Granville, S. (1993). *Language, advertising and power*. Johannesburg: Hodder and Stoughton in Association with Wits University Press.

Granville, S. (1996). *Reading beyond the text: Exploring the possibilities in critical language awareness of reshaping student teachers' ideas about reading and comprehension*. Johannesburg: Unpublished Masters thesis, University of the Witwatersrand.

Granville, S. (1997). Transforming literacy practice: Surviving collisions and making connections. *Teacher Development*, 1(3), 463–478.

Granville, S. (2001). Comprehension or comprehending: Using critical language awareness and interactive reading theory to teach learners to interact with texts. *Southern African Linguistics and Applied Language Studies*, 19, 13–21.

Janks, H. (1990). Contested terrain: English education in South Africa 1948–1987. In I. Goodson & P. Medway (eds.), *Bringing English to order: The history and politics of a school subject*, pp. 242–261. London: Falmer Press.

Janks, H. (1992). Critical language awareness and people's English. *Southern African Journal of Applied Language Studies*, 1(2), 64–76.

Janks, H. (1993a). *Language and position*. Johannesburg: Hodder and Stoughton in Association with Wits University Press.

Janks, H. (1993b). *Language, identity and power*. Johannesburg: Hodder and Stoughton in Association with Wits University Press.

Janks, H. (1996). Why we still need critical language awareness in South Africa. *Stellenbosch Papers in Linguistics Plus*, 29, 172–190.

Janks, H. (2000). Domination, access, diversity and design: A synthesis for critical literacy education. *Educational Review*, 52(2), 175–186.

Janks, H. (2001a). Critical language awareness: Curriculum 2005 meets the TRC. *Southern African Linguistics and Applied Language Studies*, 19(3–4), 241–252.

Janks, H. (2001b). Identity and conflict in the critical literacy classroom. In B. Comber & A. Simpson (eds.), *Negotiating critical literacies in classrooms*, pp. 137–150. Mahwah, NJ: Lawrence Erlbaum Associates.

Janks, H. (2010). Language, power and pedagogy. In N. Hornberger & S. McKay (eds.), *Sociolinguistics and language education*, pp. 40–60. Clevedon: Multilingual Matters.

Janks, H. (2012). The importance of critical literacy. *English Teaching: Practice and Critique*, 11(1), 150–163.

Janks, H. (2014a). Critical literacy's ongoing importance for education. *Journal of Adolescent & Adult Literacy*, 57(5), 349–356.

Janks, H. (2014b). Xenophobia and constructions of the other. In M. Prinsloo & C. Stroud (eds.), *Educating for language and literacy diversity*, pp. 193–205. London: Palgrave Macmillan.

Janks, H. & Adegoke, R. (2011). District 9 and constructions of the other: Implications for heterogenous classrooms. *English Teaching: Practice and Critique*, 10(2), 39–48.

Janks, H., Dixon, K., Ferreira, A., Newfield, D. & Granville, S. (2014). *Doing critical literacy: Texts and activities for students and teachers*. London: Routledge.

Kajee, L. (2018). 'You do not throw away history, you fight': Conversations about justice. In R. Kaur Chhina (ed) *Cambridge Conference Series* (pp. 38–46). FLE Learning Ltd. Cambridge Conference Series.

Kajee, L. & Balfour, R. (2011). Students' access to digital literacy at a South African university: Privilege and marginalisation. *Southern African Linguistics and Applied Language Studies*, 29(2), 187–196.

Kiguwa, P. (2017). How and why do we disturb? Challenges and possibilities of pedagogy of hope in socially just pedagogies. In R. Osman & D. Hornsby (eds.), *Transforming teaching & learning in higher education: Towards a socially just pedagogy in a global context*, pp. 99–118. Cham: Springer.

Kress, G. (2000). Multimodality. In B. Cope & M. Kalantzis (eds.), *Multiliteracies: Literacy learning and the design of social futures*, pp. 182–202. South Yarra, Australia: Macmillan.

Kress, G. & Van Leeuwen, T. (1996). *Reading images: The grammar of visual design*. London & New York: Routledge.

Kress, G. & Van Leeuwen, T. (2001). *Multimodal discourses: The modes and media of contemporary communication*. London: Arnold.

Kumashiro, K. (2002). *Troubling education: Queer activism and antioppressive pedagogy*. New York and London: Routledge Falmer.

Lloyd, G. (2016). Are we teaching critical literacy? Reading practices in a township classroom. *Reading & Writing-Journal of the Reading Association of South Africa*, 7(1), 1–6.

Makoni, S. & Pennycook, A. (2006). *Disinventing and reconstituting languages*. London: Multilingual Matters.

McKinney, C. (2004). 'A little hard piece of grass in your shoe': Understanding student resistance to critical literacy in post-apartheid South Africa. *Southern African Linguistics and Applied Language Studies*, 22(1 & 2), 63–73.

McKinney, C. (2011). Asymmetrical relations of knowing: Pedagogy, discourse and identity in a de(re)segregated girls' school. *Journal of Education*, 51, 29–51.

McKinney, C. (2014) The (in)visibility of children's linguistic and cultural resources in education in African contexts. Paper presented at AILA World Conference, Brisbane.

McKinney, C. (2016). *Language and power in post-colonial schooling: Ideologies in practice*. New York & London: Routledge.

Mendelowitz, B. (2017). Conceptualising and enacting the critical imagination through a critical writing pedagogy. *English Teaching: Practice & Critique*, 16(2), 178–193.

Milani, T. & Shaikjee, M. (2013). A new South African man? Beer, masculinity and social change. In L. Atanga, S. Ellece, L. Litosseliti & J. Sunderland (eds.), *Gender and language in sub-Saharan Africa: Tradition, struggle and change*, pp. 131–148. IMPACT: Studies in Language and Society, Vol. 33. John Benjamins Publishing.

Mnyanda, L. & Mbelani, M. (2018). Are we teaching critical digital literacy? Grade 9 learners' practices of digital communication. *Reading & Writing*, 9(1), a188. doi:10.4102/rw.v9i1.188

Morgan, W. (1997). *Critical literacy in the classroom*. London & New York: Routledge.

New London Group. (1996). A pedagogy of multiliteracies: Designing social futures. *Harvard Education Review*, 66(1), 60–92.

Newfield, D. (1993). *Words and pictures*. Johannesburg: Hodder and Stoughton in Association with Wits University Press.

Newfield, D. (2011). From visual literacy to critical visual literacy: An analysis of educational materials. *English Teaching: Practice and Critique*, 10(1), 81–94.

Ngwenya, T. (2006). Introducing critical language awareness in IsiZulu: The why and the how. *Southern African Linguistics and Applied Language Studies*, 24(2), 165–173.

Orlek, J. (1993). *Languages in South Africa*. Johannesburg: Hodder and Stoughton in Association with Wits University Press.

Pillay, A. (2015). Transformative and critical education praxis in a teacher education lecture room. *Education as Change*, 19(3), 4–23.

Pillay, A. & Wasserman, J. (2017). Espoused and enacted values of student teachers interrogating race, class and gender in literary texts. *Educational Research for Social Change*, 6(2), 29–44.

Prinsloo, J. & Janks, H. (2002). Critical literacy in South Africa: Possibilities and constraints in 2002. *English Teaching: Practice and Critique*, 1(1), 20.

Reid, J. (2011). 'We don't Twitter, we Facebook': An alternative pedagogical space that enables critical practices in relation to writing. *English Teaching: Practice and Critique*, 10(1), 58–80.

Rule, P. (1993). *Language and the news*. Johannesburg: Hodder and Stoughton in Association with Wits University Press.

Steyn, M., Burnett, S. & Ndzwayiba, N. (2018). Mapping capacity to deal with difference: Towards a diagnostic tool for critical diversity literacy. *African Journal of Employee Relations*, 42, 1–23.

South Africa. (1998). *Truth and reconciliation commission of South Africa report*. (1998). Cape Town: Juta & Co.

Tuck, E. & Yang, K. (2012). Decolonization is not a metaphor. *Decolonization: Indigeneity, Education & Society*, 1(1), 1–40.

Walton, E. (2012). Using literature as a strategy to promote inclusivity in high school classrooms. *Intervention in School and Clinic*, 47(4), 224–233.

Chapter 8

Becoming a Proficient Reader in Taiwan

Hwawei Ko

Summary of Chapter

- Written Chinese is notably different from alphabetic scripts.
- Characters are the fundamental units of written Chinese and are morphosyllabic.
- Considering this difference, the author describes the research and pedagogical practice of learning Chinese and discusses the view of universality on literacy development.

Vignette

Ms. Lin, a third grade Chinese language arts teacher, was facing a dilemma of adopting the Textbook-based Approach to Reading Instruction (TARI) in her class. She had just returned from a three-day workshop of teaching reading comprehension strategies, and worked with her colleagues on this semester's lesson plans. Ms. Lin knew very well that as long as her students learnt these strategies they would be self–directed learners. Yet the class hour was limited (in Taiwan's elementary schools, a class duration is 40 minutes – it is named a class hour); it might affect those low achievers who need more practice in order to get acquainted with Chinese characters. Nevertheless, she decided to give it a try.

After a class hour spent on the whole class reading aloud the text and the presentation of the new words and characters, Ms. Lin asked her class to read the text again silently. Then she asked: who can summarize the text? Silence. Ms. Lin recalled the strategy to summarize a passage is to delete sentences of similar meaning. She asked again, "Did you observe any similar meaning among the sentences?" Silence, and then two girls whispered. She looked at one of the girls, and said, "Do you have the answer?" The girl pointed to the text. Ms. Lin felt relieved and smiled, "That is correct." She returned to the whole class and saw puzzlement in many students' eyes. She dismissed the class. In the teachers' room, Ms. Lin wanted to know what to do next. Her colleague encouraged her to try again and have a group discussion since the two girls showed their understanding. The next day, Ms. Lin had the class read the same text again and repeated yesterday's question and presented the girls' answer as an example, then asked the students to discuss whether there were similarities in the text in groups. About a week later, Ms. Lin overheard one student tell friends from another class, "our teacher is different now. The Chinese lessons have become very interesting. We have to use our brain to think."

Education in Taiwan

Taiwan is an island with a population of 23 million. The population includes a highly trained workforce that is considered a crucial factor for Taiwan's economic development. Accordingly, Taiwanese people value education. A survey revealed that 59.1% of parents wanted their fourth-grade children to have a college (university) degree and that 34% of parents expected their children to have a postgraduate degree (Mullis, Martin, Foy, & Hooper, 2017).

Under this social and cultural phenomenon, learning virtues such as diligence, perseverance, and concentration are highly enforced among teachers and parents. A parent–teacher contact booklet enables teachers to communicate the daily homework and students' learning progress and difficulties to parents in order to maintain students on the learning track from kindergarten to junior high school. In particular, expending considerable effort is considered a moral duty (Fwu, Wei, Chen, & Wang, 2014). Students who have made additional effort tend to receive praise from parents and teachers for fulfilling their moral duties in learning. Fwu and colleagues (2014) developed two scenarios separately portraying junior high school students' high effort and low effort in learning mathematics; they investigated the students' as well as their parents' and teachers' agreement with moral image statements, such as "Minghua (a pseudo name) fulfills his duty," and assessed their credit assignment by using specific items, such as "Minghua should be praised by his parents (teachers)." The results clearly demonstrated that level of effort, moral image, and credit assignment were highly and positively correlated with all groups. All praised the moral worth of effort in learning.

Teachers themselves are laborious and are regarded as learned scholars (Fwu & Wang, 2002) in charge of learning and knowledge dissemination, and they have a high social status and are respected by students in Taiwan (Fwu & Wang, 2002; Global Teacher Status Index, 2018). Teachers' Day is celebrated every year in Confucius temples throughout Taiwan to pay tribute to all teachers.

Taiwan used to be almost entirely homogeneous and orderly. Such homogeneity was pervasive in not only the political domain but also the school sector; specifically, in schools, students' outfits, the curriculum, textbooks, the examination system, and the teacher training system were all identical. Academic performance constituted the primary criterion for teacher recruitment. Individuals who passed the college entrance examination and entered normal universities were immersed and cultivated in a "teachers are made" mode (Wang & Fwu, 2007). A package of tuition waiver, free accommodation and boarding, and guaranteed employment attracted capable and talented high school graduates. After four years of training, the graduates were obligated to teach for at least five years. Otherwise, they would have to return all the benefits received while at normal university. Once they decided to pursue a career in education, they secured work placement with a generous salary and retirement pension (Fwu & Wang, 2002; Wang & Fwu, 2007, 2014).

In the 1980s, bottom-up grassroots opposition movements began to challenge all signs of uniformity, including social and economic aspects, as well as questioning the Nationalist Party's authoritarianism. The teacher education system was among the criticized entities, considered controlling and conservative. All opposition forces became a powerful pressure in favor of deregulation, diversification, and free-market competition on all fronts, including textbooks and teacher education. A new Teacher Education Act passed in 1994, allowing all comprehensive universities to set up teacher training programs (TTPs), with each university having its own selection mechanism. Nevertheless, 60% of new TTPs were reported to admit students came from the top 30% in their home departments' academic rankings (Wang & Fwu, 2007). Although TTP students have no free tuition or subsidies and must compete for jobs after graduation, many college students still consider teaching as a career choice. Part of the incentive is from the remuneration and benefits package received by teachers, including salary, insurance, and pension, compared with those received by people with similar qualifications in other occupations (Wang & Fwu, 2014). In addition, teachers are encouraged to obtain a higher degree. If they successfully obtain a degree, their salary would be raised. A teacher's report revealed that 58% of elementary school teachers hold a bachelor's degree as their highest degree and that 42% of them have a postgraduate degree (Mullis et al., 2017). Moreover, teachers enjoy public respect and receive parents' trust and support. Most teachers consider teaching as a lifelong job. The Progress in International Reading Literacy Study (PIRLS)[1] developed a Teacher Career Satisfaction scale based on teachers' degree of agreement with the following five statements: "I am content with my profession as a teacher"; "I find my work full of meaning and purpose"; "I am enthusiastic about my job"; "My work inspires me"; and "I am proud of the work I do." The results of PIRLS 2016 indicated that in Taiwan, 47% of fourth-grade teachers were very satisfied with their careers and that only 12% were less than satisfied with their job (Mullis et al., 2017). Most teachers work until retirement and seldom leave the profession (Wang & Fwu, 2014).

Language Environment

In Taiwan, Mandarin is the official language and medium of instruction. Most Taiwanese students speak fluent Mandarin. On average, among fourth-grade students in Taiwan, 39% speak Mandarin at home, 20% regularly do, and 40% sometimes do (Mullis et al., 2017). Nevertheless, Taiwan is a multilingual society. In addition to Mandarin, students are required to study one local language such as Taiwanese, Hakka, or other aboriginal languages from the first grade through the sixth grade. Students also learn English at school and after school; some of them start very early in kindergarten, even though English is obligatory in the national curriculum starting from the third grade (Ministry of Education, 2017). This creates a wide range of individual differences among students from different socioeconomic status (SES) or ability groups. There is no sufficient evidence-based policy to lessen the anxiety and tension of learning English in Taiwan.

Learning Chinese

Characters are considered the basic units of written Chinese. Each character is pronounced as a syllable, and most Chinese characters represent a morpheme that carries an independent meaning. Scholars have thus considered Chinese a morphosyllabic language (DeFrancis, 1989).

Many characters are organized by components, and components are composed of relatively straight strokes, and some can also be curved. Many components are independent characters themselves. A separate semantic component (also named radical) is often associated with the meaning of a character, and another phonetic component functions as a phonetic reminder of the character's pronunciation. Such characters are labeled compound characters. For example, *mā* 媽 ("mother") is composed of two characters: *nǚ* 女 ("female," semantic radical component) and *mǎ* 馬 ("horse," phonetic component). Both components are independent characters, and each has an independent meaning. In Mandarin Chinese textbooks, 79%–91% of the characters learned from the first grade to the sixth grade are compound characters (Lee, 2011). Beginning in the second grade, students learn character components and use them to memorize characters (Anderson et al., 2013).

Although readers can use the information from the phonetic and semantic components of a character to guess the pronunciation and meaning of the character, such information from components is not reliable. For example, phonetic components are used in approximately 80% of Chinese characters, but the reliability of this information depends on the degree of transparency of the component's meaning and on the consistency of the component's pronunciation with the character (Lee, 2011; Shu & Anderson, 1997; Shu, Chen, Anderson, Wu, & Xuan, 2003). Shu and colleagues (2003) estimated that only 23%–26% of the compound characters could be read accurately by using the phonetic components. Nevertheless, students start using phonetic components to sound new characters they encounter (Anderson et al., 2013; Lee, 2011) as early as the second grade (Ko & Wu, 2003).

Additionally, spoken Chinese is highly homophonic. A single syllable can be represented by several different characters. On average, 11 characters share a single pronunciation (Lee, 2011). For example, *yi* could correspond to several characters such as 一 ("one"), 衣 ("dress"), 醫 ("medical"), 伊 ("she"), and 揖 ("bow"). Hence, students are more likely to err when identifying phonologically similar characters, particularly when these characters are also visually similar. As students grow older, the error rates decrease, but those phonologically and visually similar characters still easily cause errors (Ko & Wu, 2003). Therefore, differentiating graphic forms is useful when beginning to read Chinese. However, since most Chinese words are formed by characters, learning the meaning of characters by morphological analysis of characters and words has proved helpful. This topic is discussed in the "Roles of Phonological and Morphological Awareness in Reading Chinese" section of this chapter.

Although most Chinese characters include a phonetic component, Chinese orthography does not have the transparent correspondence between script and speech, as demonstrated by alphabetic orthographies. Reading common Chinese texts may necessitate learning approximately thousands of characters. According to estimates, with knowledge of about approximately 2700 characters, one can read daily media such as newspapers and public announcements in Taiwan. Therefore, in the fourth grade, students are expected to have learned the number of characters required to read daily media and texts (Wang, Hung, Chang, & Chen, 2008).

Wang and colleagues (2008) studied the development of the number of familiar characters recognized by students from the first grade to the ninth grade. They created a list of 40 randomly selected characters ranked from most familiar to least familiar; and provided the list to students, instructed them to write the pronunciation and meaning (or definition) of each character. The average number of characters recognized by the students from the first grade to the ninth grade ranged from 683.23 (standard deviation [SD], 250.46) to 4067.00 (SD, 540.04). The number of characters recognized increased with grade. In the fourth grade, the average number of characters recognized was 2649.13 (SD, 453.45). Thus, learning thousands of characters in a short period is a difficult task. Therefore, in China and Taiwan, phonetic systems were developed to accompany characters for people learning how to read Chinese.

In China, *pīnyīn*, an alphabetic script, is adopted, whereas in Taiwan, *zhùyīn fúhào*, 37 Chinese phonetic symbols based on subsyllabic elements are used to denote character pronunciations. Taiwan's national curriculum states that in early elementary school, students are taught these phonetic symbols. However, 80%–90% of students were reported to recognize *zhùyīn fúhào* before entering elementary school (Mullis et al., 2017).

In elementary school, each character in all textbooks for the first grade to the fourth grade has corresponding *zhùyīn fúhào* symbols beside it to help students read the texts. After the fourth grade, the texts comprise only characters. This implies that most students have learned the necessary amount of characters to read any subjects after the fourth grade. This is consistent with the character development reported by Wang and colleagues (2008).

After students learn *zhùyīn fúhào*, approximately 60% of the classroom time is focused on character instruction and practice. In character instruction, a common practice entails the teacher specifying the semantic radical component and then writing the character on the blackboard. Students model the teacher's writing by "writing" it in the air to memorize the graphic form of the character (Chern, 1999). Learning the radical component is intended to help students learn the meaning of the character. However, researchers observed that students did not learn the function of semantic components until the fourth and fifth grades (Ko & Wu, 2003). In sum, numerous teachers believe that without adequate knowledge of the characters, students cannot fully comprehend the texts. Therefore, teachers spend nearly two-thirds of their class hours on character and word instruction (author observation), and little time remains for comprehension instruction.

Roles of Phonological and Morphological Awareness in Reading Chinese

The correlation between phonological awareness (PA) and word reading is a universally acknowledged phenomenon. A meta-analysis indicated that PA correlated significantly with reading accuracy and fluency and that it did not vary as a function of task type, whether complex tasks such as tone perception or easy tasks such as syllable deletion (Song, Georgiou, Su, & Su, 2016). In alphabetic writing systems, differentiating and manipulating speech sounds at the phoneme level are crucial to reading development (Fowler et al., 1995). In Chinese, because characters are morphosyllabic, each character is pronounced as a single syllable. Chinese PA tasks are thus designed at the sub-syllabic level, which could be represented by *zhùyīn fúhào*. Naturally, a relationship exists between *zhùyīn fúhào* learning and character recognition (Huang & Hanley, 1994). Studies have confirmed the role of PA in reading Chinese in Taiwan (Hu & Catts, 1998), Hong Kong (McBride-Chang & Ho, 2000), and mainland China (Song et al., 2016).

Regarding the role of morphological awareness (MA) in reading Chinese, most studies have focused on exploring the unique contribution of PA versus MA. In general, researchers observed that both PA and MA are essential in learning to read Chinese (Li, Anderson, Nagy, & Zhang, 2002). Nevertheless, a regression analysis revealed that even after PA and vocabulary size were controlled, MA predicted a unique variance in Chinese character recognition (McBride-Chang, Shu, Zhou, Wat, & Wagner, 2003). A longitudinal study followed 294 children from ages 4 to 11 years in Beijing, China, and demonstrated the role of MA in Chinese reading (Pan et al., 2016). The study showed that preliterate children's (ages 4–6 years) PA predicted postliterate children's (ages 7–11 years) MA and that they jointly predicted character reading and writing. Postliterate children's MA predicted character reading, fluent reading, and reading comprehension. The authors concluded that MA is more beneficial to reading Chinese as the child grows older. A large-scale intervention and longitudinal study (from first grade to third grade) also provided evidence supporting that theory; according to the study, MA instruction substantially improved children's MA and literacy measures such as paragraph reading comprehension, reading fluency, character recognition, and word making (Wu et al., 2009). MA instruction emphasizes the radical analysis of characters and morphological analysis of words and the application of such knowledge when students encounter new characters and words. The underlying reason for MA's contribution agrees with the Chinese writing system. One character is mapped into a syllable, and a morpheme is considered as a whole syllable. Character highlights the syllabic and the meaning unit of Chinese and helps children access the meaning and segment the string of Chinese characters into words.

Reading Chinese

Chinese words comprise one or more characters. A word can also be an individual character with an independent meaning (morpheme). For example, nǚ 女 ("female") and yi 醫 ("medical") are two characters and words by themselves; together, they mean female physician. In printed format, each character is presented in an equal-sized square space, without word boundaries or spaces between characters. In modern alphabetic writing systems, spaces are used to guide the next eye movement as word recognition proceeds (Rayner, 1998). Thus, comprehending Chinese text first involves word segmentation, which must be completed before lexical identification (Li, Rayner, & Cave, 2009; Shen et al., 2012). Nevertheless, because most words are composed of two (approximately 65%) or more characters, research showed that second graders, similar to skilled Chinese readers, adopt word-based processing when they read (Chen & Ko, 2011).

Ko and colleagues studied students from the second grade to college as they read narratives and informational texts, and analyzed their eye movements during online reading. The characters and words used in both types of texts were considered to be comprehensible by fourth graders. A developmental trend was observed. As expected, the older the student was, the more characters he or she read in one minute. The fixation durations of fifth- and sixth-grade students were near those of adults. This result implies that by the fifth grade, students could read as adults do (Chen & Ko, 2011). However, knowing the meanings of the individual characters of a word does not guarantee understanding the general meaning of that word. For example, Jian and Ko (2014) collected physics texts from a popular science magazine and studied college students whose major was not physics. The scientific texts contained familiar words and unfamiliar academic terminology, whereas the character frequency in both physics terminology and familiar words was relatively similar. No statistical difference in first fixation duration was observed between reading physics words and reading familiar words; the first fixation durations for both were 220–250 milliseconds (Jian, Chen, & Ko, 2013; Jian & Ko, 2014). While reading scientific texts, students seemed to succeed at decoding each fixation's meaning but failed to access the meaning of the physics terminology (e.g., *ànwùzhí* 暗物質 "dark matter" and *zhōngxìngbànzǐ* 中性伴子 "neutralino"). The properties of Chinese characters and the nature of the formation of Chinese words might account for why fluent reading of characters does not necessarily imply comprehension of the Chinese words.

Teaching Chinese

In elementary school, teachers are required to teach most of the subjects and serve as classroom teachers to take care of students. In most cases, teachers of Chinese language arts are trained in Chinese or Chinese literature departments that emphasize learning Chinese classics. Most of the courses offered in college do not include the instruction of reading strategies. As mentioned, teachers are regarded as learned scholars. To ensure appropriate knowledge dissemination, most school language arts teachers follow a set of procedures and instructional activities provided by textbooks and workbooks. For example, in the first grade, lessons always begin with a warm-up activity, which mostly involves choral reading or questioning to preview the new lesson and review lessons. This stage is followed by a variety of activities to consolidate learning, especially practicing the writing of characters, and the lesson ends with individual desk work. The rationale behind the writing practice is to have students be familiar with the forms, structures and meanings of characters in order to read texts. In the third grade and higher, teaching procedures are similar, although with more extended and integrated activities as the focus of the lessons. Activities are used to reinforce the lexical or linguistic focus of the lesson or to elaborate the text (Chern, 1999). Less is observed of the instruction of morphological analysis of words. After elementary school, Chinese classics are introduced for students to learn more about Chinese culture. Many students appear to be distressed by learning classics, because of a lack of related background knowledge and the difficulty in comprehending the ancient style of writing and words used.

The aforementioned teaching methods are, in fact, a common practice across subjects. For example, Fwu and Wang (2006) observed three mathematics teachers in two junior high schools for the duration of a mathematics lesson that lasted three to four class hours. They gathered common steps used among these teachers: review of previous materials, presentation of the topic of the day, definition of terms and rules, demonstration with examples, practice on the blackboard and at the seat, and assignment of homework. During blackboard practice, teachers checked worksheet answers to ensure students had learned. In sum, learning is a refined process through the constant effort of repeated practice under the supervision of a teacher as the authority figure. Repeated practice was also previously observed in Mainland China's reading and writing instruction (Wu, Li, & Anderson, 1999).

After the National Reading Panel released its report that clearly stated that teaching reading strategies can improve reading achievement (National Reading Panel, 2000), scholars in Taiwan have advocated the implementation of strategy instruction in class.

Because most elementary school language arts teachers were trained in Chinese literature departments, Taiwan's Ministry of Education has launched the TARI program to help teachers familiarize themselves with reading strategies. To implement the instruction of reading comprehension strategies, it starts in textbooks. One reason is that teachers are familiar with the content of the textbooks. The other reason is that using textbooks to enforce reading strategies could minimize teachers' time and effort in organizing teaching plans other than textbooks. Stakeholders in this program developed a framework and guidelines for teaching reading comprehension strategies, provided exemplar lesson plans for teachers to follow or use as a reference, and convened workshops at the request of local schools (Ko, 2017). However, changing teachers' instructional practice is challenging. To ensure that change occurs, academic researchers familiar with reading theories and teaching practices worked closely with elementary schools to provide the necessary scaffolding support. They established a school–university collaboration (Lu, Yeh, Huang, & Guo, 2017), and these elementary schools eventually served as examples for neighboring schools.

After ten years of implementation of the TARI program, a visible trend demonstrates teachers are more frequently teaching reading strategies. In the PIRLS teachers' questionnaire, teachers were asked the following question: "How often do you ask students to apply the following nine strategies to help develop their reading comprehension skills?" The nine strategies are outlined as follows: identify the main ideas of what they have read; locate information within the text; explain or support their understanding of what they have read; compare what they have read with experiences they have had; compare what they have read with other things they have read; make predictions about what will happen next in the text they are reading; make generalizations and draw inferences based on what they have read; describe the style or structure of the text they have read; and determine the author's perspective or intention. The average percentage of teachers applying these strategies every day or almost every day had increased among fourth-grade teachers, especially with respect to strategies such as explaining or supporting their understanding of what they have read, making predictions, making generalizations and drawing inferences, and describing the style and structure of text read (Mullis et al., 2017; Mullis, Martin, Kennedy, & Pierre, 2007).

Apart from Teaching

Factors other than teaching influence a child becoming literate. Among such factors, home environment is considered the most critical. The relationship between family and children's reading skills is adequately documented in the Western literature (Rowe, 1991; Sénéchal & LeFevre, 2002). For example, in Australia, reading-related activities at home (e.g., read alone, being read to by others, read to others, and discuss reading) were associated with a child's attitude toward reading and his or her reading achievement (Rowe, 1991). Being in contact with storybooks at home during one's childhood was significantly associated with vocabulary development, listening comprehension, and phonological awareness, and children who had been taught to decode printed words at home made the most literacy progress in the first grade (Sénéchal, LeFevre, Thomas, & Daley, 1998).

The early home literacy activities advocated by the PIRLS are as follows: to read books, tell stories, sing songs, play with *zhùyīn fúhào* toys, play word games, and read aloud signs and labels. Of Taiwanese parents, 17% reported to have often organized these activities for their child, 75% declared to have sometimes organized these activities, and 7% disclosed to have never organized these activities at home. The parents were also asked questions pertaining to how often they enjoyed reading. Of the parents, 29% reported reading every day/almost every day, 43% reported reading once/twice a week, 19% reported reading once/twice a month, and 9% reported never reading (Mullis et al., 2017). Compared with the international average or with those of their Western counterparts, Taiwanese parents' reading behavior and early home reading activities are not outstanding.

A study examined the relationship between family environmental factors and students' reading achievements in Chinese communities (Hong Kong, Singapore, and Taiwan) and non-Chinese communities compatible to Chinese communities with respect to students' reading achievements. The analysis revealed that non-Chinese parents engaged in more parent–child reading activities, provided more books at home and for their children, and had a more positive attitude toward the importance of reading than did their Chinese counterparts. Most parents in the Chinese communities identified themselves as having medium-strength reading attitudes compared with those of parents from non-Chinese communities (Ko & Chan, 2009).

Although differences existed between these two communities concerning family reading activities, the main effects of family factors on reading achievements were similar. A hierarchical multiple regression analysis showed that children's early literacy skills at the beginning of primary school explained a significant 4% to 21% of the variance of children's reading attainment across the communities. After children's early literacy skills were controlled for, children's books and books at home explained a significant 1% to 9% of the variance in students' reading achievements. In the Chinese community, parental attitudes toward reading did not independently explain students' reading achievements, but they made a statistically significant explanation of 1% to 2% of the variance in students' achievement scores in the non-Chinese community (Ko & Chan, 2009).

In summary, children's early literacy skills and the number of books at home are the most relevant predictors of later reading achievement. In Chinese communities, these two factors are particularly critical. Apart from these two factors, other family factors made little to no contribution to students' reading achievement.

Another study supported that family factors such as parental educational level, home library, parental reading attitude, early home literacy activities, and current home reading activities were all associated with Taiwanese fourth graders' reading practice, reading attitude, and reading attainment to various extents. However, for reading achievement, parental educational level was the best predictor, followed by reading attitude, home library, early home literacy activities, gender, and current home reading activities (Chen, Chang, & Ko, 2011). These results suggest that among all factors, family SES, such as parental educational level, plays a key role in academic attainment, including becoming literate.

Conclusion

Learning to read is a complex process. For beginning reading, it seems clear that decoding efficiently should be a primary learning objective. Yet, to be a proficient reader of Chinese requires more than knowing thousands of characters. This chapter attempts to provide an overview of learning and teaching Chinese. It both refers and reports data in the context of historical and cultural background in education. First it reports Taiwanese teachers' training and their teaching practices. Subsequently, the author presents the psycholinguistic characteristics and the instruction of Chinese language. The nature of Chinese language differs from that of the alphabetic scripts, from its outlook to the structure of words. The study of Chinese structure and reading acquisition could provide additional information and data with existing theories on achieving literacy.

According to the mentioned literature, research on learning Chinese language has followed the paradigm of research on learning alphabetic scripts. Most cognitive factors related to reading alphabetic scripts have been investigated in the Chinese context. The social factors of cultivating reading such as family resources and SES have also been used in studies on factors that influence reading Chinese. The findings of these studies parallel those obtained in the alphabetic language (Ko & Chan, 2009; Pan et al., 2016). They have revealed a general universality with minor differences. The difference lies in the weight of the contributing factors, which pertain to the uniqueness of each language. Despite the differences in the nature of languages and in pedagogical practices, the mechanisms of reading different orthographies appear to be similar. Regarding instruction, Chinese teaching methods are relatively conservative. Teachers spend many class hours teaching characters and new words. Following NRP's suggestions, comprehension instruction and comprehension-monitoring strategies were introduced to language arts class in Taiwan, yet, change of teaching behavior does not occur overnight. For example, when children begin to master basic reading skills, MA is more useful when reading Chinese, and language arts teachers should consider this psycholinguistic aspect and design their teaching plans accordingly. Still, intervention study observed that teachers had difficulties in implementing MA instruction (Wu et al., 2009). Applying research to teaching practice will be challenging for future preservice and in-service teachers. For now, advocating reading in the family and encouraging teaching comprehension strategies at schools maintain the top priority of promoting literacy in Taiwan.

Implication for Future Research

Taiwanese teachers are diligent and have earned the respect of students and Taiwanese society because of the belief that effort counts and that practice makes perfect. Their efforts have promoted Taiwanese students' achievements on international assessments such as TIMSS, PISA (Fwu et al., 2014), and PIRLS (Mullis et al., 2017). Questions relating to this belief have been raised: Will this mindset become an obstacle to change? The crucial point is that the teacher should have the particular knowledge of cognitive processes of language learning and use them to adapt their teaching to the needs of students of different abilities and family SES. Furthermore, because of China's booming economy, Chinese language has become one of the most in-demand languages in the world (Tong & Yip, 2015). Research on how native Chinese learn Chinese could serve as a base for the research and teaching of students of Chinese as a foreign language (CFL) (e.g., Shen,

2005; Tong & Yip, 2015). Studies on CFL learner can support theories of literacy development in more than one language. Still, are teachers of CFL sensitive to the unique role of different orthographies and the mechanism of learning for both native Chinese and CFL students? These questions warrant follow-up research and cross-languages studies.

Recommendation for Globally Minded Literacy Teachers

As discussed, there are differences in the nature of languages and in pedagogical practices, yet, the underlying mechanisms of reading different orthographies appear to be similar. For example, the roles of phonological and morphological awareness to reading are acknowledged across languages. Still, the nature of each language should be emphasized for instructional purposes. Learning to read Chinese besides learning individual character and practicing writing characters in context, MA instruction has proved to be effective. It emphasizes the character component analysis and morphological analysis of words. The instructor needs to encourage and provide opportunity for students' application of this knowledge when they encounter new characters and words. Teachers should bear in mind that reading characters does not imply comprehension of words. Thus, applying comprehension strategies might be helpful for a better understanding of Chinese texts.

Discussion Questions Application

1. Describe two characteristics of Chinese characters. What is the nature of Chinese characters and Chinese words?
2. Share your experience of teaching comprehension strategies with Taiwan language arts teachers. How can they best develop instructional approaches at various levels of reading comprehension?
3. When family factor accounts for children's reading achievement, what can a language arts teacher do when facing students from different SES or ethnic and culture background?

Note

1 The PIRLS is one of IEA's (International Association for the Evaluation of Educational Achievement) projects and is meant to measure fourth-grade children's reading achievement every five years. In addition, the PIRLS collected extensive information on students' families and school experiences (student questionnaire), family socioeconomic conditions, parental engagement with the child in various literacy activities (parental questionnaire), various school characteristics (school questionnaire), and instructional practices (teacher questionnaire) to explain the conditions of students' reading achievement and behavior.

References

Anderson, R., Ku, Y.-M., Li, W., Chen, X., Wu, X., & Shu, H. (2013). Learning to see the patterns in Chinese characters. *Scientific Studies of Reading, 17*, 41–56.

Chen, M.-L. & Ko, H.-W. (2011). Exploring the eye movement patterns as Chinese children read texts: A developmental perspective. *Journal of Research in Reading, 34*(2), 232–246.

Chen, S. Y., Chang, Y. J., & Ko, H. W. (2011). The influence of parental education level, parental reading attitude, and current home reading activities on students' reading attainment: Findings from the PIRLS 2006. *Bulletin of Educational Psychology, 43*, 357–376.

Chern, C.-L. (1999). Literacy instruction in Taiwan: Teachers beliefs and their classroom practices. In C. Y. Mee & N. S. Moi (Eds.), *Language instructional issues in Asian classrooms* (pp. 16–28). Newark, NJ: International Reading Association.

DeFrancis, J. (1989). *Visible speech: The diverse openness of writing systems.* Honolulu, HI: University of Hawaii Press.

Fowler, A. E., Liberman, A. M., Shankweiler, D., Crain, S., Katz, L., Thornton, R., … Shaywitz, B. A. (1995). Cognitive profiles of reading-disabled children: Comparison of language skills in phonology, morphology, and syntax. *Psychological Science, 6*(3), 149–156.

Fwu, B. J. & Wang, H. H. (2002). The social status of teachers in Taiwan. *Comparative Education, 38*(2), 211–224.

Fwu, B. J. & Wang, H. H. (2006). Practice makes perfect on the blackboard: A cultural analysis of mathematics instructional patterns in Taiwan. *International Journal on Mathematics Education (Zentralblatt für Didaktik der Mathematik [ZDM]), 38*(5), 368–375.

Fwu, B. J., Wei, C. F., Chen, S. W., & Wang, H. H. (2014). Effort counts: The moral significance of effort in the patterns of credit assignment on math learning in the Confucian cultural context. *International Journal of Educational Development, 39*, 167–172.

Global Teacher Status Index. (2018). [PDF file]. www.varkeyfoundation.org/media/4867/gts-index-13-11-2018.pdf

Hu, C.-F. & Catts, H. W. (1998). The role of phonological processing in early reading ability: What we can learn from Chinese. *Scientific Studies of Reading, 2*, 55–79.

Huang, H. & Hanley, R. (1994). Phonological awareness and visual skills in learning to read Chinese and English. *Cognition, 54*, 73–98.

Jian, Y.-C., Chen, M.-L., & Ko, H.-W. (2013). Context effects in processing of Chinese academic words: An eye tracking investigation. *Reading Research Quarterly, 48*(4), 403–413.

Jian, Y.-C. & Ko, H.-W. (2014). Investigating the effects of background knowledge on Chinese word processing during text reading: Evidence from eye movements. *Journal of Research in Reading, 37*(1), 71–86.

Ko, H.-W. (2017). Promoting textbook base reading comprehension strategy instruction in Taiwan. Presented in Annual Conference of Association for Reading and Writing in Asia. The Education University of Hong Kong, Hong Kong, 24–25 February, 2017.

Ko, H.-W. & Chan, Y.-L. (2009). Family factors and primary students' Reading achievement: A Chinese community perspective. *Chinese Education and Society, 42*(3), 33–48.

Ko, H.-W. & Wu, C.-F. (2003). The role of radical awareness in reading Chinese. In C. McBride-Chang & H. Chen (Eds.), *Reading development in Chinese children* (pp. 73–79). Westport, CT: Praeger.

Lee, C.-Y. (2011). The statistical learning perspective on Chinese reading. In P. McCardle, B. Miller, J.-R. Lee, & O. J. L. Tzeng (Eds.), *Dyslexia across languages: Orthography and the brain-gene-behavior link* (pp. 44–61). Baltimore: Brookes Publishing.

Li, W., Anderson, R. C., Nagy, W., & Zhang, H. (2002). Facets of metalinguistic awareness that contribute to Chinese literacy. In W. Li, J. S. Gaffney, & J. L. Packard (Eds.), *Chinese children's reading acquisition: Theoretical and pedagogical issues* (pp. 87–106). Norwell, MA: Kluwer Academic Publishers.

Li, X., Rayner, K., & Cave, K. (2009). On the segmentation of Chinese words during reading. *Cognitive Psychology, 58*, 525–552.

Lu, I.-C., Yeh, Y., Huang, B., & Guo, Y.-C. (2017). A school-university collaboration for the implementation of the textbook-based approach to reading instruction (TBRI). Presented in Annual Conference of Association for Reading and Writing in Asia, The Education University of Hong Kong, Hong Kong.

McBride-Chang, C. & Ho, C. S. H. (2000). Developmental issues in Chinese children's character acquisition. *Journal of Educational Psychology, 92*(1), 50–55.

McBride-Chang, C., Shu, H., Zhou, A., Wat., C. P., & Wagner, R. (2003). Morphological awareness uniquely predicts young children's character recognition. *Journal of Educational Psychology, 95*(4), 743–751.

Ministry of Education. (2017). *Education in Taiwan 2017–2018*. https://english.moe.gov.tw/cp-16-17192-F34D2-1.html

Mullis, I. V. S., Martin, M. O., Foy, P., & Hooper, M. (2017). *PIRLS 2016 international results in Reading*. Boston: Boston College, TIMSS & PIRLS International Study Center.

Mullis, I. V. S., Martin, M. O., Kennedy, A. M., & Pierre, F. (2007). *PIRLS 2006 international report: IEA's progress in international reading literacy study in primary schools in 40 countries*. TIMSS & PIRLS, International Study Center. Chestnut Hill, MA: Boston College.

National Reading Panel. (2000). Teaching children to read: An evidence-based assessment of the scientific research literature on reading and its implications for reading instruction. Reports of the subgroups [PDF file]. www.nichd.nih.gov/sites/default/files/publications/pubs/nrp/Documents/report.pdf

Pan, J., Song, S., Su, M., McBride, C., Liu, H., Zhang, Y., Li, H., & Shu, H. (2016). On the relationship between phonological awareness, morphological awareness and Chinese literacy skills: Evidence from an 8-year longitudinal study. *Developmental Science, 19*(6), 982–991.

Rayner, K. (1998). Eye movements in reading and information processing: 20 years of research. *Psychological Bulletin, 24*, 372–422.

Rowe, K. J. (1991). The influence of reading activity at home on students' attitudes towards reading, classroom attentiveness and reading achievement: An application of structural equation modeling. *British Journal of Educational Psychology, 61*(1), 19–35.

Sénéchal, M. & LeFevre, J-A. (2002). Parental involvement in the development of children's reading skills: A five-year longitudinal study. *Child Development, 73*(2), 445–460.

Sénéchal, M., LeFevre, J. A., Thomas, E. M., & Daley, K. E. (1998). Differential effects of home literacy experiences on the development of oral and written language. *Reading Research Quarterly, 33*, 96–116.

Shen, D., Liversedge, S., Tian, J., Zang, C., Cui, L., Bai, X., Yan, G., & Rayner, K. (2012). Eye movements of second language learners when reading spaced and unspaced Chinese Text. *Journal of Experimental Psychology: Applied, 18*(2), 192–202.

Shen, H. H. (2005). An investigation of Chinese-character learning strategies among non-native speakers of Chinese. *System, 33*(1), 49–68.

Shu, H. & Anderson, R. (1997). Role of radical awareness in the character and word acquisition of Chinese children. *Reading Research Quarterly, 32*(1), 78–89.

Shu, H., Chen, X., Anderson, R., Wu, N., & Xuan, Y. (2003). Properties of school Chinese implications for learning to read. *Child Development, 74*(1), 27–47.

Song, S., Georgiou, G. K., Su, M., & Shu, H. (2016). How well do phonological awareness and rapid automatized naming correlate with Chinese reading accuracy and fluency? A meta-analysis. *Scientific Studies of Reading, 20*(2), 99–123.

Tong, X. & Yip, J. H. Y. (2015). Cracking the Chinese character: Radical sensitivity in learners of Chinese as a foreign language and its relationship to Chinese word reading. *Reading and Writing: An Interdisciplinary Journal, 28*(2), 159–181.

Wang, C.-C., Hung, L.-Y., Chang, Y.-W., & Chen, H.-F. (2008). Yī dào jiǔ niánjí xuéshēng guó zì shìzì liàng fāzhǎn [Number of characters school students know from Grade 1 to Grade 9]. *Jiàoyù xīnlǐ xuébào [Bulletin of Educational Psychology], 39* (4), 555–568 (in Chinese).

Wang, H. H. & Fwu, B. J. (2007). In pursuit of teacher quality in diversity: A study of the selection mechanisms of new secondary teacher education programmes in Taiwan. *International Journal of Educational Development, 27*, 166–181.

Wang, H. H. & Fwu, B. J. (2014). "Once hired, seldom gone": The deliberation process of beginning teachers in Taiwan in deciding to stay in teaching. *Teaching and Teacher Education, 37*, 108–118.

Wu, X., Anderson, R. C., Li, W., Wu, X., Li, H., Zhang, J., Zheng, Q., Zhu, J., Shu, H., Jiang, W., Chen, X., Wang, Q., Yin, L., He, Y., Packard, J., & Gaffney, J. S. (2009). Morphological awareness and Chinese children's literacy development: An intervention study. *Scientific Studies of Reading, 13*(1), 26–52.

Wu, X., Li, W., & Anderson, R. C. (1999). Reading instruction in China. *Journal of Curriculum Studies, 31*, 571–586.

Chapter 9

Becoming a Proficient Writer in New Zealand's Primary Schools

Murray Gadd

Summary of Chapter

- This chapter examines New Zealand as a culturally diverse country with varying degrees of classroom achievement in relation to student age, gender and ethnic background.
- This chapter shares key approaches to the teaching of writing in New Zealand primary classrooms. Note that primary classrooms in the New Zealand context are classrooms in which 5 to 13-year-old students are taught. Teachers regard writing primarily as a socio-cultural activity with a strong communicative intent. They mainly use a workshop approach to teaching writing.
- This chapter provides a description of what writing instruction looks like in a New Zealand classroom.

Vignette

A teacher of nine-year-old students walks into the classroom and inquires of his students, 'What shall we write about today? What's been happening in our lives that's worth sharing with other people? Have a think … Now talk to a buddy'. Having decided on 'a recent market day operated by students' as a good topic, the teacher enquires further, 'What do you want your readers to know about market day? Shall we record some ideas all together?' He later encourages them to form groups according to self-selected purposes for writing and continues, 'So your group wants to tell your readers what happened. Anyone in particular? You'd be writing a recount. You know how to write a recount don't you? Look at those examples on the wall if you're stuck' and

> Ooh, so your group wants to write an informational report about Market Day. Who would your readers be? Yes, it could go in the school

newsletter … Now, do you remember how to write an informational report? Maybe I'll bring one to school tomorrow and we could work together and begin to construct one …

This teacher appreciates the importance of knowing his students well, ensuring that topics are purposeful for students, involving them in topic and task selection, providing them with direct instruction about text types and differentiating their learning according to interests and needs.

Historical, Cultural and Political Context

New Zealand is a relatively small country (its current population is 4.8 million) and its schooling context is one educational jurisdiction approximately the size of a small state like Vermont in the United States. Its classrooms are culturally, linguistically and ethnically diverse. The most recent statistics from the Ministry of Education suggest that 50.1% of the school population identify as New Zealand European (NZE); 18.5% as Maori (the indigenous population of New Zealand); 16.3% as Pasifika (being of Pacific Island descent); 15.1% as 'Other' (www.educationcounts.govt.nz/statistics/schooling/studentnumbers/6028). The fastest growing sector are those who identify as 'Other', with students principally originating from China or India. It is predicted that by 2038, the proportion of the New Zealand population that identifies as Asian will have more than doubled from what it is in 2018; from 541,300 to 1,272,200 (www.stats.govt.nz/topics/population). Much of the population that is non-New Zealand European state that they speak a language other than English fluently. In a recent reasonably representative survey of attitudes to writing by 449 upper primary age students, 42.8% stated that they spoke a language other than English with 'reasonable fluency', naming 39 languages (Gadd et al., 2019).

New Zealand's schools are self-governing. School leaders and community representatives interpret a national curriculum statement (*New Zealand Curriculum*, Ministry of Education, 2007a) and apply its details judiciously to their local context. The statement requires that primary schools deliver a programme in eight essential learning areas (including English, which contains an outline of writing skills needed by proficient writers at each level of schooling) and encourages schools to seek and utilise further guidance in the teaching of writing from nationally available support documents and tools. These include the *Literacy Learning Progressions* (Ministry of Education, 2010), which nuance the writing skills and strategies needed for writing proficiency; research-based handbooks on the effective teaching of literacy (*Effective Literacy Practice in Years 1 to 4*, Ministry of Education, 2006; *Effective Literacy Practice in Years 5 to 8*, Ministry of Education, 2007b); and a diagnostic writing assessment tool (*e-asTTle writing*) that enables normative comparisons in writing proficiency to be made because of its links to the levels of the *New Zealand Curriculum* (Ministry of Education and New Zealand Council for Educational Research, 2012). But primary schools (and teachers) can select 'what to teach', 'how to teach' and 'how to measure' in their writing programmes from these broad guidelines and this range of support material. They are encouraged to make 'overall teacher judgements' about the progress of their 5 to 13-year-old students in writing as guided by the support material, but there is no mandated testing in New Zealand primary schools.

The range of 'overall teacher judgements' in writing reported in 2017 by New Zealand primary schools indicates that almost three-quarters (71.1%) of primary students are achieving at a level that is 'at' or 'above' national expectations for their particular year cohort, as established by the *New Zealand Curriculum*. This is comparatively better than the picture presented in the most recent *Report Card* from the United States indicating that almost three-quarters of American students in their final year of middle schooling achieved slightly below or well below an expected level of proficiency (National Council for Education Statistics, 2012) and the conclusion reached in the United Kingdom's Department for Education achievement report in 2012 that 'writing is the subject with the worst performance compared with reading, maths and science' (p. 3).

But New Zealand primary teachers also recognise that there is significant variability within the relatively high overall achievement level (71.1%). They recognise, for example, that the proportion of older primary-age students (aged 9–13) achieving 'at' or 'above' national achievement expectations is 4.3% lower than the proportion of younger students (aged 5–8); that there is a significant gap (of approximately 15%) between boys' and girls' achievement levels; and that Maori and Pasifika students score roughly 10–20% lower than other ethnic groups, especially students who identify as NZE (Ministry of Education, 2017). Furthermore, they recognise that these levels of disparity have not been reduced significantly since the collection of national data in 2013.

Hence there is an ongoing drive amongst New Zealand primary teachers to enhance the achievement level of all of their students (but especially older primary-age students) as developing writers and to reduce the achievement gap between boys and girls and between Maori/Pasifika and NZE students. Teachers recognise that this means engaging some cohorts more in writing than they are currently engaged – for they understand that achievement is only enhanced if engagement is strengthened (Gibbs & Poskitt, 2010; Joselowsky, 2007) – as well as accelerating the progress of those under-achieving cohorts in order to narrow some worrying levels of disparity in writing.

The drive is contingent on the research finding that 'what teachers do matters'. On the back cover of the previously mentioned literacy handbooks for teachers is the widely accepted maxim, 'It is what teachers actually do, moment by moment in their classrooms, that makes a difference to student achievement'. This emanates from conclusions made by Adrienne Alton-Lee (2003) in her synthesis of findings to the New Zealand Ministry of Education on what constitutes quality teaching for diverse learners: 'Quality teaching … is the most influential point of leverage on student outcomes' (p. 2) and high achievement for diverse groups of learners is 'an outcome of the skilled and cumulative pedagogical actions of a teacher in creating and optimising an effective learning environment' (p. 1). Accepting that effective teachers iteratively inquire into the effectiveness of their practice on the engagement, progress and achievement of their students (Ministry of Education, 2007a, p. 35), New Zealand primary teachers continually inquire into what aspects of their practice work best for which of their students in their classrooms for all aspects of their teaching.

Historical and Philosophical Underpinnings: Key Approaches to the Teaching of Writing

New Zealand primary teachers primarily regard writing as a *socio-cultural* activity in which writers aim to communicate clearly and proficiently for a range of purposes (though principally to inform, entertain or persuade others) and on information or ideas that are generally important to them (Barnard & Campbell, 2005; Cherry, 2018; Vygotsky, 1978). They principally recognise that being a good writer is contingent on 'having something to say' (Graves, 1983, 1994).

Most primary teachers employ a *workshop approach* to the teaching of writing (Atwell, 1987; Calkins, 1994). Acknowledging that writers move between a range of processes and strategies (such as planning, composing and revising) as they construct texts (Flower & Hayes, 1981), they encourage their students to work independently or collaboratively over time at deciding on writing topics, purposes and audiences; planning for writing through gathering and ordering possible content; recording ideas clearly by using their graphophonic, semantic and syntactic knowledge to construct a range of sentences; re-reading, reflecting, re-crafting and presenting their writing by thinking about the possible reader and reviewing their work accordingly (Ministry of Education, 2006, pp. 138–141, 2007b, pp. 150–158).

In their survey of writing instructional practices that teachers utilise, Parr and Jesson (2016) conclude that New Zealand primary teachers spend almost three hours per week on average teaching writing and that students spend on average almost five hours per week writing in the classroom. They contend that this is considerably more than American students spend on writing per week at school. Cutler and Graham (2008) reported that grade 1–3 students in the United States write for a median of 1.75 hours per week.

New Zealand primary students are generally encouraged to learn to write and learn about writing through the construction of extended texts; namely, texts comprising connected sentences on a selected topic (Kellogg & Raulerson, 2007). This contrasts with students receiving writing instruction through isolated or discrete exercises, not always related to a particular writing topic and often on points of grammar, which appears to be a reasonably common instructional approach in the United States and the United Kingdom (Parr & Jesson, 2016). When New Zealand primary students are taught about writing – whether at the whole class, small group or individual level – this is almost always within the context of composing a real text for an authentic purpose (Gadd, 2017).

But New Zealand teachers also recognise that students develop at varying rates and need varying levels of support as they construct texts. This support can come from 'expert others', whether they be authors of model texts, other students, or themselves as teachers who demonstrate, question, explain and give feedback and feed-forward to students about aspects of their writing (Vygotsky, 1978). They understand that their role involves making learning tasks as achievable and manageable as possible for their students by altering the cognitive load that students must carry as they undertake tasks (Hmelo-Silver, Duncan, & Chinn, 2007; Wood, Bruner, & Ross, 1976). They also understand that this means 'knowing your students well' (Hamre & Pianta, 2001) so that they can ascertain 'who needs what support and when' and 'what this support needs to look like' (Gadd, 2017).

Most literacy research that is writing-focussed in New Zealand aims at helping teachers determine 'who needs what support and when' and 'what this support needs to look like'. An important question that New Zealand literacy researchers and teachers continually ask is: 'What makes the difference?' if issues of achievement disparity are to be addressed satisfactorily (Gadd, 2014).

Theory and Research Base: A Summary of Writing-Focussed Research in New Zealand 2000–2018

A considerable amount of writing-focussed research has been undertaken in New Zealand over the past two decades, much of it within the context of older primary-age students (aged 9–13) because of previously mentioned issues of under-achievement within this cohort. Analysis of this research has led to the identification of a set of broad effective practice dimensions and related instructional strategies that appear to be associated with enhanced student engagement and progress in writing within the New Zealand context. These are synthesised in Parr and Jesson's (2016) article on mapping the landscape of writing instruction in New Zealand primary classrooms, and in Parr and colleagues' two-year inquiry (2018) into what makes a difference for under-achieving older primary-age students in New Zealand classrooms. The New Zealand-based research collectively suggests that effective teachers of writing:

- Hold a good knowledge of their students as unique and culturally-centred learners and as developing writers (Bishop, Berryman, Cavanagh, & Teddy, 2007; Fletcher, Parkhill, & Fa'afoi, 2005; Parr & Limbrick, 2010; Si'ilata, 2014; Si'lata, Samu, & Siteine, 2017).
- Develop writing tasks with and for students that are closely aligned to strategically selected learning goals (Gadd, 2014, 2017; Gadd & Parr, 2016, 2017; Parr & Limbrick, 2010; Timperley & Parr, 2009).
- Provide direct and explicit instruction at the time of need. This includes giving targeted feedback and feed-forward to students (Gadd, 2014, 2017; Gadd & Parr, 2017; Glasswell, 2000; Glasswell, Parr, & McNaughton, 2003; Jesson & Cockle, 2014; Parr & Hawe, 2017; Parr & Jesson, 2016; Parr & Timperley, 2010).
- Differentiate instruction according to the needs of students (Gadd, 2014, 2017; Gadd & Parr, 2017; Glasswell, 2000).
- Scaffold self-regulation and independence for writers (Gadd, 2014; 2017; Gadd & Parr, 2017; Glasswell & Parr, 2009; Parr & Timperley, 2010).

In the inquiry undertaken by Parr and colleagues (2018) there is evidence that proficient operationalisation of these dimensions of effective practice and related instructional strategies is strongly associated with significantly greater than expected progress by under-achieving students. Using the norm-referenced e-asTTle writing assessment tool to measure the progress of a large group of 9–13-year-old students (n = 449) over two years, data indicated that more students (but particularly boys, Maori students and Pasifika students) were achieving 'well below' national expectations than were achieving 'above', 'at' or 'just below' them at the beginning of the inquiry. But by the end, more were achieving in the 'above' expectations achievement band than in any other band. Furthermore, boys made twice the progress of girls, though their achievement levels continued to be lower than those for girls; and Maori students made twice the progress of NZE students, though their achievement levels continued to be lower than those for NZE students.

Many of the conclusions in the previously mentioned research are not unique to the New Zealand context – most of these dimensions feature in the summary discussions of much international writing research by (for example) Applebee and Langer (2011); Cutler and Graham (2008); Gilbert and Graham (2010); Graham and Perin (2007); Graham, Capizzi, Harris, Hebert, and Morphy (2014); Grossman, Loeb, Cohen, and Wyckoff (2013); Langer (2001); Medwell, Wray, Poulson, and Fox (1998); Pressley, Wharton-McDonald, Mistretta-Hampson, and Echevarria (1998) – but the local findings generate a particular and unique picture of what effective writing instruction 'looks like' in New Zealand.

Holding a Good Knowledge of Students as Culturally-Centred Learners

Effective teachers of writing recognise the importance of knowing their students well as *unique and culturally-centred learners* (Bishop et al., 2007; Parr & Limbrick, 2010; Si'ilata, 2014; Si'lata et al., 2017). They understand that knowing their students well as culturally centred learners can influence (for example) topic and task choice, selection of teaching and learning strategies, the nature of teacher–student learning conversations, and approaches to grouping; all key factors for enhancing the engagement of students in writing (Gadd, 2014; Gadd & Clueard, 2018). When interviewed about knowing their under-achieving students (referred to as touchstone students) in the Parr et al. (2018) inquiry, participating teachers emphasised relationships as particularly important with these diverse students. As one teacher commented:

> It's funny when we chose the touchstone kids at the beginning of the year we didn't really know them and as the year progresses you see the things that are influencing factors for them … [You need to] notice their attitudes and writing-related behaviours by watching, sitting alongside, talking about writing and what they think about it.
>
> (p. 7)

Because New Zealand classrooms are culturally and linguistically diverse (as discussed previously) and because of the achievement disparity between NZE and Maori/Pasifika achievement, much of the New Zealand research on 'knowing students well' focuses on the importance of teachers knowing their Maori and Pasifika students well. In their widely published research on engagement and achievement by Maori students in secondary school classrooms, Bishop et al. (2007) conclude that teachers who 'care for their students as culturally located human beings above all else' (which they refer to in the Maori language as Manaakitanga), who 'are able to create a secure, well-managed learning environment' (Whakakapiringatanga), who 'are able to engage in effective teaching interactions with Maori students as Maori' (Wananga) and who 'can use a range of strategies that promote effective teaching interactions and relationships with their learners' (Ako) contribute significantly to positive outcomes by learners. They advocate that these are some key elements of a 'culturally responsive teacher' and their accompanying professional learning programme suggest pedagogical actions that teachers can utilise to achieve these goals (http://tekotahitanga.tki.org.nz/About/The-Development-of-Te-Kotahitanga/Effective-Teaching-Profile).

In her unpublished doctoral thesis on ways of enhancing the literacy achievement levels of Pasifika students, Si'ilata (2014) explores how teachers can enable Pasifika students to connect their learning at school with the worldviews, languages, literacy practices and experiences of their homes through the strategic use of culturally responsive pedagogies. This involves ensuring that Pasifika students' languages, cultures and identities are represented in the valued knowledge of the school and utilised as a normal part of language and literacy learning in the classroom (Si'lata et al., 2017). In her thesis, she demonstrates how effective operationalisation of these pedagogies can enhance Pasifika students' linguistic and literacy achievement beyond expected achievement levels.

Holding a Good Knowledge of Students as Developing Writers

Effective teachers of writing also recognise the importance of knowing their students well as *developing writers* (Clarke, Timperley, & Hattie, 2003; Symes & Timperley, 2003; Timperley & Parr, 2009). They understand that this requires them to hold a comprehensive knowledge of what their students should be able to achieve and demonstrate as developing writers as outlined in the *New Zealand Curriculum* and its related documents. This also requires them to be able to notice their students' strengths and needs as developing writers in relation to what they should be achieving. Teachers need to be able to analyse student texts efficiently and keep manageable records of these analyses that can be used for planning and teaching purposes. Ultimately, they need to be able to demonstrate that their teaching of writing is informed by student learning needs. Much professional development and learning for New Zealand teachers in writing has focussed on how to get to know students well and understand their needs as developing writers (Meissel, Parr, & Timperley, 2016; Poskitt & Taylor, 2008).

This was a challenge for some of the teachers in the Parr et al. inquiry (2018). All acknowledged that 'keeping track of individual needs' was an essential component of knowing their students as developing writers; but some admitted that they were not doing this satisfactorily at the beginning of the inquiry. As one stated, 'I could see objectively that [noting strengths and needs] was a good idea, but I just didn't quite, I don't know why, it hadn't quite gelled for me' (p. 7). By the end of the inquiry, this same teacher stated, 'I think I'm [now] keeping a real track of who I'm seeing … I've actually been using a document I've devised for this' (p. 7). This document, which became a key planning and teaching tool for the teacher, contained a list of the writing skills and strategies the teacher's year level cohort should be able to achieve, space for recording students' names beside items that were identified as needs from regular analyses of texts, and space for combining names in order to form needs-based workshop groups.

Developing Purposeful and Authentic Writing Tasks

Effective teachers have always understood that 'what students write about' affects their engagement and ultimately their achievement in writing (Ames,

1992; Blumenfeld, 1992). When asked what strategies their teachers used that most engaged them in writing, senior primary students in the previously mentioned survey of attitudes to writing (Gadd et al., 2019), overwhelmingly nominated 'the teacher selected a topic that was interesting for me' and 'the teacher gave me some choice in topic or how I wrote' as the top-ranked strategies. One 12-year-old boy stated, 'I like writing if I have a choice in what I write or if the topic is one that I enjoy' (p. 8). This student acknowledged that the nature of writing tasks, including what he wrote about, had the power of engaging or disengaging him as a writer at school.

In his unpublished doctoral thesis on what is critical in the effective teaching of writing in relation to eight dimensions of pedagogical practice (expectations; learning goals; learning tasks; direct instruction; responding to students; motivation and challenge; organisation and management; self-regulation), Gadd (2014) confirmed the critical importance of *learning tasks* in New Zealand primary classrooms by determining a significant correlation (using Spearman's *rho*) between teacher effectiveness around learning tasks and high learner gains ($r_s = .73$, $p<.05$) in his study of nine effective teachers of writing. Furthermore, he determined a significant correlation for two instructional aspects of task orientation and high learner gains: teachers' capacity to devise learning tasks that students can identify as purposeful ($r_s = .76$, $p<.05$) and their capacity to involve students in the selection or construction of learning tasks ($r_s = .68$, $p<.05$). Further investigation into this data reinforced the importance of task purposefulness, authenticity and student involvement (Gadd, 2017; Gadd & Parr, 2016, 2017). As one teacher in the study (2014) stated, teachers and students 'have to seize the moment ... because topic is so essential ... I find the best writing is the writing that's, you know, got real purpose'. This teacher did not have a predetermined plan of topics 'because that would not allow us, as a class, to go off and write on the things that we want to write about'. She added that 'having something to say ... something to write about ... is of paramount importance to me as a teacher of writing' (pp. 110–111).

Even though Gadd (2014) concluded that 'the dimensions and strategies of effective pedagogy needed for [under-achieving students] are those needed for success by all learners' (p. 184), he acknowledged that some differentiation of pedagogical strategies was needed for generating particular progress by boys in writing. This mainly involved selecting writing tasks and topics that engaged the interest of boys. Through professional learning, New Zealand teachers have taken on the suggestion that boy writers respond particularly well to writing (for example) 'imaginative narratives ... recounts of events that are significant to them ... reports and explanations of phenomena that are important to them ... structured poetry' and creating story books for other students, especially younger students ... caption writing for 'real life' digital images ... [devising] Power Point presentations of research topics with key points noted ... writing and recording digitally rap songs, short scenes, jokes, jingles and advertisements ... [undertaking] drama or role play that leads to writing.

(http://motivatingboywriters.blogspot.co.nz/2010/01/23-top-tips-for-boys-writing-research)

Teachers in the Parr et al. (2018) inquiry, whose boy students had made twice the progress of their girl students, actively reflected on the selection of tasks and topics for boys from this research when planning and implementing their writing programmes.

Providing Direct and Explicit Instruction

Previous New Zealand research around the importance of providing students with direct and explicit instruction in writing (Glasswell, 2000; Glasswell, Parr, & McNaughton, 2003; Jesson & Cockle, 2014; Parr & Limbrick, 2010) has led to a description of classroom routines and structures that many New Zealand teachers would recognise: 'whole class modelling, including the reading and exploring of text often as part of shared writing, followed by independent or guided writing by small groups, with in-task teacher support of writers through feedback within writing conferences' (Parr & Jesson, 2016, p. 988). In addition, Parr and Timperley (2010) demonstrated a statistically strong relationship between teachers' ability to give high quality feedback and students' progress in writing.

But in his unpublished doctoral thesis and in subsequent articles, Gadd (2014) not only confirmed the critical importance of providing direct and explicit instruction in New Zealand primary classrooms but also nuanced several aspects of the above description. Just as he did with *learning tasks*, he determined a significant correlation (using Spearman's *rho*) between teacher effectiveness at providing *direct and explicit instruction* and high learner gains ($r_s = .67$, $p<.05$).

But a close examination of variation between proficiency levels of participating teachers at the instruction they were providing generated some interesting conclusions. Even though all teachers were regarded as exemplary, students in some classrooms appeared to make greater progress than others. Those teachers whose students made the greatest progress were the teachers who wrote actively with their students. All teachers utilised *receptive modelling* (instructing through exemplar or existing texts) but only those whose students made the greatest progress also utilised *active modelling* (co-constructing texts with students and using teacher think-alouds as they did so) (Gadd, 2014, pp. 121–129). This finding reinforces the pedagogical importance of demonstrating learning processes and outcomes actively to students (Regan & Berkeley, 2012).

In addition, those teachers whose students made the greatest progress asked three times more high cognitive-demand questions in their discussions with students about writing than the others did. High cognitive-demand questions are those that require students to analyse, evaluate and synthesise text-related issues and think deeply and metacognitively about them (Bloom, 1956). They are often 'how?' and 'why?' questions rather than 'what?' questions (Gadd, 2014, pp. 129–130).

In addition, many teachers in the Parr et al. (2018) inquiry into what works best for touchstone students talked about the importance of breaking writing tasks into manageable components. As one teacher explained:

> It is overwhelming for my touchstone students to think of completing a whole piece of writing … I make sure that I chunk the task down to achievable bites. This means, for example, breaking up the brainstorming associated with planning. I am trying to structure planning by … chunking it, by having brainstorms for each specific bit rather than just one big brainstorm.
>
> (p. 9)

Others in the inquiry talked about the benefits of using scaffolds (such as graphic organisers, mnemonics, word banks and sentence starters) as temporary supports for touchstone students during writing (p. 9).

Differentiating Instruction according to the Needs of Students

In their discussion of classroom routines and structures, Parr and Jesson (2016) suggested that lesson patterns that include whole class modelling sometimes 'constrain teachers' and students' ability to incorporate diverse learners' existing textual and communicative repertoires of expertise' (p. 988). This signals the need for teachers to differentiate their instruction in order to address diverse and changing needs amongst students as developing writers. They need to constantly inquire, 'Who needs what teaching, when and what does it need to look like?'

Grouping is at the heart of differentiated instruction but using a workshop approach (as many New Zealand primary teachers do) means that grouping needs to be flexible and based on emerging needs rather than ability levels (Calkins, 1994). This links with the previous discussion about the importance of analysing students' writing regularly and noting strengths and needs as developing writers as a means of forming workshop groups.

Teachers across the Gadd study (2014, 2017) and across the Parr et al. inquiry (2018) rarely undertook direct writing instruction with the whole class; they worked instead with small groups for short periods, sometimes co-constructing texts with them, sometimes discussing their writing with them and getting them to respond to each other's writing, sometimes teaching them a writing skill or strategy through the collaborative re-construction of one student's text. One of the teachers in the Gadd study (2017) suggested that the concept of differentiated instruction was critical to her. She explained:

> I've got ... almost beginning writers through to some really quite advanced writers in my class this year. One size just doesn't fit all ... I have to look for ways of doing things that allow each of my kids to learn or make progress at their own level ... Otherwise I'm going to lose some of them ... and I don't just mean my [under-achieving] kids ...
>
> (p. 42)

However, a challenge related to differentiation emerged amongst some of the teachers in the Parr et al. inquiry (2018) in that some under-achieving students resisted being part of small group instructional sessions. Investigation into this suggested that they equated small group instruction with a visible reminder to their class-mates (as well as themselves) that they needed more support than others. This reinforced a self-perception that they were 'dumb'. Discussions with teachers about this during the inquiry encouraged them to ensure that grouping was always flexible, that students were sometimes invited rather than directed to be part of a group, and that under-achieving students received regular opportunities to work independently or with a buddy rather than just with the teacher. One teacher in the inquiry who felt that her instructional grouping was effective suggested that mixed ability grouping (based on needs rather than ability) made some of her less-confident writers more aware of 'some of the good stuff they were doing' and understand that 'some of the students that they regard as good writers struggle with aspects of writing too' (p. 8).

Scaffolding Self-Regulation and Independence

One of the key goals of the *New Zealand Curriculum* is to ensure that students become independent, motivated, metacognitive and self-regulated learners. The curriculum statement suggests that students who manage their learning well can 'establish personal goals, make plans, manage projects and set high standards' (Ministry of Education, 2007a, p. 12). Much research has been undertaken on the pedagogical actions that teachers can implement to support primary students to meet this goal satisfactorily.

Gibbs and Poskitt, in their review of engagement and motivation amongst older primary students as learners (2010), conclude that students 'who have been taught how to use self-regulation processes and are provided with opportunities to use them, demonstrate high levels of engagement and achievement' (p. 20).

Gadd, in his 2014 study, explores what this conclusion might look like in an effective writing classroom. He signals the importance of *self-regulation* as a key dimension of effective writing practice by noting a significant correlation between teacher effectiveness at promoting self-regulation by students and a decrease in achievement variance amongst students ($r_s = .67$, $p<.05$). He also calculates that self-regulation is the dimension with the greatest operational proficiency difference between teacher participants whose students made the greatest learning gains and other teachers.

He notes several instructional actions that the most proficient teachers made. He notes, for example, that they provided opportunities for independent (as well as instructional) writing. Some timetabled independent writing sessions; others merely encouraged students to write in their own time. Some allowed for total self-selection of topics; others offered topics that students could choose from. Students' independent writing was not assessed as such, but teachers were always willing to respond to writing if asked. One of the teachers in the Gadd study (2014) explained why independent writing was so important to her and her students:

> I want writing to be a real-life thing for my students ... It's not just something you do between 9 and 10; it's something you do because you've got something to say ... and you want to get it out of you ... I want them to think of themselves as writers and understand that writing isn't just something you do in writing time.
>
> (p. 140)

Several teachers in the Parr et al. (2018) inquiry spoke of the implementation of *lightning writing* or *quick writes* (when students write for a short time on anything they want to) as a means of building enthusiasm, confidence, risk-taking and independence in students as developing writers.

Gadd (2014) also notes that highly proficient teachers in his study encouraged students to write collaboratively from time to time and assume responsibility for self-monitoring their progress and seeking the support they perceive as necessary to overcome problems and challenges in their writing. Students could (for example) be invited rather than directed to attend workshops; they could 'book in' for workshops they felt they needed to attend.

Applying the Research to the Classroom

So what does a synthesis of this research *look like* in a set of typical instructional writing sessions in a New Zealand primary classroom? The following is an outline of a set of three writing sessions (each lasting approximately 45 minutes) that the author led with a class of 10–11-year-old students. A monarch butterfly had just emerged from a chrysalis in the classroom and the students were very excited about this. Discussion of what they had observed led to a decision to write about it.

Introductory Session

The steps, in order, were:

- *Decide on a topic to write about.* This was an easy decision to make because of the students' excitement around the natural phenomenon being observed. If such an obvious topic was not available, the teacher might have (for example) told or read a story to students, discussed a picture or video clip with them or provided a story starter as a means of motivating or engaging students in a possible topic.
- *Develop content around the topic.* The teacher elicited students' understanding of what they had observed (through close questioning) as well as their prior knowledge about the life cycle of a monarch butterfly. He recorded key information on a whiteboard (steps in the process; order of steps; related vocabulary) that students could access in their writing. If the students did not hold this knowledge, further research would have been required.
- *Decide on a writing task.* Recording of key information on the life cycle led students to decide that the task would be *to explain how a monarch butterfly is formed for readers with little knowledge about this that could be incorporated into a school display.* They could have decided instead to (for example) *describe* the butterfly, *recount* what they had observed or *write a poem* about it; or the teacher could have allowed them to select their own task.
- *Establish some success criteria.* The teacher asked: 'So what will we need to be good at to do this task well?' Through guided questioning and prompting, it was decided that they would need to be good at 'including detail in the explanation', 'putting the steps in the correct sequence and using some sequence words' and 'using the topic words correctly', as well as reflecting on the generic skills (such as sentence formation, punctuation, spelling) required of good writers. Each student knew which of these generic skills to reflect on from previous teacher feedback, but the emphasis would be on the co-constructed success criteria for this particular task.
- *Invite students to move off and write independently.* Sufficient scaffolding had been provided for students and most felt confident about moving off to explain the life cycle. Five students who felt less confident or requested support remained with the teacher and co-constructed an opening sentence with him from the available information. This involved articulating the sentence before recording it, re-reading it for clarity and accuracy and checking it off in relation to the success criteria (which had been focused on strategically by the teacher in the co-construction process). Some others watched and listened from a distance as the teacher worked with the small group. Students in the

small group were subsequently invited to compose their own opening sentence/s and use what had been co-constructed if they wished. Most decided to use part of what had been co-constructed in their own writing.

- *Rove amongst students working independently.* The teacher roved and questioned students about what they had composed so far, prompted them to think about the next sentence or sentence, and fed back to them on their effectiveness so far in demonstrating the indicators of success.
- *Share and celebrate writing.* Students (including those who had co-constructed with the teacher) were encouraged to share and comment on their first drafts with each other, particularly on success with the criteria. This was done at the whole class level, though could have been done in pairs or small groups.

Subsequent Sessions

Prior to the subsequent two sessions, the teacher had read each student's first draft and noted strengths and needs demonstrated by each student and across the cohort of students. He particularly noted that many students were having difficulty 'including detail in the explanation'. At the beginning of the first of the subsequent sessions, all students were invited to re-read and reflect on what they had written so far and decide whether they should continue writing or begin to revise what they had written so far. Some teacher guidance for some students was needed on this. Students were also invited to attend one of three workshops that the teacher was offering on 'including detail' over the next two sessions. Most chose to attend a workshop at a time that they selected. At each workshop:

- The teaching point was identified at the beginning.
- Teaching and learning within the workshop was contextualised within a text that one of the workshop group had generated. The student had to agree to his/her text being used for this purpose.
- Other students in the group applied new learning acquired during the workshop to their writing as soon as possible afterwards.

As workshops were occurring, other students worked independently at the stage of the writing process (planning; crafting; re-crafting; presenting) that was most appropriate for them.

At the end of each of the subsequent sessions, all students were again encouraged to share and comment on their writing with each other. At the end of the three sessions, students were invited to contribute their writing (as a finished product) to a display and celebration of writing that was to be presented in the school foyer.

Recommendations for Globally Minded Teachers

The above set of writing sessions was devised and implemented as a deliberate attempt to illustrate the key points of the previously discussed research. It contextualises what a globally minded literacy teacher should adopt when striving for effectiveness as a teacher of writing. The teacher should utilise his/her *knowledge of students* meaningfully; ensure that topics and tasks are *purposeful* to students; provide meaningful opportunities for *student involvement*, especially in topic and task selection; provide instruction that is *direct and explicit*; *differentiate instruction* in terms of student needs; include opportunities for *independence and self-regulation* by students. Students should not just be learning to write; they should be learning *how to be* writers.

The instructional processes described above are very different to processes used by many New Zealand primary teachers in the 1980s and 1990s. Writing programs were then driven more by genres and text-types than topics and tasks; direct instruction was more often undertaken with the whole class rather than with needs-based groups; teaching skills were generally taught in isolation, not within the context of crafting and re-crafting authentic and purposeful texts. Globally minded teachers should reflect on what set of instructional processes best encapsulate their current practice – processes prevalent in the 1980s and 1990s or processes prevalent in today's world – and make changes to their practice accordingly.

Future Directions

As indicated previously, a considerable amount of writing-focussed research has been undertaken in New Zealand over the past two decades. But some research omissions remain evident.

The most obvious of these relates to the rapidly changing demographics of the New Zealand student population. As mentioned previously, one sector of the population ('Other'; students of mainly Chinese and Indian descent) is growing more rapidly than the others, with the population of this sector predicted to more than double by 2038. But writing research in relation to this sector is relatively scarce, especially in comparison with research on the literacy under-achievement of many Maori and Pasifika students (for example, Bishop et al., 2007; Fletcher et al., 2005; Si'ilata, 2014; Si'lata et al, 2017). This omission needs to be attended to, especially in that many students in the 'Other' sector are English language learners.

Some research has been undertaken on the teaching and learning of writing within content areas (for example, Locke, 2015; Locke & Hawthorne, 2017). But research on what the teaching and learning of writing looks like within, for example, science, mathematics and social studies classes, is also relatively scarce. Attending to this omission is also especially important, given that the *New Zealand Curriculum* indicates that 'success in [writing] is fundamental to success across the curriculum' (Ministry of Education, 2007a, p.18).

It is also suggested that ongoing research could be undertaken on other areas that have been comparatively under-served by the New Zealand literacy research community. These include the continued achievement gap between boys and girls in writing classrooms, links between reading and writing that teachers might make to generate stronger student engagement and achievement in writing, the utilisation of technological tools to help students become more effective writers, and of course any other issues that emerge from the ongoing analysis of New Zealand writing data.

Discussion Questions and Application

1. Do I know my students well, both as culturally centred individuals and as developing writers? Do I use what information I hold meaningfully for teaching and learning purposes? Do I need to collect and record more information?
2. Is the writing programme that I devise and deliver purposeful for my students, particularly in terms of topic and task selection? What can I do to make it more purposeful?
3. Do I involve my students sufficiently in (for example) topic and task selection, decisions about indicators for success and what they need to work on to be more successful? How could I involve them more?
4. Is the instruction that I provide (especially my demonstrating and questioning) direct and explicit? How could I make it more direct and explicit? What changes would I need to make to it?
5. Do I differentiate my teaching sufficiently for my students' different learning needs? Do I ask myself continually: 'Who needs what teaching, when, and what does it need to look like?' What changes would I need to make to my programme to differentiate my teaching more effectively?
6. Do I give my students sufficient opportunities to write independently and in a self-regulated way by encouraging them (for example) to select their own topics and tasks from time to time, write collaboratively from time to time and decide what help and support they believe as developing writers? How might I promote independence and self-regulation more for my students?

References

Alton-Lee, A. (2003). *Quality teaching for diverse students in schooling: Best evidence synthesis.* Wellington, New Zealand: Ministry of Education.

Ames, C. (1992). Classrooms: Goals, structures, and student motivation. *Journal of Educational Psychology, 84*(3), 261–271.

Applebee, A.N. & Langer, J.A. (2011). 'EJ' extra: A snapshot of writing instruction in middle schools and high schools. *The English Journal, 100*(6), 14–27.

Atwell, N. (1987). *In the middle: Reading, writing and learning with adolescents.* Portsmouth, NH: Heinemann.

Barnard, R. & Campbell, L. (2005). Sociocultural theory and the meaning of process writing: The scaffolding of learning in a university context. *The TESOLANZ Journal, 13,* 76–88.

Bishop, R., Berryman, M., Cavanagh, T., & Teddy, T. (2007). *Te Kotahitanga Phase 3 Whanaungatanga: Establishing a culturally responsive pedagogy of relations in mainstream secondary school classrooms.* Wellington, New Zealand: Ministry of Education.

Bloom, B. (1956). *Taxonomy of educational objectives: The classification of educational goals: Handbook I. Cognitive domain.* New York, NY: Longmans Green.

Blumenfeld, P.C. (1992). Classroom learning and motivation: Clarifying and expanding goal theory. *Journal of Educational Psychology, 84*(3), 272–281.

Calkins, L. M. (1994). *The art of teaching writing.* Portsmouth, NH: Heinemann.

Cherry, K. (2018). What is sociocultural theory? *Verywellmind.* Retrieved from www.verywellmind/what-is-sociocultural-theory-2795088

Clarke, S., Timperley, H., & Hattie, J. (2003). *Unlocking formative assessment: Practical strategies for enhancing students' learning in the primary and intermediate classroom* (New Zealand edition). Auckland, New Zealand: Hodder Moa Beckett.

Cutler, L. & Graham, S. (2008). Primary grade writing instruction: A national survey. *Journal of Educational Psychology, 100*(4), 907–919.

Department for Education (2012). *What is the research evidence on writing?* (Research Report DFE-RR238). Retrieved from www.gov.uk/government/uploads/system/uploads/attachment_data/file/183399/DFE-RR238.pdf

Fletcher, J., Parkhill, F., & Fa'afoi, A. (2005). What factors promote and support Pasifika students in reading and writing. *SET: Research Information for Teachers, 2,* 2–8.

Flower, L. & Hayes, J.R. (1981). A cognitive process theory of writing. *College Composition and Communication, 32,* 365–387.

Gadd, M. (2017). What does an effective teacher of writing do that makes a difference to student achievement? *SET: Research Information for Teachers, 1,* 37–45.

Gadd, M. & Clueard, T. (2018). Turning non-writers into writers: A case study. *Literacy Forum NZ, 33*(3), 27–33.

Gadd, M. & Parr, J.M. (2016). It's all about Baxter: Task orientation in the effective teaching of writing. *Literacy, 50*(2), 93–99.

Gadd, M. & Parr, J.M. (2017). Practices of effective writing teachers. *Reading and Writing, 30*(7), 1551–1574.

Gadd, M., Parr, J.M., Robertson, J., Carran, L., Ali, Z., Gendall, L., & Watson, K. (2019). Portrait of the student as a young writer: Some student survey findings about attitudes to writing and self-efficacy as writers. *Literacy.* doi:10.1111/lit.12178

Gadd, M.O. (2014). *What is critical in the effective teaching of writing? A study of some Year 5 to 8 teachers in the New Zealand context.* Unpublished PhD thesis, University of Auckland.

Gibbs, R. & Poskitt, J. (2010). *Student engagement in the middle years of schooling (years 7–10): A literature review.* Wellington, New Zealand: Ministry of Education.

Gilbert, J. & Graham, S. (2010). Teaching writing to elementary students in grades 4–6: A national survey. *The Elementary School Journal, 110*(4), 1–15.

Glasswell, K. (2000). *The patterning of difference: Teachers and children constructing development in writing.* Unpublished PhD thesis, University of Auckland.

Glasswell, K. & Parr, J.M. (2009). Teachable moments: Linking assesment and teaching in talk around writing. *Language Arts, 86,* 352–361.

Glasswell, K., Parr, J.M., & McNaughton, S. (2003). Four ways to work against yourself when conferencing with struggling writers. *Language Arts, 80,* 291–298.

Graham, S., Capizzi, A., Harris, K.R., Hebert, M., & Morphy, P. (2014). Teaching writing to middle school students: A national survey. *Reading and Writing, 27*(6), 1015–1042.

Graham, S. & Perin, D. (2007). A meta-analysis of writing instruction for adolescent students. *Journal of Educational Psychology, 99*(3), 445–476.

Graves, D. H. (1983). *Writing: Teachers and children at work.* Portsmouth, NH: Heinemann.

Graves, D. H. (1994). *A fresh look at writing.* Portsmouth, NH: Heinemann.

Grossman, P.L., Loeb, S., Cohen, J., & Wyckoff, J. (2013). Measure for measure: The relationship between measures of instructional practice in middle school English language arts and teachers' value-added scores. *American Journal of Education, 119,* 445–470.

Hamre, B. K. & Pianta, R. C. (2001). Early teacher–child relationships and the trajectory of children's school outcomes through eighth grade. *Child Development, 72*(4), 625–638.

Hmelo-Silver, C., Duncan, R., & Chinn, C. (2007). Scaffolding and achievement in problem-based and inquiry learning: A response to Kirschner, Sweller, and Clark (2006). *Educational Psychologist, 42*(2), 99–107.

Jesson, R.N. & Cockle, V. (2014). The opportunities to build on existing expertise in writing classrooms: A study of writing lessons in New Zealand primary schools. *Education 3–13, 44*(6), 604–616.

Joselowsky, F. (2007). Youth engagement, high school reform, and improved learning outcomes: Building systematic approaches for youth engagement. *National Association of Secondary School Principals' Bulletin, 91*(3), 257–276.

Kellogg, R.T. & Raulerson, B.A. (2007). Improving the writing skills of college students. *Psychonomic Bulletin and Review, 14*(2), 237–242.

Langer, J. A. (2001). Beating the odds: Teaching middle and high school students to read and write well. *American Educational Research Journal, 38*(4), 837–880.

Locke, T. (2015). The impact of intensive writing workshop professional development on a cross-curricular group of secondary teachers. *New Zealand Journal of Educational Studies, 50*(1), 1–15.

Locke, T. & Hawthorne, S. (2017). Affecting a high school culture of writing: Issues and dilemmas in participatory action research. In L. Rowell, C. Bruce, J. Shosh, & M. Riel (Eds.), *The Palgrave international handbook of action research* (pp. 527–544). New York, NY: Palgrave Macmillan.

Medwell, J., Wray, D., Poulson, L., & Fox, R. (1998). *Effective teachers of literacy.* A report commissioned by the UK Teacher Training Agency. Exeter, England.

Meissel, K., Parr, J.M., & Timperley, H. (2016). Can professional development of teachers reduce disparity in student achievement? *Teaching and Teacher Education, 58,* 163–173.

Ministry of Education. (2006). *Effective literacy practice in years 1 to 4.* Wellington, New Zealand: Learning Media.

Ministry of Education. (2007a). *The New Zealand Curriculum*. Wellington, New Zealand: Learning Media.

Ministry of Education. (2007b). *Effective literacy practice in years 5 to 8*. Wellington, New Zealand: Learning Media.

Ministry of Education. (2010). *Literacy learning progressions: Meeting the reading and writing demands of the curriculum*. Wellington, New Zealand: Learning Media.

Ministry of Education. (2017). *National standards results 2016*. Retrieved from https://www.educationcounts.govt.nz/topics/pai/other-achievement-profiles#

Ministry of Education and New Zealand Council for Educational Research (2012). *e-asTTle: Writing (revised)*. Retrieved from http://e-asTTle.tki.org.nz/user-manuals

National Center for Education Statistics. (2012). *The nation's report card: Writing 2011 (NCES 2012-470)*. Washington, DC: Institute of Education Sciences, US Department of Education.

Parr, J.M., Gadd, M., Carran, L., Robertson, J., Watson, K., Gendall, L., & Ali, Z. (2018). *Generating positive outcomes by years 5 to 8 priority learners in writing: An inquiry into effective teacher practice*. A report for the Teaching and Learning Research Initiative. Retrieved from www.tlri.org.nz/sites/default/files/projects/TLRI%20Summary%20Report_Parr%20andGadd.pdf

Parr, J.M. & Hawe, E. (2017). Facilitating real-time observation of, and peer discussion and feedback about, practice in writing classrooms. *Professional Development in Education*, *43*(5), 709–728.

Parr, J.M. & Jesson, R. (2016). Mapping the landscape of writing instruction in New Zealand primary school classrooms. *Reading and Writing*, *29*(5), 981–1011.

Parr, J.M. & Limbrick, L. (2010). Contextualising practice: Hallmarks of effective teachers of writing. *Teaching and Teacher Education*, *26*(3), 583–590.

Parr, J.M. & Timperley, H. (2010). Feedback for writing, assessment for teaching and learning and student progress. *Assessing Writing*, *15*, 68–85.

Poskitt, J. & Taylor, K. (2008). *National education findings of Assess to Learn (AtoL)*. Wellington, New Zealand: Ministry of Education.

Pressley, M., Wharton-McDonald, R., Mistretta-Hampson, A., & Echevarria, J. (1998). Literacy instruction in 10 fourth and fifth grade classrooms in upstate New York. *Scientific Studies of Reading*, *2*(2), 159–194.

Regan, K. & Berkeley, S. (2012). Effective reading and writing instruction: A focus on modelling. *Intervention in School and Clinic*, *47*(5), 276–282.

Si'ilata, R. (2014). *Va'a Tele: Pasifika learners riding the success wave on linguistically and culturally responsive pedagogies*. Unpublished PhD thesis, University of Auckland.

Si'lata, R., Samu, T.W., & Siteine, A. (2017). The Va'atele framework: Redefining and transforming Pasifika education. In E.A. McKinley & T. Smooth (Eds.), *Handbook of indigenous education* (pp. 1–30). Singapore: Springer.

Symes, I. & Timperley, H. (2003). Using achievement information to raise student achievement. *SET: Research Information for Teachers*, *1*, 36–39.

Timperley, H. & Parr, J.M. (2009). What is this lesson about? Instructional processes and student understandings in the writing classroom. *Curriculum Journal*, *20*, 43–60.

Vygotsky, L.S. (1978). *Mind in society: The development of higher psychological processes*. Harvard, MA: Harvard University Press.

Wood, D., Bruner, J.S., & Ross, G. (1976). The role of tutoring in problem-solving. *Journal of Child Psychology and Psychiatry*, *17*(2), 89–100.

Chapter 10

Visible Learning for Adolescents in the USA

Joanna Schaefer, Nancy Frey, and Douglas Fisher

Summary of Chapter

- The history of U.S. education has been one of struggle regarding local control and has a long history of changes as citizens and immigrant populations have shaped educational policies.
- The visible learning research has provided clarity in identifying effective literacy approaches that foster the kind of critical thinking necessary for global citizenship.
- The alignment of literacy strategies to phases of learning (surface, deep, and transfer) can increase precision and deepen critical thinking.

Vignette

Tenth grade World History students Milo and Saahirah are ready with their opening statement as the class debate begins. The topic is mandatory community service for high school graduation. The class has been examining global communities, and see the value in giving back, but some teeter on whether requiring service is a form of involuntary servitude, and question whether caring can be mandated. Milo and Saahirah will be supporting the affirmative side, which is that globally oriented community service should be mandatory for youth in order to build the habits of altruism and cross-border interconnectedness. They will be paired with another set of students who will be presenting the opposing side of the debate. The task at hand has required a great deal of preparation, reading, fact checking, notetaking, public speaking, and feedback. Students not only need to be well versed on their side, but be prepared to receive criticism for their claims, and craft a rebuttal of the opposing team's argument. In order to do so, students must have multiple cognitive and metacognitive tools to effectively plan and participate in a meaningful debate. These literacy processes are highlighted in the Visible Learning database as being highly effective

learning approaches. As the debate opens, Milo and Saahirah shake hands
with their opponents and begin their opening statement.

Historical, Cultural, and Political Context

Beliefs about public education in the United States were formed at the birth
of the nation itself and continue to exert influence on policies and practices
today. The earliest (and perhaps most enduring) arguments have centered on
the tension between States rights and federal oversight. The 10th amend-
ment of the Bill of Rights to the U.S. Constitution, written in 1791, captures the essence of this principle: "The powers not delegated to the United
States by the Constitution, nor prohibited by it to the states, are reserved to
the States respectively, or to the people." Educational policies up until the
latter half of the twentieth century reflected this position. State and local
government determined the taxes needed to fund schools and developed
curricular guidelines that mirrored the cultural values and norms of the
community. However, what emerged were intolerable inequities about fundamental elements of schooling. One notable change occurred in 1954,
with the U.S. Supreme Court's landmark ruling, *Brown v. Board of Education*.
The inferior education of African-American children in underfunded schools
would no longer be tolerated. The Court established an important precedent
that continues to influence policy today: separate is not equal.

In the decades since then, the federal government has taken a more outsize role in educational policy as it applies to protected categories of students: those with disabilities, underserved racial and language groups, and
students living in poverty. The federal Elementary and Secondary Education
Act (ESEA) of 1965 ushered in a new perspective on the role of federal
government in matters of schooling. This legislation provided supplemental
Title 1 funding for students living in poverty, and new programs, especially
the early education Head Start program for preschool-aged children in
underserved committees. With these programs came a need for accounting
for how monies were being utilized, and to what effect.

Historical and Philosophical Underpinnings

While states continue to lead educational policy at the local level, federal oversight for underserved categories of students has greatly influenced local practice
in this century. The 2002 renewal of the ESEA, known commonly as No
Child Left Behind, shepherded in a higher degree of accountability in the form
of standardized tests. It is important to note that educators and educational systems have long measured student outcomes through testing. But the emphasis
on demonstrating that federal categorical monies were being used to effect

positive growth for students signaled a sea change in terms of interest in instruction of reading and mathematics, the two subject areas measured. With increased accountability mandates (and the punitive repercussions of not meeting these benchmarks), states' interest now focused for the first time on *how* these subjects were taught. With this shift came a series of state-directed policies about processes for professional learning, assistance, and interventions for schools failing to make expected progress. But despite a decade of increased fiscal and human resources, reading achievement remained essentially unchanged (National Center for Educational Statistics, 2011). Educators and researchers continued to seek ways to identify effective instructional and curricular approaches.

Standards for Literacy Learning

In 2010, faced with stagnant testing results, the National Governors Association sponsored the development of the Common Core State Standards (CCSS) for the English Language Arts and Mathematics (2010). For the first time, states worked together to agree on a set of standards held in common such that local and state educational agencies could work in concert to share resources and research. Some have argued that a byproduct of the CCSS has been a resurgence in the role of local control and influence in education, after decades of increasing federal presence (Marsh & Wohlstetter, 2013). However, the CCSS has also been fraught with political overtones from its inception, and there has been a retreat in some states from these standards since their initial adoption (Friedberg et al., 2018).

Best Practices in Disciplinary Literacy

A lasting effect of the CCSS, regardless of whether a state has formally adopted these standards or not, has been its influence on the field of adolescent literacy. Students in grades 6–12 are expected to use literacies to acquire, investigate, and present knowledge in all subject areas, including science, history, mathematics, and technical and career education. These disciplinary literacies require that teachers engage in direct instruction and also to foster dialogic learning through discussion and debate (Goldman et al., 2016). This emphasis on argumentation in discourse and writing is intended to foster the kind of critical and analytic thinking representative of meaningful learning, as students are apprenticed in to the formal reasoning and logic utilized by scientists and historians (Goldman et al., 2016). Therefore, secondary teachers in all content areas (not only in the subject of English literature) are expected to engage students with instruction about how the literacies of reading and writing, speaking, listening, and viewing are leveraged within specific disciplines.

The field of adolescent literacy has further recognized the crucial role of fostering global perspectives among youth. The intersection of globalization and literacy education is newer in US education, but its outward-facing orientation on matters that are of inherent interest to people across the world is one that has strong appeal for teachers in many disciplines, especially in history and civics education. Yoon, Yol, Haag, and Simpson (2018), propose a critical global literacies framework that encompasses many of the ideals of disciplinary literacy and its associated standards:

- Global awareness with an interconnected world concept.
- Connections from a personal to global level.
- Text analysis and critique from global and cross-cultural perspectives.
- Actions on global and multicultural issues.

The ability for students to think critically about global events requires that they be equipped with the literacy tools to read, investigate, question, craft formal arguments, and communicate through writing and multimedia platforms. Yet the forces that influence educational practice in the U.S. are not completely in alignment. These tensions include those discussed previously in this chapter: ongoing debate about local control, the emergence of more rigorous standards and related measures, and the rise of global information economies that are shaping the future. As if these were not complex enough, U.S. educational practices are greatly impacted by policies related to immigration and learning English as a subsequent language.

Immigration and Language and Literacy Learning

The educational thrust in the United States is that all students learn English. There are many bilingual or dual immersion programs that students can enroll in throughout the country to learn other languages besides English. However, the primary orientation, and thus the accountability measures that schools must achieve, is English proficiency in the school setting. This purports to prepare students to function in a society that predominantly uses English: careers, banking, car loans, and political debate. Command of English in the U.S. is more than an issue of access, however—it is an issue of power and what counts as literacy (e.g., Rubinstein-Ávila, 2007). It must be recognized that it is crucial for immigrant students to possess

> competent levels of multiple literacies that enable immigrant groups to manage literacy not only for social representation but also to obtain health and economic stability, among other qualities of life, within multiple and complex social systems.
>
> (Soto Huerta & Pérez, 2014, p. 498)

Proficiency in English, therefore, is as much a social justice issue as it is an educational one, especially in an anti-immigration political climate that negatively impacts health and wellbeing (Wallace & de Trinidad Young, 2018).

To foster literacy knowledge in English, educators need to provide a greater opportunity for immigrant students to navigate society in the United States, and also to equip youth with opportunities to examine their own cultures—a pathway suggested by Yoon et al. (2018) as necessary in order to move from personal to global perspectives. Educators must see their immigrant students and learn their stories because that can be a barrier to learning English and learning about the world. Irizarry and Kleyn (2011) remind us of the "critical importance of educators having knowledge of opportunities available for immigrant youth as they navigate the challenges of the educational system" (p. 23). Immigrant students quickly learn the struggle of the system, but educators who are ready to help them and provide culturally relevant material, ultimately support that transition to read, write and speak in English.

In summary, U.S. educators have been buffeted by educational policies and societal tensions that are profoundly shaping secondary schooling. Globalization has heightened awareness that while "all politics are local," we put our students and ourselves at risk if we continue to ignore issues that impact people throughout the world. In point of fact, classrooms across the country are filled with adolescents whose experiences, language, and cultural referents differ from the adult leading the class. That said, these challenges have caused American educators to look for evidence-based research that has an international orientation. The *Visible Learning* body of research, developed by an Australian scholar using studies from throughout the world, offers a way for literacy educators to understand what works, and when it works.

Theory and Research Base for Visible Learning

The publication of the Visible Learning database (Hattie, 2008) represented a critical shift in the way teaching and learning are understood in the U.S. Hattie's meticulous quantitative research utilizes meta-analysis as a tool for understanding the influence of a variety of policy, instructional, and curricular practices on measures of student achievement. A meta-analysis is a statistical tool for comparing quantitative measures across multiple studies, even when the measures themselves vary (Glass, 1976). Meta-analyses are used to generate an effect size, which connotes the magnitude (effect) of an intervention. Hattie pioneered an innovative means for performing a meta-analysis *of* meta-analyses, thus providing a means for understanding large datasets gathered across time and under different conditions (Hattie, 2008). Now numbering nearly 1400 meta-analyses involving 300 million students, Hattie has calculated effect sizes for nearly 250 influences on student achievement, grouping them into six major categories: the student, the home, the school, the curricula, the teacher, and teaching and learning approaches. It should be noted as well that the meta-analyses represent research from across the globe, and are not assigned to an individual country or culture.

The reported effect size data have proven to be instructive in determining what matters in learning. Noting that 95% of approaches have *some* effect, Hattie wanted to know if the effort was worthwhile. His synthesis of all the meta-analyses revealed that 0.40 represents a year's worth of progress for a year in school, and dubbed this "the hinge point" (Hattie, 2008, p. 17). Therefore, this hinge point has served as a means for identifying promising policies and practices. These high-yield practices offer educators a guide for making instructional and curricular decisions.

Phases of Learning

Hattie's work has been further aligned to phases of learning, from surface acquisition of knowledge and skills, to deeper consolidation, to transfer of learning (Biggs, 1993; Marton & Säljö, 1976). Surface learning focuses on one skill or concept at a time. This is a necessary starting point for all learning, and should not be mistaken for superficial learning. Unfortunately, surface learning is too often emphasized over deeper learning, and too often consumes an outsize portion of classroom instruction (Frey, Fisher, & Hattie, 2017). A goal, therefore, is to deepen learning through consolidation. In this phase of learning, students see connections between related concepts and skills, and are better able to develop analogies and metaphors to represent complex relationships. Learning is furthered through transfer, as students apply knowledge and skills in increasingly novel situations. Transfer of learning represents true ownership of knowledge (National Research Council, 2005). The scenario that opened this chapter is a case in point. Students who are able to engage in extended critical discourse about a debate topic are displaying evidence of their transfer of learning. They have gained initial factual knowledge crucial to their position (surface learning), engaged in critical reading and investigation of the claims and counterclaims surrounding the issue (deep learning), and are applying their learning by analyzing conceptual similarities and differences (transfer of learning). A chart of literacy approaches aligned with phases of instruction can be found in Table 10.1. However, it should be noted that these phases of learning are iterative, and should not be narrowly interpreted as being strictly time-bound. Rather, they describe how people move from acquisition to transfer.

Table 10.1 High-impact literacy approaches at each phase of learning

Surface Learning		Deep Learning		Transfer Learning	
Strategy	ES	Strategy	ES	Strategy	ES
Wide reading (exposure to reading)	0.42	Questioning	0.48	Extended writing	0.44
Phonics instruction	0.54	Concept mapping	0.60	Peer tutoring	0.55
Direct instruction	0.59	Close reading (study skills)	0.63	Problem-based learning	0.61
Note-taking	0.59	Self-questioning	0.64	Synthesizing information across texts	0.63
Comprehension strategy instruction	0.60	Metacognitive strategy instruction	0.69	Formal discussions (e.g., debates)	0.82
Annotation (study skills)	0.63	Reciprocal Teaching	0.74	Transforming conceptual knowledge	0.85
Summarizing	0.63	Class discussion	0.82	Organizing conceptual knowledge	0.85
Leverage prior knowledge	0.65	Organizing and transforming notes	0.85	Identifying similarities and differences	1.32
Vocabulary instruction	0.67				
Repeated reading	0.67				
Spaced practice	0.71				

Cooperative learning 0.59

Student–teacher relationships 0.72

Teacher clarity 0.75

Feedback 0.75

Teacher credibility 0.90

Assessment-capable learners 1.44

Collective teacher efficacy 1.57

Teacher estimates (expectations) of student learning 1.62

Fisher, D., Frey, N., & Hattie, J. (2017). Teaching Literacy in the Visible Learning Classroom, 6-12 (p. 15). Thousand Oaks, CA: Corwin. Used with permission.

Surface Learning

Initial surface learning is critical for acquiring knowledge about a subject. Hattie's database reveals a number of literacy approaches that work especially well at for acquisition and early consolidation of information. Vocabulary instruction ($d = 0.67$) is critical at this phase, as command of the academic terminology of a discipline is predictive of comprehension of written materials (Cain, Oakhill, & Lemmon, 2004). Another strong literacy approach during surface learning is note-taking ($d = 0.59$), in which students summarize knowledge in written form. These practices contribute to a learner's ability to build schema, as they initially consolidate information through early conceptual pattern recognition (Rumelhart, 1980). However, students move from acquisition to consolidation, and then further to deep learning, by further formalizing these patterns through techniques such as concept mapping ($d = 0.60$). Teachers in practice integrate techniques after initial acquisition to promote deep learning.

Sasha steps into her high school World History classroom. She takes out her interactive notebook, which is decorated with stickers and her name. The interactive notebook holds her cumulative notes from lectures, the textbook, quickwrites and concept maps. Her notes not only contain factual information, but her ideas, summaries, and opinions of her peers. The teacher asks Sasha and her classmates to review the concept map they are developing about the start of the French Revolution. It is divided into three sections: First Estate (clergy), Second Estate (nobility), and Third Estate (the people). As Sasha opens her concept map, there are notes she has previously composed about each estate, including taxing rights, and examples of political and social power. The teacher asks the table partners to turn and talk about each estate as key influences in the French Revolution. After a few minutes, the teacher poses two questions that the students will discuss and record in their notebook and then share with their table. "How does fairness and injustice play out in this society?" asks the teacher. "What predictions can you make about each of these groups?" Sasha and the other four students at her table write their thoughts down on the concept map, then launch into a discussion about the questions. The notes Sasha develops are not simply for the purpose of encoding information. Rather, they are meant to serve as a launching point for engaging in critical thinking and questioning.

Deep Learning

The ability to critically analyze text is a hallmark of deep learning, as students read first with the text to gain an understanding of its major messages, then read against the text to unpack and interrogate alternative perspectives and differential power structures (Janks, 2010). Close and critical reading ($d = 0.60$) is an essential literacy process for content area teachers, especially history teachers. Wineburg describes historical thinking, which is to say deep learning, as the nexus of cognitive and meta-cognitive practices that include close reading of primary texts, corroboration of the accuracy of the text, and contextualization of the text as it is situated in the historical milieu (1991). Related literacy processes for deepening learning include the use of discussion ($d = 0.82$), and questioning that provokes critical response, rather than recall and reproduction ($d = 0.48$). Close reading involves surface learning to grasp the literal meaning of the text, before moving into structural and inferential meanings that are not as easily gleaned from the reading. The questions that scaffold deep learning, and the related discussions it generates, are crucial for promoting critical thinking.

> Students sit in groups of four with a copy of the Franklin D. Roosevelt's Infamy Speech in front of them. Students have highlighters and pens in their hands as they wait for instructions from the teacher. The teacher explains the purpose of the day, "To analyze the purpose and repercussions of Roosevelt's speech" after the attack on Pearl Harbor. The teacher also has success criteria posted on the board, "I know I am successful when: (1) I can annotate my speech with my thoughts and write down findings when we have class discussion. (2) I can discuss the impact of the speech with evidence." Students read through the text on their own first to get a general understanding, making notes of confusing words and highlighting main points, and discuss elements of the speech to examine it for historical context and the president's use of rhetorical structures. The teacher's questions move the group to critical analysis, as she asks them to identify "emotional and polarizing words" and to consider unintended consequences. This proves to be a turning point for the class, as they move to discussion about the internment of Japanese-American citizens two months after the speech in response to mounting fear of espionage and sabotage, as well as the role of racism in American society. "It was a call to action," said one student, "but it also made it harder for Americans to trust their neighbors."

Transfer of Learning

A major outcome of education is transfer of learning, as people utilize knowledge to develop new solutions to pressing problems. Innovation and creativity depend on transfer, such that both require a deep understanding of existing rules and structures, coupled with the skills and dispositions to manipulate constraints in an effort to find new solutions. Learning sciences theorists (e.g., Biggs, 1993; Marton & Säljö, 1976; National Research Council, 2005) have proposed that evidence of transfer of learning occurs when a learner can apply knowledge, skills, and concepts to new and novel situations, rather than a close replication of what has been taught. This is termed *far transfer* is used to describe a learner's application that bears only some overlap to the conditions under which the information was previously taught. The transfer stage of learning is not easily achieved, and it is important to note that not all content taught must necessarily move to this level of learning.

As with the other phases of learning, literacy approaches must be aligned to facilitate the kind of cognitive and metacognitive thinking necessary to deepen learning. Formal discussions, such as the debate featured in the opening scenario, are one such approach. Another is problem-based learning (PBL), a student-centered method that encourages students to investigate a problem not easily solved (see Wilder, 2015 for a systematic review). The roots of PBL can be traced to education in medical school, where students are challenged to apply specialized knowledge to complex, real world cases. Problem-based learning differs from its closely related pedagogical, project-based learning. The requirement that the learner propose a possible solution is the element that separates this approach from project-based learning. PBL in K–12 education lends itself especially well in fostering globally minded students to surface longstanding problems for people across the world. However, PBL is often misapplied in these same classrooms. Hattie reports that the overall effect size for problem-based learning is 0.15, suggesting that students gain little in terms of learning. However, the phase of learning in which it is utilized is a mitigating factor. The use of an inquiry approach during the surface phase of learning is ineffective because students don't possess enough knowledge to be able to properly investigate and propose solutions. However, when deployed later in the learning process, when students possess a deeper understanding of the factors that influence the problem, the effect size increases to 0.61, well above Hattie's hinge point of 0.40. Illustrative examples of problem-based learning projects with a global perspective include:

- How did an inadequate public health care and government oversight contribute to the Flint, Michigan water crisis?
- Why do 1.1 billion people worldwide still not have electricity in 2018?
- Is there a relationship between totalitarianism in government and economic downturns?
- What does democracy need to survive in the twenty-first century?

However, the success of students in investigating these topics and proposing solutions is dependent on the knowledge the can leverage to engage in informed study. In an age where information, including suspect propaganda and fake news can be readily found on the internet, it is crucial that students using a PBL approach are taught to thoroughly analyze and interrogate the veracity of their sources. The close reading model Wineburg (1991) proposed, and discussed in the previous section, serves history students well in examining problems using a critical lens.

In sum, the literacy skills described in the visible learning research are essential for adolescents to acquire, consolidate, and apply essential content knowledge. But beyond knowledge building is the larger question that presses all educators: how can we best equip our students to thinking closely and critically about the issues that impact their local and global community? The work capture in this body of research challenges the very notion of school as a place where the learning is passive and without controversy. In the same way that the history of U.S. education has been one of struggle and at times competing perspectives, so should our classrooms, as we seek to problematize issues of yesterday and today, in order to build the global citizens we need tomorrow.

Implications for Future Research

As we have noted, literacy is an essential aspect of the curriculum for adolescents and is not the sole responsibility of English language arts teachers. As Fisher, Frey, and Hattie (2017) noted, literacy makes your life better and is among the best antidotes for poverty that we have at our disposal. The Visible Learning database makes clear that some instructional routines work better than others. The database also makes clear the need to align the right strategy, at the right time, for the right kind of learning. The challenge, though, is to go to scale with this knowledge. Future translational research is warranted, namely how to create large-scale change in schools such that teachers align their instructional tools with students phases of learning. Continuing to use effective surface learning strategies when students need deep learning will not result in positive outcomes and will likely hinder students' future development. It is no longer the case that "we did know" because the evidence is clear. Instead, it is the proverbial knowing/doing gap that stimies so many professions. Evidence on effective approaches to overcome that gap would be most welcome.

In addition, there is a need to continue to generate knowledge and aggregate that knowledge through meta-analyses so that the Visible Learning database remains current and relevant. Toward that end, researchers need to continue to investigate effective approaches that impact students' learning and provide effect size information. No longer should researchers simply say that their findings were "statistically significant." Given a large enough population, very small impacts will be result in statistical significance. The world needs to how much learning resulted from the intervention. There is a difference in value when a specific approach results in the equivalent of nine months increased learning compared with two months.

Focusing on translational research will provide school systems with evidence-based ways to implement change, which are by-and-large missing from the world. Focusing on effect sizes will provide teachers and leaders with information that they can use to identify the return on investment. The logical question should be, "If I implement this new approach, how much additional learning should I expect based on the investment of time and other resources?"

Recommendations for Globally Minded Literacy Teachers

There are several recommendations for globally minded teachers that arise from the Visible Learning database. The first of which is to know your impact. Teachers should always consider the impact that they have on students' learning. This is one of the enduring lessons from Hattie: know thy impact. And, if the strategies being used are not having the desired or necessary impact, change the strategy. We should never hold an instructional strategy in higher esteem than students' learning. Instead, we should determine the impact that the strategy has and then make decisions about the continued use of that strategy.

The second recommendation centers on the phases of learning discussed previously. Globally minded teachers would be well served to recognize that learning occurs in phases, and that our goal is to teach for transfer. Having said that, it's important to note that learning starts at the surface level, and there's nothing wrong with that. The error is to leave students at the surface level and not changing the instructional approaches to ensure that students move from surface to deep to transfer. Changing strategies to ensure the transitions between phases is important for every teacher to consider.

And third, globally minded teachers who guide the learning of adolescents must always remember that learning is based in language. Human beings learn best when they read, write, speak, listen, and view. As such, classrooms should be filled with literacy tasks and those tasks should span the literacy processes. Spending 55 minutes listening to the teacher is not likely to result in deep levels of learning. That doesn't mean that lecture must be eliminated, but rather that students also need opportunities to talk, read, write, and view as part of their learning experiences.

Discussion Questions and Application

1. In what ways are the strengths and experiences of immigrant students leveraged in your classroom or school?
2. What additional language approaches are necessary in order for immigrant students to participate fully in challenging content?

3. How might alignment of literacy strategies to phases of learning (surface, deep and transfer learning) change practices in your classroom or school?

4. Are educators equipped to teach culturally relevant content to promote global citizenship?

References

Biggs, J. (1993). What do inventories of students' learning processes really measure? A theoretical review and clarification. *British Journal of Educational Psychology, 63*, 3–19.

Cain, K., Oakhill, J. V., & Lemmon, K. (2004). Individual differences in the inference of word meanings from context: The influence of reading comprehension, vocabulary knowledge, and memory capacity. *Journal of Educational Psychology, 96*(4), 671–681.

Frey, N., Fisher, D., & Hattie, J. (2017). Surface, deep, and transfer? Considering the role of content literacy instructional strategies. *Journal of Adolescent & Adult Literacy, 60*(5), 567–575.

Friedberg, S., Barone, D., Belding, J., Chen, A., Dixon, L., Fennell, F., Fisher, D., Frey, N., Howe, R., & Shanahan, T. (2018). *The state of state standards post-Common Core* [PDF file]. Thomas Fordham Institute. Retrieved at http://edex.s3-us-west-2.amazonaws.com/publication/pdfs/(08.22)%20The%20State%20of%20State%20Standards%20Post-Common%20Core.pdf

Glass, G. V. (1976). Primary, secondary, and meta-analysis of research. *Educational Researcher, 5*(10), 3–8.

Goldman, S. R., Britt, M. A., Brown, W., Cribb, G., George, M., Greenleaf, C., Lee, C., Shanahan, C., & Project Readi5. (2016). Disciplinary literacies and learning to read for understanding: A conceptual framework for disciplinary literacy. *Educational Psychologist, 51*(2), 219–246.

Hattie, J. (2009). *Visible learning: A synthesis of over 800 meta-analyses relating to achievement.* New York: Routledge.

Irizarry, J. G., & Kleyn, T. (2011). Immigration and education in the "Supposed Land of Opportunity": Youth perspectives on living and learning in the United States. *New Educator, 7*(1), 5–26.

Janks, H. (2010). *Literacy and power.* New York: Routledge.

Marsh, J. A., & Wohlstetter, P. (2013). Recent trends in intergovernmental relations: The resurgence of local actors in education policy. *Educational Researcher, 42*(5), 276–283.

Marton, F., & Säljö, R. (1976). On qualitative differences in learning: I – Outcome and process. *British Journal of Educational Psychology, 46*(1), 4–11.

National Center for Education Statistics. (2011). *Contexts of elementary and secondary education* (Table 36-2). Washington, DC: Institute of Education Sciences. Retrieved at https://nces.ed.gov/pubs2011/2011033_5.pdf.

National Governors Association Center for Best Practices & Council of Chief State School Officers. (2010). *Common core state standards for English language arts and literacy in history/social studies, science, and technical subjects.* Washington, DC: Authors.

National Research Council. (2005). *How students learn: History, mathematics, and science in the classroom.* Committee on *How People Learn*, A Targeted Report for Teachers, M.S. Donovan and J.D. Bransford (Eds.). Division of Behavioral and Social Sciences and Education. Washington, DC: The National Academies Press.

Rubinstein-Ávila, E. (2007). From the Dominican Republic to Drew High: What counts as literacy for Yanira Lara? *Reading Research Quarterly, 42*(4), 568–589.

Rumelhart, D. E. (1980). Schemata: The building blocks of cognition. In R. J. Spiro, B. C. Bruce, & W. F. Brewer (Eds.), *Theoretical issues in reading comprehension: Perspectives from cognitive psychology, linguistics, artificial intelligence, and education* (pp. 33–58). Hillsdale, NJ: Lawrence Erlbaum.

Soto Huerta, M., & Pérez, B. (2014). Second-language literacy, immigration, and globalization. *International Journal of Bilingual Education and Bilingualism, 18*(4), 1–16.

Wallace, S. P., & de Trinidad Young, M. E. (2018). Immigration versus immigrant: The cycle of anti-immigrant policies. *American Journal of Public Health, 108*(4), 436–437.

Wilder, S. (2015). Impact of problem-based learning on academic achievement in high school: A systematic review. *Educational Review, 67*(4), 414–435.

Wineburg, S. S. (1991). Historical problem solving: A study of the cognitive processes used in the evaluation of documentary and pictorial evidence. *Journal of Educational Psychology, 83*(1), 73–87.

Yoon, B., Yol, Ö., Haag, C., & Simpson, A. (2018). Critical global literacies: A new instructional framework in the global era. *Journal of Adolescent & Adult Literacy, 62*(2), 205–214.

Chapter 11

Digital Literacies in Canada

Cheryl McLean and Jennifer Rowsell

Summary of Chapter

- Overview of digital literacies within Canada's education system.
- Current connections to policy, research and pedagogical trends.
- Recommendations for theory and practice based on research.

Vignette

In Mrs. Turcotte's[1] grade 3/4 split classroom at her elementary school in St. Catharines, she purposively, meaningfully, and naturally embeds technology into her language arts programs. A typical lesson moves from brainstorming and curating information on the Internet displayed on a SMART board to writing down initial ideas on a sheet of paper to the option of writing, drawing, and designing on chrome books a response to a book, topic, or movie clip. Children have autonomy with technology, so they are often seen signing out a Chromebook and working on an assignment. When they finish, they return the Chromebook and grab a reader or chapter book in the class' library. Across all subject areas, children do not differentiate between digital tasks and analogue tasks, rather they move in and out of digital domains as the task sees fit. In other words, children's digital literacy practices are tacit and part of the fabric of their everyday learning.

In the opening vignette, we profile Mrs. Turcotte's elementary classroom in Canada's Niagara area as a way to illustrate a grounded and integrated model of digital literacy. Even so, in highlighting the rich experiences that such an integrated approach to literacy and digital technology provide these children, we also acknowledge that Mrs. Turcotte's classroom is not the norm for many Canadian students. Within Canadian classrooms and schools, disparities in opportunities to access, use, and learn with digital and technological resources, reflect the inequities that persist across the education system. With this in mind, the goal of this chapter is to explore the multiple ways in which digital literacies are understood, taken up, and practiced in diverse spaces in Canadian contexts. Having collaborated together in the area of digital literacies for over a decade and having conducted research together in Canada and the United States, we have come together as authors to foreground digital literacy research in Canada and to consider what we can learn from it. We regard digital literacy as literacy practices that are digitally mediated, as children access, use, analyze, produce, and share texts and other artifacts (Marsh, 2005; Merchant, 2015; Pahl & Rowsell, 2010; Sheridan & Rowsell, 2010; Walsh, 2011). We also acknowledge that these digitally-mediated literacy practices, by their very nature, encompass the multiple spaces and contexts that make up these learners' everyday lives.

In the past 20 years, on the global stage, the technological and digital have come to heavily inform ways of learning and working–both at school and in the workplace. Canada is no exception, with digital technologies having transformed the nature of work skill development of the Canadian workforce. With these changes come increased demands on the education system to prepare a digitally literate future workers and citizens. This call for digitally literate and skilled workers has, in turn, been met by an education policy response. In 2013, The Council of Ministers of Education, Canada (CMEC, 2013) issued a press release stating that literacies for the twenty-first century are multiple (e.g., text literacy, number literacy, visual literacy, digital literacy), dynamic, as well as "essential for full participation in the social and economic life of the modern world. Citizens need to be able to understand and engage with multiple technologies along with mastering the foundational skills of reading, writing, and mathematics." Here, the Ministry of Education's move to expand the definition of foundational literacy skills to include technology and digital literacy, while signaling the increasingly pivotal roles of technology and digital in our everyday lives, was by no means specific to Canada. The Canadian policy is consistent with the National Council of Teachers of English position statement (NCTE, 2013) in the U.S. that "technology has increased the intensity and complexity of literate environments such that the twenty-first century demands that a literate person possess a wide range of abilities and competencies, many literacies." Thus, these policy changes and related schooling practices reflect North American efforts to respond to and keep pace with technological changes and corresponding knowledge and skill demands in their respective countries. Even further, the commitment to better meet these demands is also evident in funding efforts such as the Canadian federal government's recent commitment to increase funding aimed at teaching basic digital skills, advancing digital literacy, and inclusion along with coding, and computer skills (Huynh & Do, 2017).

Historical, Cultural, and Political Context

Since the 2000s, Canadian researchers have begun noted efforts to explore digital literacies in Canadian classrooms as a way to understand how digital literacy mediates children and adolescents' literacy learning. One such earlier study by Courtland and Paddington (2008) involved 8th grade students' blog entries for a student-produced teen e-zine. At the time, Courtland and Paddington noted that digital literacy was a relatively recent "newcomer" to the existing vast array of sign systems. More recently, however, the awareness of the centrality of digital technologies in schools, workplace, and everyday lives, has garnered an increased focus on understanding the skills and competencies that need to be taught and learned for deep learning and understanding. With the solidified presence and use of digital technology and tools to communicate and learn, literacies are now conceptualized as all the skills, strategies, mind-sets, and dispositions students need to be able to read and create digital texts, and participate in digital spaces (Hagerman, 2017, p. 320; Kress, 2003; Leu, Kinzer, Coiro, Castek, & Henry, 2013) and to use technological tools to critically understand content and problem-solve (Huynh & Do, 2017).

In Canada, policies on digital literacy vary across provinces. Based on the Canadian system, education is governed provincially and territorially, not nationally. The mandate for all Canadian provincial and territorial educational jurisdictions is to ensure equitable access to education for all students, with each province and territory having evolved policies and approaches to literacy education that respond to their specific needs (Government of Canada, 2018). Accordingly, each of the ten provinces and three territories have developed curricula and/or standards documents that describe the learning outcomes that students should attain within a given grade or year of education. These curricula or standards reflect each province's policies, context, and resources (Gallagher & Rowsell, 2017). But, provincial perspectives on digital literacies can vary greatly—with some of the strongest, multimodal pedagogies (in our view) in Prairie provinces and in Eastern Canada—based on Indigenous pedagogies in the Prairie provinces (Honeyford & Trussler 2020) and on early childhood methods of inquiry (Whitty, 2017).

Despite some of these noted efforts to put Canada on the map in terms of digital literacy, there is a tendency to go back to basics and to adopt more monomodal approaches to literacy with an overlay of twenty-first century ideologies ("old wine in new bottles"—again this comes from our perspectives based on international audits of digital literacy such as Burnett, Merchant, Davies, & Rowsell, 2014). Some recent publications on the topics are position statements by task forces that delineate twenty-first century learning skills and that put out a call to attend to how students acquire twenty-first century learning skills. Two recent task forces are: *Future Tense: Adapting Canadian Education Systems for the Twenty-First Century* (Boudreault,

Haga, Paylor, Sabourin Thomas, & van der Linden, 2013) and *Shifting Minds: A Twenty-First Century Vision of Public Education for Canada* (Canadians for twenty-first Century Learning & Innovation, 2012). The former illuminates the need for Canada to have a "cohesive national strategy with respect to twenty-first century learning" (p. 3) and the latter offers a vision, guidelines and competencies for twenty-first century learning that are referenced by several Canadian provinces and territories. In the context of this chapter, and the proceeding discussion that situates some of the policy history and research perspectives and foci of digital literacy in Canada, the former report substantiates our rationale and the latter report provides our analytical framework.

Historical and Philosophical Underpinnings of Expectations for Teachers

Looking across Canadian curricular documents, there is explicit acknowledgement of the need to develop innovative approaches to educational practices and the inclusion of digital technologies. Viewed as a twenty-first-century challenge, there have been explicit efforts to integrate/incorporate digital tools and devices in schools, use multimedia links to open possibilities for digital literacy development. It is not uncommon now to have curriculum and pedagogy expand to be inclusive of (a) online/virtual learning, (b) screen and digital platforms and mobile devices, (c) view learners as collaborators, producers/designers, and users of such texts. More so, within this educational context, is the need to have teachers now accommodate and facilitate learners' complex digital media knowledge, literacy practices, and support students' interface with and access to such digital texts. In keeping with the emphasis on a social constructivist approaches to teaching and learning, the interactive and social nature of instruction places the teacher in the critical role of facilitating these learning experiences in the classroom. These digital and technological pedagogical expectations placed on teachers, as it applies to the teacher's role in designing and executing curriculum, speak to the gaps and needs in classroom practice that have persisted. While the history of K-12 policy and curricular efforts in Canada acknowledges the central role of the education system in developing the necessary digital and technical skills and competencies necessary for all high school graduates and at the post-secondary levels, the practice falls short. As Hadziristic (2018) points out, to date, there is no common consensus on what teaching digital literacy in schools should look like, and consequently, schools are not organized to promote digital competence. To support her claim, Hadziristic points to the lack of unified curricula in digital literacy, along with the lack of teacher training and qualified teachers. Here, the recurring criticisms about teacher knowledge arise particularly when teachers are unable to use the full potential of technologies in innovative ways and in ways that reflect their understanding of how digital technologies have changed the nature of learning and teaching, and how technology interacts with knowledge (i.e. foundational, meta, and humanistic) (see Kereluik, Mishra, Fahnoe, & Terry, 2013 in Erstad, Eickelmann, & Eichhorn, 2015). What this points to is the lack of focus on preparing and training teachers so that they can effectively teach content using digital technology.

Education policy intended to develop learners' digital knowledge and skills have not been limited to traditional classrooms and learner populations. There have been more focused efforts out of school to develop digital literacies among youth and adults. For example, Canada ABC created the ABC Internet Matters workbook to help older Canadians without digital literacy skills. Added to this, Massive Open Online Courses (MOOCs) and Afterschool training programs have helped to bridge what Hadziristic (2018) and others (e.g., Ipsos Public Affairs, 2015) have identified as a digital divide. Nonetheless, the common argument made among many policy reviewers, practitioners, and teacher–educators is that the comprehensive digitization and technological proliferation (both in-and-out-of-school) can only occur through consistent, quality technological support, access to digital literacy training, robust internet service, and internet-enabled devices (Hadziristic, 2018).

Immigration and Literacy Learning

Refugee children and parents who arrive in Canada are accustomed to engaging in different cognitive processes shaped by culturally influenced learning experiences that are often distinct from Western practices and texts (DeCapua & Marshall, 2015). In turn, such cultural and linguistic dissonances can directly impact success in their new lives in Canada. Settlement is informed by a sometimes-jarring induction into discourses and modalities that are not transparent and that can confound newcomers.

Canadian studies on mapping language use (Dagenais, Moore, Sabatier, Lamarre, & Armand, 2009) have similarly investigated the importance of "linguistic landscapes" awareness with specific attention to diversity, religion, culture, and ethnicity. Other scholars based in Montreal, have used mapping language tools to identify such educational matters as language anxiety (Godfrey-Smith, 2017) and multilingualism practices in youth (Lamarre, 2013). Technologies and digital literacies played a role in these research studies, but in an allusive way—rather they helped children and participants piece together the ways that multiple linguistic systems flow through pedagogical spaces through visual modes, which are themselves inherent to digital literacies.

In Zaidi's research (2019) in Calgary with resettled families, she talks about using technology and resources, such as Google translate, Google images, and online databases/encyclopedia to foster an inquiry-based mindset in students. Zaidi explores instances with newly arrived Canadians when digital literacy has served as a powerful vehicle for language learning. For instance, she has observed how teachers can plan a mini lesson on how to find reliable resources, what kind of research can be done to supplement interviews conducted at home, and how to present the show and tell online (Prezi, PowerPoint, and blogs are good examples).

Finally, for a research study that took place in the Niagara region from January 2018 until May 2018 with resettled, newcomer families, Gallagher, Di Cesare, and Rowsell discussed with resettled families their stories of digital lives/digital divides (Gallagher, DiCesare, & Rowsell, 2019). What resulted from the six-month research study is a confirmation of two emerging findings within digital literacy: (1) that digital lives are variable and strongly influenced by culture, linguistic systems, social class, ethnicity and race, and personal beliefs; and, (2) that there are clear and present digital divides manifested not only in terms of access, but also and potentially more importantly in terms of literacy practices applied to digital engagements.

Language Learning

Given its national dual language identity of English and French, Canada's experience with language learning offers insights into how the privileging of English affects indigenous and minority-language learners' and speakers' literacy education. In their case study of teacher's expressions of their literacy-related professional development needs in a First Nations school in a reserve in a small Ontario town in Canada, Heydon and Stooke (2012) address the privileging of English—and its effect on indigenous education and implications for teachers and children. The authors argue that in this particular context, literacy teaching is "complex and tied to an ongoing legacy of colonialism" (Heydon & Stooke, 2012). While addressing many salient issues related to teaching and literacy in First Nations schools, the article explores the tensions between English and Indigenous languages. They do so against the backdrop that Aboriginal languages are sacred to Aboriginal people, and English is deemed to be a "killer language" that is learned at the cost of smaller (Indigenous) languages rather than being learned "in addition to" small languages (Skutnabb-Kangas, Maffi, & Harmon, 2003, p. 33, in Heydon & Stooke, 2012, p. 13). It is worth noting that Heydon and Stooke (2012) point to the neocolonial lens in teacher professional development (PD) where the dominant group redefines another as deficient, restricts choices and resources, and normalizes certain skills, viewpoints, and languages so that they become entrenched as what counts as the norm.

Issues of language and its role in literacy learning are pervasive in the context of Hagerman's (2017) maker project in a Francophone minority school. In fact, Hagerman notes, "linguistic francophone minority community in Canada rarely sees itself reflected in online and mainstream media" (Hagerman, 2017). Thus, teachers and students experience an additional barrier to learning and teaching particularly when attempting to integrate literacies practices to support content learning—particularly in science, technology, engineering, and mathematics (STEM). As a result, in these research sites and school contexts, there is the central issue of the language of instruction and its negative impact on learners in all aspects of their education. In this case, the privileging of English as the dominant and/or sole language of instruction contradicts any meaningful and socially constructed approach to learning and teaching, and weaponizes the language against minoritized Other/minority groups.

Digital literacy and Indigenous perspectives

In the Canadian landscape, given the aforementioned discriminatory approaches to language and literacy, more consideration is being given to the ongoing reciprocal relationships between literacies, spaces and land, particularly in efforts to decolonize literacies through creative multidimensional and digital means (Doucet, 2018; Tuhiwai Smith, Tuck, & Yang 2018; Whitty, 2017). These social justice initiatives can be addressed by respecting traditional lands and integrating digital literacy practices in storytelling and reversing dominating settler discourses (Barton & Barton, 2017; Doucet, 2018; Styres, 2018). Posthuman Indigenous research looking at the more-than-human dimensions of literacies and place (Nxumalo & Rubin, 2018) have laid the ground for further research in areas that extend early literacy childhood. Other recent studies aimed to provide wider unrestricted access to literacy resources all the while working with materialities with concerns for access and equity in university settings (Lemieux & McLarnon, 2018). Across these empirical studies, there is an unrelenting will to restore social justice in established and existing systems, whether these are embedded in materialities and in immaterialities at play. The work towards social justice not only needs to permeate ideologies, but also the materialized results of oppressive systems that need to be untangled through such effective means as digital literacies.

Digital Literacy as Transformative

The trend derived from increased emphasis on the digital as the primary vehicle for learning/teaching is not without its affordances and limitations. On one hand, the growing push for content, pedagogy, and teaching philosophy, results in students' proficiency *and* the normalization of such schooling practices. On the other hand, through the sedimentation of such practices as a distinct character of schooling/teaching and learning, there is the risk that *because* of their proficiency with the digital, students then become indifferent to practices that are then viewed as rote or typical.

Many researchers have long since examined the risks and benefits of digital literacies as a defining characteristic of schools. For example, O'Mara and Laidlaw (2011) caution that such tools and texts that students use out of school, once translated into classrooms, tend to be "domesticated" by practices that resist the transformative affordances of these tools, thereby becoming barriers to student engagement and practice. The ongoing work of Harwood in Canadian contexts (Harwood, 2015, 2017) promises heightened investigations into the lives of children who engage with ecoliteracies and digital worlds in situated learning spaces and places. As such, play in the twenty-first century embeds a logic that surpasses kinesthetic assemblages, and considers the environment, musings, and contextually relevant pedagogy-in-the-making. Exploration, trial-and-error, decision-making, and creativity occupy a determining role in these digital literacy pedagogies. Wohlwend and Rowsell (2017) have also studied children's interactions with digital applications to elucidate and understand how they enact different types of digital literacy practices. Drawing from empirical research, they established six concrete and useful aspects of participatory literacies: multiplayer, productive, multimodal, open-ended, pleasurable, and connected. These six dimensions can be measured from levels of "low" to "high", with specialized insights into the literacy practices of youth as they engage with digital apps. These dimensions have concrete repercussions in and implications for classroom-based practices, including how teachers negotiate their own approaches to digital app use with students and, more importantly, how students negotiate their own learning and engagement practices with apps.

When considering the application and implementation of digital literacies across various contexts, design-based research offers insights into digital learning in real-world educational settings. The cutting edge research of Lacelle (Lacelle et al., 2015, 2017) in Quebec has two main objectives in the areas of multimodality and digital literacy: (1) to document the digital and multimodal resources mobilized by students in the context of documentary research or artistic creation (art and literature) in school and out-of-school contexts; (2) construct, validate, and implement, in collaboration with teachers and students, a research-design model (DBR) including devices for the realization of scholarly research work or artistic creation that take into account the skills in LMM developed in school and out-of-school digital contexts. Design-based research is rooted in educational technology and in research-teacher collaboration, which together develops learning experiences (phase design) and then studies their impact on learners (implementation and iterative stages) in authentic contexts. This research aims mainly to propose a model of accompaniment in school tasks in language, art and social studies disciplines (documentary research and artistic creation).

Theory and Research Base

Theoretical Approaches

Literacy pedagogy has been explored from a range of theoretical perspectives in order to explore the value of multimodal literacy practices. Heydon and O'Neill (2016), for instance, used poststructural theory to engage in critical deconstruction of the concept of literacy and well-being. Underscoring this theoretical approach is the view/stance that there is never one dominant conception of the term; rather conflicting and multiple understanding co-exist at any given point in the history of the concept. Even further, Heydon (2013) drew on Bakhtin's (1986) notion of the dialogic to explore the intersection of communicative practices, meaning-making and cognitive development of children. In this study, the social interactions took precedence in supporting learning.

Courtland and Paddington (2008) use a social constructivist and reader-response framework to explore representation via print literacy and multiliteracies as sign systems. Using Foucault's (1982) theory of power, Burkholder, Makramalla, Abdou, Khoja, and Khan (2015) address four levels of power dynamics with regard to (1) participants and society (2) researcher vs. researched, (3) participants, and (4) ethics of dissemination. These researchers also draw on Freire's (2010) codifications that allow participants to "externalise a series of sentiments and opinions about themselves they would not express under different circumstances" (Freire, 2010, p. 219). Honeyford's (2013) design of her ethnographic case study of students' digital storytelling was informed by narrative and artifactual literacies theories that allowed her to simultaneously privilege children's narratives and their multimodality. In another study, Simon and Kalan (2016) use practitioner inquiry as an epistemological and methodological stance—one that is grounded in the view of educational research as in insider position. From this grass-roots, action research approach, the practitioner is viewed as knower and agent of educational and social change.

These research studies push for what we might think of as more nuanced perspectives on digital literacy that complicate the old wine and in new bottles syndrome (2003). The old wine in new bottles syndrome allude to the ways that "many researchers have identified the old wine in new bottles' syndrome, whereby longstanding school literacy routines have a new technology tacked on here or there without in any way changing the substance of the practice" (Lankshear & Knobel, 2003, p. 5). The research in this section approaches the digital as differing in logic to the monomodal and analogue—a logic based on the notion of multimodality as two or more modes of expression or representation in play.

Sociocultural Approaches

The link between the pivotal/central role of digital technology in cognitive and social development of young children is addressed/explored in O'Mara,

Laidlaw, and Blackmore's (O'Mara, Laidlaw, & Blackmore, 2017) article where the authors reflect on the technological texts that children use in their out-of-school worlds. Heydon and O'Neill's (2014) study of intergenerational multimodal programs involving preschoolers and elderly participants highlights the value of multiple modes in facilitating meaning making. What stands out for Heydon and O'Neill's approach is that the value of privileging multiple cultural interactions communities differences, among diverse learners—generational, economic, and ethnically. The authors argue that when teaching and learning are grounded in the sociocultural dimensions of literacy, the benefits are salient. Similarly, Heydon's (2013) literacy-focused study of an art program involving intergenerational groups of children media (age 4), and adult participants (median age 85) looks at the intersection of semiotics and engagement. Using Bakhtin's (1983) notion of the dialogic to emphasize the heterogeneity of texts, the author (Heydon, 2013) asserts that learners (children's) meaning-making practices and cognitive development.

Teaching and Learning in the Digitally Mediated Classroom

A number of researchers have explored ways of using digital story-telling as a way of ushering identities into classroom spaces. In Honeyford's (2013) study in Manitoba, artefacts are viewed as forms of representation—signs and symbols of meaning and a process of becoming. By having students play with narrative modes and genres, the process and product act as a way to "make sense of and communicate their experiences, dreams, and social critiques" (Honeyford, 2013, p. 24). Heydon and Stooke (2012) take the notion of identity in literacy practice even further in their study of teachers' practices and curricular content from an indigenous perspective. In this study, these authors highlight the ameliorating or standardized packaging of content that minimizes or negates teacher strengths, knowledge, and identities, and the unique nature of First Nations schools, while defaulting to an implied one-right way or normative "best practices." They call for an approach that views teachers as "knowledgeable professionals who can entertain sophisticated notions of literacy that consider its relationship to situation including culture" (Heydon & Stooke, 2012, p. 11).

Collier's (2017) research in Newfoundland focused on how social class dimensions enfolded as white, working-class elementary school children engage with cosmopolitan practices when they created digital posters as part of their English Language Arts classroom. The findings pointed to increased engagement with humor, masculinities and femininities as they materially represented their identities. Broadly viewed, cosmopolitanism was an inherent, pervasive part of their performed identities in the study. Such research on children's digital literacies encourages researchers to start to examine not only degrees of access, but also the kinds of literacy practices that children engage in. Engagements with popular culture shape children's and adolescents' identity constructions, sense of performed genders (masculinities/femininities), and desires and pleasures as students (Collier, 2015). The implications of social class for digital literacies surpass patterns of reception and production with regards to digital texts in classroom settings. In particular, we find that educational policies need to address more specifically how digital literacy practices can serve as a repertoire for stereotyping categories embedded in social class (van Leeuwen, 2018). In classroom and pedagogical settings, this means prioritizing opportunities to deconstruct social classes and relationships with access to digital tools, critical readings, and adequately surveying the affordances of certain modes over others. For instance, one may ask: is sound paired with video a better outlet to address social class in comparison to sound paired with moving image and kinesthetic touch? What are the affordances of digital consumption and digital production in situated early childhood contexts? To teach digital literacies responsibly, we must all take these types of questions into account as we prepare children for future literacy landscapes.

In the Eastern Canadian context, recent applied research has framed eco-sustainability and digital ecologies around children working with iPads (Rose, Fitzpatrick, Mersereau, & Whitty, 2017). Specifically, this study revitalized the relationships between the University of New Brunswick's Children Centre and local families and their children's desiring to explore digital literacies in out-of-school contexts. Exploring iPad use on the playground, the researchers along with four teachers guided four-year-old children as they engaged in playful experimentation, using iPads as tools for inquiry, and developed immersive relationships with storytelling and witch play. The authors recommend adopting such practices to foster digital engagements outside the classroom.

Engaging Learners in Digital Ecologies

Engagement as ownership and social learning (from peers, teacher support) is yet another theme running across digital literacy research in Canada. Some researchers have explored how children negotiated texts based on their literacy, home engagements, discourses etc. (e.g. Burke, Butland, Roberts, & Snow, 2013; McTavish, 2009; Wong, 2013, 2015). In Western Canada, McTavish has conducted a number of fascinating research studies in the area of digital literacy in British Columbia. Investigating the intersection of children's in and out of school literacy practices, McTavish (2009) examines how children have rich, varied and highly multimodal literacy practices outside of school that rarely find their way into more traditional schooling models. Through detailed and careful ethnographic fieldwork in homes and classrooms, McTavish celebrates the creativity young children display and how much they fade into the background when schooling practices take precedence. Wong (2013, 2015) has spent significant amounts of time conducting home ethnographies of multimodal meaning making in Edmonton, Alberta and in Melbourne, Australia. Wong focuses on data from different participants analyzing such literacy events as children's use of iPads and the ways that they motivate children and incite creativity. Informed by complexity thinking (Davis & Sumara, 2008) and Green's (1988, 2012) three-dimensional model of literacy as conceptual frameworks, Wong's work probes deeply into children's media ecologies and ways of leveraging them in schooling spaces. Textual and technology engagements as a way to connect students' literacy practices, was the focus of a study by Burke et al. (2013). The researchers looked at how the range of practices including language and cultural diversity (e.g. immigrant and linguistic backgrounds) in their respective classrooms were borne out in the ways that students engaged with diverse texts and activities.

A central character of engagement is its social nature, which often involves active participation and collaboration. In the learning/teaching context, the engagement comes in the form of teachers working with students, students with each other, researchers with teachers to create a deeper and more complex understanding of a concept, space, topic etc. Simon and Kalan's (2016) research that focuses on collaborative inquiry in teacher education classrooms with middle-school students, teacher candidates, and university researchers is one such example of collaborative learning. Simon and Kalan describe collaborative practitioner inquiry as a model of curricular and methodological development and adolescent literacy engagement. Here the authors attempt to "challenge the notion that curriculum is developed *for* students (or for teachers)" by working *with* students to meaningfully shape their understanding of the curriculum. Collaborators (teachers, students, and researchers) draw on visual motifs of the graphic novel, artwork, and painting to help work through the responses to the novel and the Holocaust. Similar to youth participatory action research (YPAR), the authors highlight the emphasis on valuing multiple perspectives and collective experiences developed through shared inquiry of history narratives in the teaching of Spiegelman's (1986) graphic novel, Maus. For the authors (Simon & Kalan, 2016), collaborative inquiries generate such qualities as empathy, activism, and risk-taking.

The maker movement has spurred more recent research on learners' use of digital literacies to create, compose, and design using digital tools and technologies. Similar to Simon and Kalan's (2016) study, Hagerman's (2017) project also emphasized the collaboration between researchers and teachers —who in this case, co-designed the maker project focused on digital literacies that support science learning. Informed by the modern maker movement that operates on the premise of the human need to craft, tinker, design, create, and invent, Hagerman (2017) describes an innovative maker project in 6th grade classrooms in a Francophone minority-language school in Canada. Even further, in a SSHRC-funded research study in the Niagara region, Rowsell, Lemieux, Swartz, Turcotte, and Burkitt (2018) work with cross-sector professionals and elementary and secondary teachers working with specific modes such as documentary filmmaking or conceptual photography with students. In their research, they spotlight relational moments as foundational to maker and design approaches to teaching and learning. Students who normally keep their preferred literacy practices outside of school, began to make their lived, preferred literacies more visible and incorporated them into multimodal compositions (Pahl et al., 2019). Rowsell and colleagues (2018) described these relational moments as the glued, or taken from the work of Ahmed (2015), sticky emotions coming to the surface, driving multimodal and digital engagements.

Social Support Mediating Digital Learning

Research on supporting students' digital and technological learning has spanned early childhood to adult learners. What is consistent is that in many of these studies, the understanding of support adopts an approach similar to a gradual release model used by the Manitoba Continuum Model for Literacy in ICT when young people build resilience, problem-solve, and engage positively with technology (Hadziristic, 2018). Schreurs, Quan-Haase, and Martin (2017), in their survey and interview study of older adults, investigate the digital skills, barriers to literacy, and the social and institutional support systems adults accessed in order to get help with technology. Findings show that age, coupled with low levels institutional and social support, plays a role in the adoption of technology by older adults. The complex relationship with technology experienced by older adults significantly hinders or precludes the development of the digital literacies.

Support for learners is not necessarily harnessed to one specific site or context as evident in Laidlaw and Wong's study of home-school connections. Laidlaw and Wong's (2016) approach to "new literacy" practices with kindergarten and young learners spanned a two-year project using drama and digital tools. Using the notion of complexity-informed approaches, the authors assert that complexity thinking can aid in provoking a deeper recognition of the collective and recursive nature of learning for both student and teacher. Based on their observations of classroom and home, the authors note the connections with increasing digital media internationally within and outside of classroom settings. Here, the approaches to technology both theoretical and practical approaches for organizing classroom learning structures.

However, when considering the opportunities for learning that the digital affords, issues of power and participation cannot be ignored. Burkholder et al. (2015) interrogated notions of power in relation to the creation and dissemination of three participatory visual methods (drawing, photovoice, and cellphilms) through digital spaces. Through the intertextuality of critical thinking and collaborative work, the authors argue that "participatory visual methods can intentionally or unintentionally influence, after, and/or transfer the voices of marginalized people in researchers' attempts to effect social change" (p. 19).

Across the body of research, one of the central themes/issues is the use and transformative roles of inquiry approach to literacy teaching and learning in general and developing digital literacies in particular. The inquiry approach is collaborative, participatory, problem solving, multimodal, and processural in nature. Hagerman and White's (2013) study involves online inquiry through collaborative reading and writing, and publishing of the digital "Wonder" project. The power of an inquiry approach to learning and teaching is later evident in Hagerman's (2017) study of a maker project in which a central feature of the collaborative nature of the maker project in which student participated was the role of investigating and questioning resources via online and physical exploration. Even further, in Burke, Butland, Roberts, and Snow's (2013) study, the transformational roles of literacy is evidenced in the (1) inclusion of home literacy practices to enhance students' understanding of a school-based texts; (2) student-centered activities via literacy circles; and (3) community-based, multimodal, and interactive discussions and comments.

Implications for Future Research

School districts, school administrators, and teachers face the challenge of keeping up with an ever-evolving technological landscape, with schools mediating complex and entangled environments that both enable and disable innovation (Malgilchrist & Böhmig, 2012; O'Mara, Laidlaw & Blackmore, 2017) when policy, curriculum as it is written and enacted, and societal and technological change intersect. Educators and curriculum developers must address the need to develop new models and structures for literacy instruction and shifting digital contexts.

In writing this chapter, we found some compelling research conducted across Canada, but on the whole, somewhat dated and at times pedestrian. As with much international twenty-first policies, there are lots of good intentions and lip service for radical changes, but alas they tend to fall short —especially in larger provinces like Ontario. As with other researchers (Gallagher & Rowsell, 2017), we found policy coverage of digital literacy fairly inconsistent and with minimal coverage of the competencies of, "Using digital resources, variety of media and technology to access information, create knowledge and create solutions" (p. 390). These competencies are integral to inquiry-based learning approaches that are in practice in many jurisdictions. Next, there are no provinces that explicitly mention in the curriculum standards that learners should be, "Developing twenty-first century competencies in the context of core subjects" (p. 390). The competency of,

"Using social media to communicate and learn" (p. 383) is absent from all of the provinces' curriculum documents. This is not surprising given the fact that the publication dates of the documents that range from 2000 to 2012 and the explosion of social media is a recent reality (Buckingham & Martinez-Rodriguez, 2013).

It is worth noting that many of the provinces have supplementary resources for teachers that provide recommendations for instructional approaches and resources that align with twenty-first century learning. This is an attempt to fill the gap between standards documents and practice. Examples of these supplementary resources include: *Digital Literacy Framework (Profiles and Learning Activities)* (Government of British Columbia, n.d.); *Technology in Education* (Prince Edward Island Education, n.d.); *Literacy with ICT Across the Curriculum* (Northwest Territories Education, 2012). As well, attempts have been made to include twenty-first-century learning principles in recent provincial and territorial education position statements. Examples of these include: *A Vision for Twenty-First Century Education* (British Columbia Premier's Technology Council, 2010); *Emerging Technologies in the Twenty-First Century: A Summary of Final Reports* (Alberta Education, 2008); *Shaping A New Vision For Public Education in Nova Scotia* (Nova Scotia School Boards Association, 2014); *Towards Defining Twenty-First Century Competencies for Ontario* (Ontario Ministry of Education, 2016). However, the curriculum documents are lagging woefully behind practices and position statements. The first province to pick up this gauntlet is British Columbia (2016) who has piloted a revised set of curricula honoring twenty-first century skills.

What is needed is a Canadian *national* policy that attends to issues of policy and infrastructure for the support of teachers' practices and the learning of their students. This needs to be well beyond the ambit of white papers and it needs to include multiple academic, pedagogic and cultural lenses across Canada. The publications, *Shifting Minds: A Twenty-First Century Vision of Public Education for Canada (2012)* and very recently, *Shifting Minds 3.0: Redefining the Learning Landscape in Canada (2015)* continue to articulate six areas that need to shift to drive systemic change: Curriculum; Pedagogy; Learning Environment; Governance; Citizen Engagement; Assessment. Among the curriculum re-design priorities (Canadians for twenty-first Century Learning & Innovation, 2012) are, "twenty-first century competencies must be infused throughout all learning outcomes" (p. 14) and "learning outcomes must be rationalized across subject areas to reduce redundancy while strengthening cross-curricular relationships" (p.14). One of the Pedagogy re-design priorities is, "learners must have individualized access to the internet and digital resources" (p. 15). A re-design priority in Learning Environment, "mobile learning opportunities should be integrated with other learning delivery models" (p. 15) suggests that educators themselves avail of media and technology to enhance their instructional methods.

Recommendations for Global-Minded Literacy Teachers

1. Be mindful of haves and have nots and can and cannots (Dolan, 2016).
2. Get beyond the tools and technologies by focusing on diversity of modes.
3. Tinker, hack, and problem-solve with students on technologies.
4. Apply inquiry models from early childhood pedagogies and open up classroom space and time for experimentation.
5. Harness interests to digital literacy practices and redefine academic literacies/school literacies around newer literacy practices.
6. Do not fight screen logic—embrace it but also critical frame it and sometimes disrupt it.
7. Keep digital literacy work open to inquiry and lots of curation time.
8. Leverage the power of social media to access facts and be activist.
9. Encourage auto-didactic practices and curating research online.
10. Do not romanticize or valorize screens—arts and crafts materials are just as effective.

Discussion Questions and Application

1. Does my classroom speak to my students' authentic, lived digital literacy practices?
2. In what ways can I shape digital literacies around my teaching philosophy?
3. How can I assess my students' levels of access and attendant digital literacy competencies (due to a lack of access)?
4. Are there ways to shift my language and literacy assessments around digital and multimodal principles?

Note

1 Melissa Turcotte is now Vice-Principal at St. Anthony Catholic School in St Catharines, ON.

References

Ahmed, S. (2015). *The cultural politics of emotion* (2nd ed.). New York: Routledge.
Alberta Education. (2008). *Emerging technologies in the 21st century: A summary of final reports.* Retrieved from https://archive.org/details/emergingtechnolo00albe
Bakhtin, M. M. (1983). *The dialogic imagination: Four essays.* Texas: University of Texas Press.
Bakhtin, M. M. (1986). The problem of speech genres. In C. Emerson & M. Holquist (Eds.), *Speech genres and other late essays* (Trans. V.W. McGee) (pp. 60–102). Austin, TX: University of Texas Press.

Barton, G. M., & Barton, R. S. (2017). The importance of storytelling for children: An exploration of Indigenous approaches to learning. In S. Garvis & N. Pramling (Eds.), *Narratives in early childhood education: Communication, sense making and lived experience* (pp. 61–74). London: Routledge.

Boudreault, F.-A., Haga, J., Paylor, B., Sabourin, A., Thomas, S., & van der Linden, C. (2013). *Future tense: Adapting Canadian education systems for the 21st century*. Retrieved from www.actioncanada.ca/project/future-tense-adapting-canad ian-education-systems-21st-century.

British Columbia Premier's Technology Council. (2010). A vision for twenty-first century education [PDF file]. Retrieved from https://premierstechnologycouncil. ca/wp-content/uploads/2016/11/PTC-Special-Report-A-Vision-for-21st-Cen tury-Education.pdf

Buckingham, D., & Martinez-Rodriguez, J. B. (2013). Interactive youth: New citizenship between social networks and school settings. *Comunicar, 40,* 10–14.

Burke, A., Butland, L., Roberts, K., & Snow, S. (2013). Using multiliteracies to "rethink" literacy pedagogy in elementary classrooms. *Journal of Technology Integration in the Classroom, 5*(1), 41–53.

Burkholder, C., Makramalla, M., Abdou, E., Khoja, N., & Khan, F. (2015). Why study power in digital spaces anyway? Considering power and participatory visual methods. *Perspectives in Education, 33*(4), 6–22.

Burnett, C., Davies, J., Merchant, G., & Rowsell, J. (2014). *New literacies around the globe*. London: Routledge.

Canadians for 21st Century Learning & Innovation. (2012). Shifting minds: A twenty-first century vision of public education for Canada [PDF file]. Retrieved from www.c21canada.org/wp-content/uploads/2012/05/C21-Canada-Shifting-Version-2.0.pdf

Collier, D. R. (2015). I'm just trying to be tough, okay: Masculine performances of everyday practices. *Journal of Early Childhood Literacy, 15*(2), 203–226.

Collier, D. R. (2017). Rescripting classed lives and imagining audiences as online cosmopolitan practice. In R. Zaidi & J. Rowsell (Eds.), *Literacy lives in transcultural times* (pp. 136–154). New York: Routledge.

Council of Ministers of Education. (2013). Ministers of Education highlight 21st-century literacies on international literacy day [Press release]. Retrieved from www.cmec.ca/278/Ministers_of_Education_Highlight_21st-Century_Literacies_o n_International_Literacy_Day.html?id=641

Council of Ministers of Education, Canada (2018). *Quality education for all: Canadian report for the UNESCO ninth consultation of member states on the implementation of the convention and recommendation against discrimination in education.* Canada: UNESCO.

Courtland, M. C., & Paddington, D. (2008). Digital literacy in a grade 8 classroom: An e-zine webquest. *Language and Literacy: A Canadian E-journal, 10*(1), 1–23.

Dagenais, D., Moore, D., Sabatier, C., Lamarre, S., & Armand, F. (2009). Linguistic landscape and language awareness. In E. Shohamy & D. Gorter (Eds.), *Linguistic landscape: Expanding the scenery* (pp. 253–269). New York: Routledge.

Davis, B., & Sumara, D. (2008). The death and life of great educational ideas: Why we might want to avoid a critical complexity theory. *Journal of the Canadian Association for Curriculum Studies, 6*(1), 163–176.

DeCapua, A., & Marshall, H. W. (2015). Implementing a mutually adaptive learning paradigm in a community-based adult ESL literacy class. In M. G. Santos & A. Whiteside (Eds.), *Low educated second language and literacy acquisition: Proceedings of the ninth symposium* (pp. 151–171). San Francisco, CA: Lulu Publishing.

Dolan, J. E. (2016). Splicing the divide: A review of research on the evolving digital divide among K–12 students. *Journal of Research on Technology in Education*, *48*(1), 16–37.

Doucet, A. (2018). Decolonizing family photographs: Ecological imaginaries and non-representational ethnographies. *Journal of Contemporary Ethnography*, *47*(6), 729–757.

Erstad, O., Eickelmann, B., & Eichhorn, K. (2015). Preparing teachers for schooling in the digital age: A meta-perspective on existing strategies and future challenges. *Education and Information Technologies*, *20*(4), 641–654.

Foucault, M. (1982). The subject and power. *Critical Inquiry*, *8*(4), 777–795.

Freire, P. (2010). *Pedagogy of the oppressed*. New York: Continuum.

Gallagher, T., DiCesare, D., & Rowsell, J. (2019). Stories of digital lives and digital divides: Newcomer families and their thoughts on digital literacy. *The Reading Teacher*, *72*(6), 774–778. (Digital Literacy Column).

Gallagher, T., & Rowsell, J. (2017). Untangling binaries: Where Canada sits in the "21st century debate". *McGill Journal of Education*, *52*(2), 383–407.

Godfrey-Smith, L. (2017). "Pardon my French": A non-static case-study of the social dimensions of non-classroom language anxiety in Montréal. Unpublished dissertation, McGill University, Montréal, QC.

Government of British Columbia. (n.d.). Digital literacy framework [PDF file]. Retrieved from www2.gov.bc.ca/assets/gov/education/kindergarten-to-grade-12/teach/teaching-tools/digital-literacy-framework.pdf

Government of Northwest Territories: Education, Culture and Employment. (2012). *Literacy with ICT across the curriculum* [PDF file]. Retrieved from www.ece.gov.nt.ca/sites/ece/files/resources/lwict_infusion_guide_-_2012.pdf

Green, B. (1988). Subject-specific literacy and school learning: A focus on writing. *Australian Journal of Education*, *32*(2), 156–179.

Hadziristic, T. (2018). The state of digital literacy in Canada: A literature review [PDF file]. Retrieved from https://brookfieldinstitute.ca/wp-content/uploads/Brookfiel dInstitute_State-of-Digital-Literacy-in-Canada_Literature_WorkingPaper.pdf

Hagerman, M. S. (2017). Les bricoscientifiques: Exploring the intersections of disciplinary, digital, and maker literacies instruction in a Franco-Ontarian school. *Journal of Adolescent & Adult Literacy*, *61*(3), 319–325.

Hagerman, M. S., & White, A. (2013). What's the best formula for enhancing online inquiry skills? *Reading Today*, *31*(3), 20.

Harwood, D. (2015). Crayons & iPads: Children's meaning making in the digital world. *An Leanbh Óg (The Young Child) Journal*, *9*(1), 107–120.

Harwood, D. (2017). *Crayons and iPads: Learning and teaching of young children in the digital world*. Thousand Oaks, CA: Sage.

Heydon, R. (2013). *Learning at the ends of life: Children, elders and literacies in intergenerational curricula*. Toronto: University of Toronto Press.

Heydon, R. & O'Neill, S. (2014). Songs in our hearts: Affordances and constraints of an intergenerational multimodal arts curriculum. *International Journal of Education & the Arts*, *15*(16), 1–32.

Heydon, R., & O'Neill, S. (2016). *Why multimodal literacy matters: (Re)conceptualizing literacy and wellbeing through singing-infused multimodal, intergenerational curricula.* Boston, MA: Sense Publishers.

Heydon, R., & Stooke, R. (2012). Border work: Teacher's expressions of their literacy-related professional development needs in a First Nations school. *Teaching and Teacher Education, 28,* 11–20.

Honeyford, M. (2013). The simultaneity of experience: Cultural identity, magical realism, and the artefactual in digital storytelling. *Literacy, 47*(1), 17–25.

Honeyford, M., & Trussler, P. (2020). Red dresses and sequined bras: Encountering materiality, place, and affect in pop-up installation pedagogy. In K. Lenters, & M. McDermott (Eds). *Affect, embodiment, and place in critical literacy: Assembling theory and practice.* New York: Taylor and Francis.

Huynh, A., & Do, A. (2017). Digital literacy in a digital age: A discussion paper [PDF file]. Retrieved from https://brookfieldinstitute.ca/wp-content/uploads/Brookfiel dInstitute_DigitalLiteracy_DigitalAge.pdf

Ipsos Public Affairs. (2015). *One in ten (9%) Canadians do not have internet access at home.* Retrieved from www.ipsos.com/en-ca/one-ten-9-canadians-do-not-have-inter net-access-home

Kereluik, K., Mishra, P., Fahnoe, C., & Terry, L. (2013). What knowledge is of most worth: Teacher knowledge for 21st century learning. *Journal of Digital Learning in Teacher Education, 29*(4), 127–140.

Kress, G. (2003). *Literacy in the new media age.* London: Routledge.

Lacelle, N., Boutin, J.-F., & Lebrun, M. (2017). *Applied multimodal media literacy in digital literacy in digital contexts – MML@. Conceptual and pedagogical tools.* Ste-Foy: University of Quebec Press.

Lacelle, N., Lebrun, M., Boutin, J.-F., Richard, M. & Martel, V. (2015). Multimodal Media Literacy (MML) skills at the elementary and secondary level: A transdisciplinary grid for analysis. In L. Lafontaine & J. Pharand (Eds.), *Literacy: Towards a mastery of skills in diverse environments* (pp. 168–184). Québec: PUQ.

Lacelle, N., Boutin, J., & Lebrun, M. (2017) *Multimodal media literacy applied in a digital context – LMM @. Conceptual and didactic tools.* Quebec, Canada: University of Quebec Press.

Laidlaw, L. & Wong, S. (2016). Complexity, pedagogy, play: On using technology within emergent learning structures with young learners. *Complicity: An International Journal of Complexity and Education, 13*(1), 3–42.

Lamarre, P. (2013). Catching "Montreal on the move" and challenging the discourse of unilingualism in Quebec. *Anthropologica, 55*(1), 41–56.

Lankshear, C., & Knobel, M. (2003). *New literacies. Changing knowledge and classroom learning.* Buckingham: Open University Press.

Lemieux, A., & McLarnon, M. (2018). Artful portable library spaces: Increasing community agency and shared knowledge. In E. Hasebe-Ludt & C. Leggo (Eds.), *Canadian Curriculum Studies: A métissage of inspiration/imagination* (pp. 35–47). Toronto: Canadian Scholars.

Leu D. J., Kinzer, C. K., Coiro, J., Castek, J., & Henry, L. A. (2013). New literacies and the new literacies of online reading comprehension: A dual level theory. In N. Unrau & D. Alvermann (Eds.), *Theoretical models and process of reading* (pp. 1150–1181). Newark, DE: International Reading Association.

Malgilchrist, F., & Böhmig, I. (2012). Blogs, genes and immigration. Online media and minimal politics. *Media, Culture & Society, 34*(1), 83–100.

Marsh, J. (2005). Ritual, performance and identity construction: Young children's engagement with popular cultural and media texts. In J. Marsh (Ed.), *Popular culture, new media and digital literacy in early childhood* (pp. 21–38). London/New York: Routledge Falmer.

McTavish, M. (2009). "I get my facts from the Internet": A case study of the teaching and learning of information literacy in in-school and out-of-school contexts. *Journal of Early Childhood Literacy, 9*(1), 3–28.

Merchant, G. (2015). Keep talking the tablets: iPads, story apps, and early literacy. *The Australian Journal of Language and Literacy, 38*(1), 3–11.

National Council of Teachers of English. (2013, February 28). *The NCTE definition of 21st century literacies.* Retrieved from www2.ncte.org/statement/21stcentdefinition/

Nova Scotia School Boards Association. (2014). *Shaping a new vision for public education in Nova Scotia.* Dartmouth, NS: NSSBA.

Nxumalo, F., & Rubin, J. C. (2018). Encountering waste landscapes: More-than-human place literacies in early childhood education. In C. R. Kuby, K. Spector, & J. J. Thiel (Eds.), *Posthumanism and literacy education: Knowing/becoming/doing literacies* (pp. 201–230). New York: Routledge.

O'Mara, J., & Laidlaw, L. (2011). Living in the iWorld: Two literacy researchers reflect on the changing texts and literacy practices of childhood. *English Teaching: Practice and Critique, 10*(4), 149–159.

O'Mara, J., Laidlaw, L., & Blackmore, J. (2017). The new digital divide: Digital technology policies and provision in Canada and Australia. In C. Burnett, G. Merchant, A. Simpson, & M. Walsh (Eds.), *The case of the iPad: Mobile literacies in education* (pp. 87–104). Singapore: Springer.

Ontario Ministry of Education. (2016). Towards defining 21st century competencies for Ontario [PDF file]. Retrieved from www.edugains.ca/resources21CL/About21stCentury/21CL_21stCenturyCompetencies.pdf

Pahl, K., & Rowsell, J. (2010). *Artifactual literacy: Every object tells a story.* New York: Teachers College Press.

Pahl, K., & Rowsell, J. with D. Collier, S. Pool, Z. Rasool, & T. Trzecak (2019). *Living literacies.* Boston, MA: MIT Press.

Prince Edward Island Education. (n.d.). *Technology in education.* Retrieved from www.edu.pe.ca/journeyon/index.htm

Rose, S., Fitzpatrick, K., Mersereau, C., & Whitty, P. (2017). Playful pedagogic moves: Digital devices in the outdoors. In D. Harwood (Ed.), *Crayons and iPads: Learning and teaching of young children in the digital world* (pp. 16–28). London: Sage.

Rowsell, J., Lemieux, A., Swartz, L., Turcotte, M., & Burkitt, J. (2018). The stuff that heroes are made of: Elastic, sticky, messy literacies in children's transmedial cultures. *Language Arts, 96*(1), 7–20.

Schreurs, K., Quan-Haase, A., & Martin, K. (2017). Problematizing the digital literacy paradox in the context of older adults' ICT use: Aging, media discourse, and self-determination. *Canadian Journal of Communication, 42*(2), 359–377.

Sheridan, M. P., & Rowsell, J. (2010). *Design literacies: Learning and innovation in the digital age.* London: Routledge.

Simon, R., & Kalan, A. (2016). Adolescent literacy and collaborative inquiry. In K. A. Hinchman, & D.A. Appleman (Eds.) *Adolescent literacies: A handbook of practice-based research.* (pp. 398–420).

Skutnabb-Kangas, T, Maffi L, & Harmon D. (2003). *Sharing a world of difference: The earth's linguistic, cultural, and biological diversity and companion map the world's biocultural diversity: People, languages, and ecosystems.* Paris: UNESCO.

Spiegelman, A. (1986). *Maus I: A survivor's tale. My father bleeds history.* New York: Pantheon.

Styres, S. (2018). Literacies of land: Decolonizing narratives, storying, and literature. In L. Tuhiwai Smith, E. Tuck, & K. W. Yang (Eds.), *Indigenous and decolonizing studies in education: Mapping the long view* (pp. 24–38). New York: Routledge.

Tuhiwai Smith, L., Tuck, E., Yang, K. W. (2018). *Indigenous and decolonizing studies in education: Mapping the long view.* New York: Routledge.

van Leeuwen, T. (2018). Legitimation and multimodality. In R. Wodak & B. Forchtner (Eds.), *The Routledge handbook of language and politics* (pp. 218–232). New York: Routledge.

Walsh, M. (2011). *Multimodal literacy: Researching classroom practice.* Australia: Primary English Teacher Association.

Whitty, P. (2017). Complicating literacies: Settler ways of being with story(ies) on Wabanaki lands. In R. Zaidi & J. Rowsell (Eds.), *Literacy lives in transcultural times* (pp. 17–31). New York: Routledge.

Wohlwend, K. E., & Rowsell, J. (2017). App maps: Evaluating children's iPad software for 21st century literacy learning. In N. Kucirkova & G. Falloon (Eds.), *Apps, technology, and younger learners: International evidence for teaching* (pp. 73–88). London: Routledge.

Wong, S. (2013). Hop on pop, click on Poptropica. *Early Childhood Education Journal of ATA, 41*(1), 25–30.

Wong, S. (2015). Mobile digital devices and preschoolers' home multiliteracy practices. *Language and literacy, special issue: A landscape view of literacy studies in Canada, 17*(2), 75–90.

Zaida, R. (2019). Transcultural approaches to literacy, learning, and play. In N. Kucirkova, J. Rowsell, & G. Falloon (Eds.), *The Routledge International Handbook of Learning with Technology in Early Childhood* (pp. 62–73). London: Routledge.

Part III

Case Studies

Chapter 12

Teaching to Read in English using Annotations in a High-Stakes Testing Context

A Case of Korean High School Students

Soyoung Lee

Teaching English to Korean students through English reading passages is not really the ideal way to teach English or reading. It's test prep and except for a few students they feel bombarded by the endless number of passages they have to read and comprehend. It's the wrong orientation to reading comprehension and learning a foreign language. There's no engagement with the reading materials, no back-and-forth with the author, no real reading involved. Most of them lose interest in reading in English and it certainly doesn't give them the tools to communicate in English in the global world (Ms. Kim, Korean high school English teacher).

Many Korean high school English teachers share Ms. Kim's sentiments of the Korean English education system. Teaching English in Korean high schools means teaching to the English college entrance exam and it is challenging in many ways. Teachers acknowledge that it's not the right way to teach reading comprehension and it certainly does not help students learn English, the language of international commerce, business, trade, and communication. This kind of English education does not, as Ms. Kim a high school English teacher in Korea states, help students become efficient and effective communicators in the global context.

Ms. Kim has been interested in creating learning opportunities in her English classes to help her students understand reading in English as a two-way communication event where the reader is in active conversation with the author, and as an authentic tool for written communication. However, for Ms. Kim this is not an easy process. There are a number of different social, cultural, and political contexts at play.

For one, the level of reading comprehension that is required of students for the Korean college entrance exam is relatively high meaning that it requires a level of proficiency in English that is beyond what most students are capable of comprehending as a result of their foreign language education in the public school system. Students need the extra time in English classes devoted to preparing for the exam. Teachers and students alike say, "English is preparing for the English exam."

Second, the way that high school English teachers deal with this reality is through lessons that help students focus on formulaic sequences for problem solving and lessons that work on memorizing reading passages. For instance, the question listed below is from the English portion of the 2017 Korean college entrance exam. According to Ms. Kim, because the reading passages are beyond most of the students' level of English reading proficiency and the students have limited time in answering the questions, English teachers teach a number of different formulas in approaching the questions. Ms. Kim's instructions for "fill in the blank" type questions such as the one below are as follows.

When doing "fill in the blank questions":

1. Locate the blank and just focus on the 3–4 lines above and below the blank
2. Only skim the other lines if you have time and if you must read it to answer the question
3. Answer the question

Question 33)
Grief is unpleasant. Would one not then be better off without it altogether? Why accept it even when the loss is real? Perhaps we should say of it what Spinoza said of regret: that whoever feels it is twice unhappy or twice help-less." Laurence Thomas has suggested the utility of "negative sentiments" (emotions like grief, guilt, resentment, and anger, which there is seemingly a reason to believe we might be better off without) lies in their providing a kind of guarantee of authenticity for such dispositional sentiments as love and respect. No occurrent feelings of love and respect need to be present throughout the period in which it is true that one loves or respects. One might therefore sometimes suspect, in the absence of the positive occurrent feelings, that _____.
At such times, negative emotions like grief offer a kind of testimonial to the authenticity of love or respect.
(3 points)
* dispositional: 성향적인 ** testimonial: 증거

① one no longer loves
② one is much happier
③ an emotional loss can never be real
④ respect for oneself can be guaranteed
⑤ negative sentiments do not hold any longer

For the students the other feasible method to successfully solving the com-prehension questions in a timely manner, is to actually memorize the pas-sages. The Korean Education Department is in charge of the college entrance exams and every year they publish a book with a collection of passages in conjunction with the Korean Education Broadcasting System (EBS). Each volume holds approximately 100 passages (and related questions) and 70% of that year's English exam passages will be "related" to the passages from this book. Some are straight out of the book and others are "indirectly related" passages meaning that they may cover the same topic or they are from the same author. For most students, it is impossible to read, comprehend, and answer all the reading comprehension questions during the exam in the given time. Thus, both teachers and students believe that memorizing the passages is a sure way to raise their exam scores and teachers encourage students to do a literal memorization of all 100 reading passages.

The most substantial issue related to the Korean English education situation, however, is the competitive nature of the country's college admissions process. Koreans in general place great value in education and even greater value in college admissions. It has its roots in the Korean Confusionist culture that is 5000 years old and the security that a college's name provides individuals in the Korean society (Cho, 2004; Lee, 2003, 2014). Though some claim that this over-the-top, cutthroat college admissions culture is in transition and taking a turn for the better, most people are skeptical that it will ever change given the people's cultural history. There's a strong gate-keeping mechanism in effect and the exam that is held once a year for all high school seniors and those repeating the admissions process must act as a tool to differentiate the good from the very good, and the very good from the genius. The level of difficulty of the exams, especially the English exam, comes under strong criticism from the public and experts alike every year. No one can deny the political undertones inherent in the process but at the same time, no one can do anything about it (Kim, Lee, & Lee, 2005; Kwon, Lee, & Shin, 2017; Lee, 2014).

So, the dilemma falls on the teachers and the students. Ms. Kim has been interested in doing something different in her classes and for a number of years, she has been thinking about and trying out different activities that may provide authentic reading experiences in English reading for her students. She believes that the Korean English education system is orienting students in erroneous and damaging ways for understanding what it means to learn a language and communicate using that language in reading and writing. However, she notes that the challenge is to create learning opportunities that are not unrelated to their reading comprehension exam and at the same time provide students with experiences that enable them to engage with the passages in meaningful ways. She wants students to think about the content, talk to the author, note interesting expressions, ask questions, talk back to the readings, and simultaneously gain practice in reading for the test.

She became interested in annotations while talking to a friend who is a professor of English in a Korean university (Lee) and decided to try it out in her classes this year. She adopted Lee's materials and researched how this may work with her students who have no experience with annotations.

Whole Group Lesson

According to Porter-O'Donnell (2004), annotating is "a visible record of the thoughts that emerge while making sense of the reading" (p. 82). It is active reading and it positions the reader for deep conversations with the text. The main purpose of annotations is to slow down the process of reading for self-monitoring of understanding and engagement.

model

Ms. Kim introduced annotations to her students first by showing them an annotated text (Figure 12.1). She decided to use reading passages from the exam book for annotations. She wanted them to see two things. First, annotations are about active interaction with the text and writing down those interactions, not just keeping them in one's mind. Second, there are no right or wrong answers in annotations as long as they are authentic interactions with the text.

She then introduced students to the Annotations chart (see Table 12.1) adopted and adapted from Lee. Lee created the chart for her college students

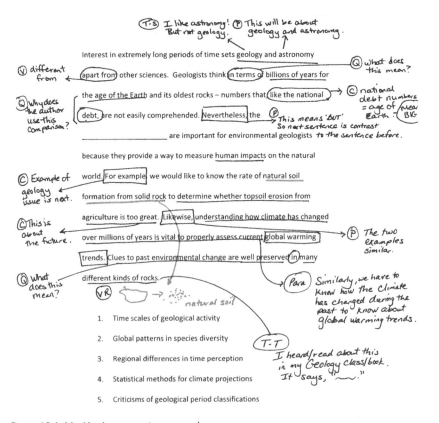

Figure 12.1 Ms. Kim's annotation example

Table 12.1 Annotations chart

Methods of Annotation	Explanation	Framing Questions
Predictions	Using the title to think about the text's content Predicting what will come next in the text	What do I think this text will be about? What will the author discuss next?
Questions	Asking questions of the text – clarifying questions, rhetorical questions, probing questions, etc.	Do I have a question about this word/sentence/paragraph? Do I have a question about this content? What does this word mean?
Vocabulary	Writing down the meaning of words	Is this a word that I want to remember and if so what does it mean?
Comments	Statements related to the content (Catch all)	Do I have anything to say about this?
Text-to-self connection	Making a personal connection to the text using one's own experience	Do I have a personal experience related to this part of the text?
Text-to-text connection	Making a connection to another text (intertextual)	Does this content relate to another text/visual/movie that I have read or seen?
Text-to-world connection	Making a connection to the larger world – social, cultural, political, etc.	How does this content relate to what is going on in the world both past and present?
Visual representation	Making a visual representation of the content when appropriate (i.e. charts, diagrams, illustrations)	Will drawing a picture or diagramming help me understand and summarize the content more effectively and if so how might I do that?
Paraphrasing	Put into one's own words content that is important	How can I say this in my own words?

who, having been through the same education system, were not used to interacting with texts in English. Using another reading passage from the exam book, Ms. Kim demonstrated a few of the methods. She started with four of the methods – predictions, questions, vocabulary, and text-to-self connection – and led the class through the annotations process. She felt that the four methods provided students with good entry points into the idea of annotations. To introduce students to predictions, she showed the students just the first sentence of the text and then used the question from the "Framing Questions" column of the Annotations Chart (Table 12.1) "What do I think this text will be about?" to help them make predictions about the text. Making predictions is

about activating prior knowledge on the topic of the text and therefore directing one's mind to the content and context of the text even before reading it.
This is an especially important process for foreign language learner in reading
comprehension. She demonstrated the other three methods using the same
process.

Students' initial reactions to annotations were marked by confusion and
wonder. They were confused about the purpose of the activity as evidenced
through the following questions: Why are we doing this? What does this do
for the exam? How will you grade this? How do I know I have the "right"
annotations? Can I really write down all the things related to the text? etc. At
the same time they also seemed enthusiastic and welcomed the opportunity to
participate in an English reading comprehension activity that had no right or
wrong answer. They genuinely looked forward to trying it out on their own.

Small Group Work

Once the students had gained orientation to what annotations are using the
four methods – predictions, questions, vocabulary, and text-to-self connection – Ms. Kim organized the students into small groups of threes and fours
and gave each group a short passage to annotate. Each group received
a passage printed on a letter-size piece of paper that was taped to a larger
piece of butcher paper. This allowed more space for the annotations. Each
student received a marker to annotate with.

Before sending them off for small group work, Ms. Kim briefly explained
the remaining five categories – text-to-text connection, text-to-world connection, visual representation, paraphrasing and comments. For the "Comments" category, she explained that it was a catch-all for statements that
they did not think belonged in other categories. In small groups, the students had different kinds of questions about annotations that were more specific and ones that were related to the logistics. For instance, some of their
questions include: Do we have to annotate in English? Can we also annotate
in Korean? How many annotations should we have? Do the annotations
have to be long? Can we use different color pens for annotations? Can we
add post-it notes if we run out of space? What kinds of annotations are
good annotations? What are bad annotations?

Ms. Kim advised the students to annotate in English when possible.
However, she also stated that the main purpose of annotations is about
engagement with text and thus when they had annotations that were longer
and complex they were welcome to annotate in Korean. For instance, she
stated that the three "text-to" categories have the potential to generate
longer and more detailed annotations and she anticipated that these categories may have more annotations in Korean. She gave the students approximately 20 minutes to work in their groups and she passionately encouraged
them to verbally interact with each other during the process.

When all the groups completed their annotations the students did a gallery walk. Ms. Kim asked the students to write down things they noticed about other groups' work during the gallery walk and to be ready to share them with the whole class.

Individual Work

Ms. Kim had another reading passage ready to hand out as an assignment after the small group work. She provided students with specific instructions for the annotations assignment. The instructions are as below.

Instructions for homework:

Remember that the main purpose of annotation is to have a DEEP conversation with the text. Think about all the things you ask, say, and think about when you are in a real conversation with an interesting person or someone who matters to you. This is the level of engagement I expect to see in writing!

1. Use all the methods of annotations listed in the chart. All 9!
2. Have at least 12 annotations for the passage
3. When you ask a question in your annotations, and you later find a response to that question in the latter part of the text, go back and answer your question
4. Respond to the predictions you made about the text after reading the whole text
5. Enjoy!

Assessment

Ms. Kim later noted that assessing annotations was both a dilemma and a challenge for her. It posed a dilemma because the main purpose of annotations was in providing her students with authentic experiences in interacting with texts, an objective that was not easy to assess. In the planning stages, she played with the idea of not assessing the students' work. How can one assess authentic interactions? However, she also knew that without assessment, both formative and summative, students would not have the guidance they would need to improve their skills.

The challenge, however, was in the time that she could actually devote to reading and responding to her students' annotations. She taught five classes, approximately 200 students, and she wanted to respond to all her students' inquiries, questions, and comments but she knew that this was practically impossible. However, she also knew that her feedback would naturally help them engage in even more diverse and meaningful ways with the passages.

In consultation with Lee, Ms. Kim adopted some of Lee's guidelines for assessment. She used two criteria for grading her students' annotations. First, she graded based on quantity – the number of annotations – and then on quality. In the beginning, Ms. Kim assigned certain numbers to count for the quantity of annotations. The quality criterion was trickier and though it took some getting used to Ms. Kim continuously encouraged her students to make annotations that contributed to understanding the text in its entirety, helped them stay on topic, figure out the main message of the author, pull together background information, and ones that moved them through the reading rather than getting them stuck. This took time for the students to understand and put into practice but Ms. Kim noticed that her students' annotations became more and more focused on the topic and the author's ideas with time and practice.

Ms. Kim also made a schedule for responding to her students' work. She looked over each student's annotated text and assigned a grade, but she focused on 50 students at a time for written feedback. She let the students know that they will not get written feedback from her every time they submit an annotated passage but she is reading every single one of them!

Navigating through the complicated terrains of reading instruction in a high stakes testing environment and negotiating the contextual tensions emerging from such a scenario as a teacher is a universal issue not limited to the unique situation of Ms. Kim illustrated. Studies report that high stakes assessment has negative and lasting effects not only on students but also on teachers (Agee, 2004; Coles, 2005). Assaf (2008) explains that teachers find themselves narrowing the scope of their literacy curriculum by teaching to the test (Smith & Fey, 2000), overusing drill-based instructional methods (Agee, 2004), and reprioritizing personal philosophies about teaching that often result in giving less attention to individual student's needs (Pennington, 2004). Though a universal problem, this issue has no universal answer. It is up to each teacher to interpret her unique classroom situation and the high-stakes ideologies mandating her reading curriculum with a critical eye and become creative in establishing research-based instructional plans that enable students to overcome their personal struggles as readers, establish themselves as sophisticated readers beyond what is measured on tests (Assaf, 2008), and most importantly, become empowered as readers and learners in the global context.

Discussion Questions and Application

1. Describe the cultural and political context of Ms. Kim's teaching situation. Are there any similar constraints in your own teaching situation?
2. Ms. Kim's challenge as an English teacher is to create learning opportunities that provide students with meaningful and authentic reading experiences while simultaneously providing them with lessons that are not unrelated to their English college entrance exam. How does Ms. Kim's teaching approach annotations bridge the gap between the two seemingly contrary goals of her class?

3. What adaptations would you make to the Annotations chart (Table 12.1) to use it in your own teaching context?

4. Ms. Kim's biggest challenge with annotations was in assessment. What are some alternative ways of assessing the students' work that Ms. Kim could adopt?

References

Agee, J. (2004). Negotiating a teacher identity: An African American teacher's struggle to teach in test driven contexts. *Teachers College Record, 106* (4), 747–774.

Assaf, L. C. (2008). Professional identity of a reading teacher: Responding to high-stakes testing pressures. *Teachers and Teaching, 14* (3), 239–252.

Cho, B. E. (2004). Issues concerning Korean learners of English: English education in Korea and some difficulties of Korean students. *The East Asian Learner, 1* (2), 31–36.

Coles, M. (2005). *Reading the naked truth: Literacy, legislation, and lies.* Portsmouth, NH: Heinemann.

Kim, J., Lee, J., & Lee, S. (2005). Understanding of education fever in Korea. *KEDI Journal of Educational Policy, 2* (1), 7–15.

Kwon, S. K., Lee, M., & Shin, D. (2017). Educational assessment in the Republic of Korea: Lights and shadows of high-stake exam-based education system. *Assessment in Education: Principles, Policy & Practice, 24* (1), 60–77.

Lee, B. M. (2003). The importance of instructional time in EFL learning environment. *Foreign Language Education, 10* (2), 107–129.

Lee, B. M. (2014). 당신의 영어는 왜 실패하는가? 대한민국에서 영어를 배운다는 것 *[Why you fail in English: What it means to learn English in Korea].* Seoul, Korea: 우리학교.

Pennington, J. L. (2004). Teaching interrupted: The effect of high-stakes testing on literacy instruction in a Texas elementary school. In F. B. Boyd & C. H. Brock (Eds.), *Multicultural and multilingual literacy and language* (pp. 241–261). New York: Guilford Press.

Porter-O'Donnell, C. (2004). Beyond the yellow highlighter: Teaching annotation skills to improve reading comprehension. *English Journal, 93* (5), 82–89.

Smith, M. L., & Fey, P. (2000). Validity and accountability in high-stakes testing. *Journal of Teacher Education, 51* (5), 334–344.

Chapter 13

Teaching Language, Literacy, and Content in a Mexico City Third Grade Classroom

A Case Study

Ann Ebe

"How can I support my students, who are at different stages of language and literacy development, as they work to learn content, language and literacy all at the same time?"

Mr. Matt, as he is called by his students, is a third grade teacher at a large American school in Mexico City. Having taught previously in San Francisco, California, Mr. Matt is experienced and comfortable in big urban cities and classrooms with students from a variety of cultural and linguistic backgrounds. The bilingual school in Mexico City provides thematic-based integrated curriculum in both English and Spanish. Well over half of the students are Mexican, seeking to develop English language proficiency through an American-style curriculum. The remaining 30 to 40 percent of the students are an international group from outside of Mexico, who speak Spanish as well as other languages. These students come from over 40 countries, including Italy, Colombia, Romania, Korea, Chile, and the United States. The bilingual model the school follows focuses primarily on English as the language of instruction with about two hours of Spanish daily.

Mr. Matt wants his students to enjoy reading and writing, to see it as fun and useful for learning. Like in all schools, the students in his classroom vary in their literacy proficiency and need varying levels of support. In addition, all of his students are emergent bilinguals or multilinguals at different stages along the continuum of language learning. Having come from the United States as an English speaker who is now learning Spanish, Mr. Matt understands the challenges of learning a new language. The question he grapples with in his teaching is how best to support his students, who are at different stages of language and literacy development, as they work to learn content, language and literacy all at the same time.

Through his instruction, Mr. Matt works effectively to draw on his students' backgrounds and interests, and to use their languages as resources for learning. In order to do this, Mr. Matt finds it essential to get to know his students well from the beginning of the year. In addition to reading information about each student passed down from previous teachers, he creates a class profile chart (Celic, 2009) to document key

Figure 13.1 Children sharing a book

information about each of his students. This chart includes their name, home language(s), country of origin, information about their language proficiency, and assessment data. With the international and often transient nature of his students, Mr. Matt finds it helpful to know where his students have lived and studied and the languages his students and their families speak. Using an adaptation of García, Johnson, and Seltzer's (2017) Bilingual Student Profile he informally interviews his students to get to know them better. He asks questions such as "What languages do you speak at home?" and "What languages do you speak with your friends?" To find out about where they have lived and attended school he asks "What are all the countries you have lived in since you were born?" "What are all the countries have you gone to school in?" and "What languages did you and your teachers speak in those schools?"

This year, 19 of the 24 students in Mr. Matt's class were born in Mexico and speak Spanish as their home language. These students are developing English proficiency in school. Diego, who arrived in first grade, was born in Venezuela and speaks both Spanish and English at home but feels more comfortable in Spanish. Kumi also feels more comfortable in Spanish. She was born in Mexico, and her parents, who were born in Japan, speak both Spanish and Japanese at home. Olivia was born in the United States and arrived in Mexico in first grade. While her schooling was previously all in English, her father is Mexican and her mother is American, so her home languages are both English and Spanish. Olivia feels much more comfortable speaking in English and is developing both conversational and academic Spanish in school. Enya arrived this year from Germany where she had attended a German–English bilingual school. Now in Mexico, she is continuing to develop English and is in the very beginning stages of Spanish language acquisition. Victor was born in France and is fluent in French, Spanish and English. His mother is French and his father is American, although he grew up speaking Spanish in Argentina.

While Mr. Matt teaches primarily in English, he realizes that his students are not monolingual. They are multilingual and bring to the classroom rich linguistic repertoires. As Garcia and Wei (2014) explain, though from a societal point of view bilinguals are said to speak two languages, from their own perspective, bilingual speakers have just one bank of language. This language repertoire includes linguistic features that are associated socially and politically with one language or another and are named as English, Spanish, French, Japanese, and so on. Bilinguals pull features from their language repertoire, or bank, to communicate in what are called different languages. When bilinguals do this, they are translanguaging (García, 2009). Rather than having his students suppress aspects of their language during the vast majority of their days, Mr. Matt works to find strategic ways for students to translanguage, to use their entire linguistic repertoires as a resource for learning.

Interactive Read Aloud: Large-Group Introduction

Mr. Matt's class sits together on the carpet in front of the white board to start literacy time. The objective for the reader's workshop is neatly written on the board along with key words and instructions for this time together. Over the past week, students had been learning about features of non-fiction text following the same daily routine. Mr. Matt begins the session by drawing the group's attention to the objective and reading it aloud "I can identify bold words and use the glossary to understand them." The words *bold words* and *glossary* are underlined and defined on the board as well. They are almost last on a list of features of text the class has been exploring. "So what are bold words?" Mr. Matt asks. "*Letras en negrita!*" one student eagerly offers in Spanish. "That's right," responds Mr. Matt, drawing the student's attention to the definition written on the board, which included the Spanish translation of this key word. "And what is the glossary ... let's see?" Mr. Matt continued. He went on to read each definition from the board and to show examples of them in the book he had been reading aloud to the class about the rainforest as part of their inquiry unit on different environments. He knows his students could easily read the definitions from the board but wants to be sure they really understand what each feature looks like in the book. He hopes this will help them find the features later in their own independent reading.

The bold words from the read aloud are also listed on the board. Mr. Matt reads them over and asks students to raise their hands when they hear them during the read aloud. As he reads hands shoot up every time he comes to a key word. Keeping in mind the different linguistic needs and language experiences of each student, Mr. Matt strategically calls on students who raise their hands and asks them to explain which words they heard. He discusses how they are important words and has the students try to describe them. Sometimes the students are able to describe the words from the context of what is being read but Mr. Matt realizes that at times he has to stop and go beyond the book. In those moments, he takes the time to tell stories from his own experiences to define the bold words and hopes that building background knowledge for the vocabulary will be helpful for his students. To describe the word *pour* he talks about the rain in Washington where he used to live and liked to surf. He also takes his coffee cup and talks about how he could pour coffee. For *mist*, he talks about how in Veracruz it was like walking in a cloud and they call it *chipichipi* in Spanish.

At one point the students notice the country Ecuador on a map in the book and are interested that it is the same as the key word *equator* in English. Mr. Matt explains this is a cognate, a word that is the same or similar in English and Spanish. The class looks at where Ecuador is located and talks about why the country might be called equator in Spanish. Students then notice that the word *tropical* is the same in English and Spanish, and Victor is excited to share that it is the same in French too. Realizing that this was a key moment to celebrate his student's bilingualism and to have them use their home languages for learning, Mr. Matt asks Enya what it is in German and the class decides that *tropisch* sounds quite a bit like tropical as well. This prompts more discussion about cognates so Mr. Matt encourages the students to continue to look for cognates in their reading and lists them next to the key words on the board as they come up. As key words are discussed throughout the read aloud, Mr. Matt also models how to use the glossary at the back of the book to look them up.

Shared and Independent Reading

Before transitioning to the next literacy activity, Mr. Matt reads over the instructions for what students would be doing on their own as he works with his small guided reading group. As part of a larger, transdisciplinary study on the environment, the third graders are beginning an animal research project and each student has to select an animal to learn about. They are to learn about the animal's habitat, and how it survives in its particular environment. To help students make their selection, Mr. Matt had checked out baskets of informational books on all types of animals from the school library, which were piled on the students' tables around the room. Mr. Matt reads the instructions from the board: *Partner read or independently read non-fiction books and identify bold words and their definitions.*

Through formal and informal reading assessments, Mr. Matt had determined earlier which reading partnerships would be helpful for students, pairing a more proficient reader with a less proficient reader for shared reading support. For this assignment, students could work in their partnerships or independently to read about an animal they were interested in and find and define bold words within their reading. Students knew they would be using the features of text they had been learning about in the animal reports they would be writing and Mr. Matt emphasizes thinking about which words are in bold and why the author had chosen to highlight and define them.

To help students focus in on this as they read in partnerships or independently, Mr. Matt provides students with a small piece of paper where they are to write three bold words they find in their books as well as the glossary definition. Mr. Matt encourages the students to write the definition of the bold words they find in their own words, rather than copying it directly from the glossary. After the exiting conversation the students had about cognates, Mr. Matt decides to also have the class try to write the key words not only in English, but in their home languages too. He realizes this would be an additional way to get the students thinking about this content-specific vocabulary. Figures 13.2, 13.3, and 13.4 show three students' work where students made an effort to list their bold words in English as well as Spanish, French, and German. While the translations are not always perfect, by having the opportunity to write the words in their home languages, students are able to further demonstrate their understanding of key vocabulary in the text.

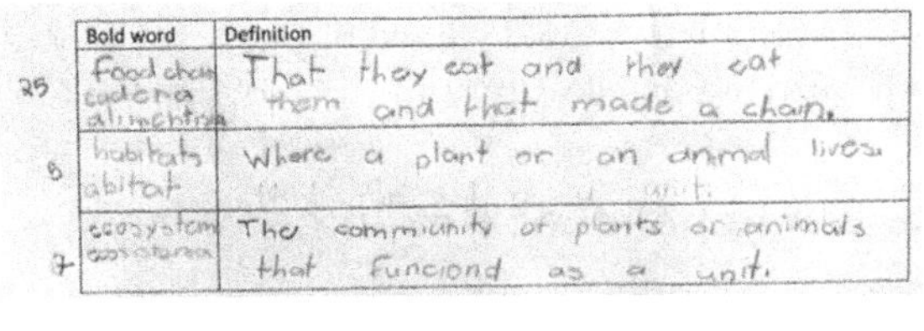

Figure 13.2 Defining bold words, Spanish

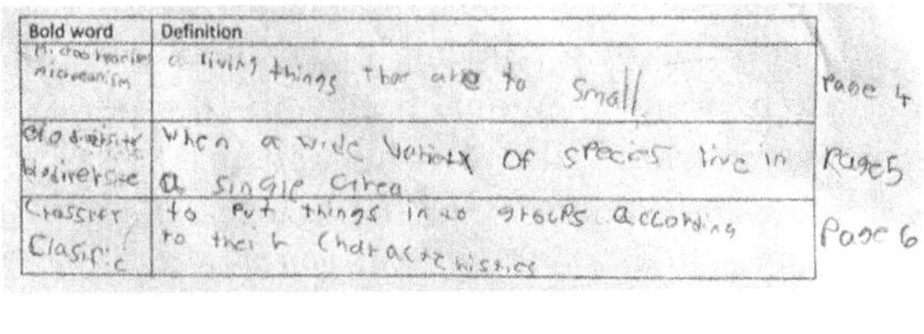

Figure 13.3 Defining bold words, French

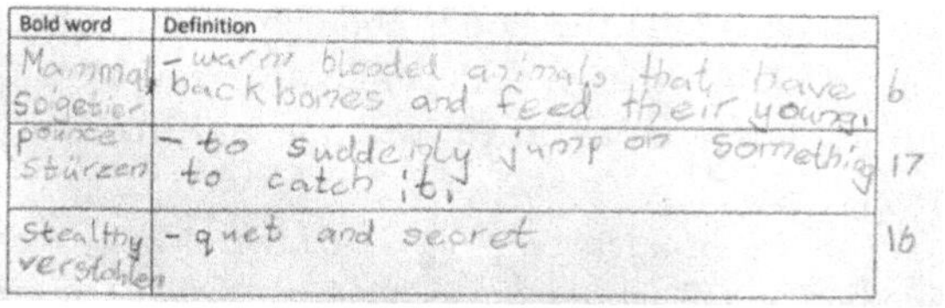

Bold word	Definition	
Mammal Säugetier	– warm blooded animals that have back bones and feed their young	6
pounce Stürzen	– to suddenly jump on something to catch it.	17
Stealthy verstohlen	– quiet and secret	16

Figure 13.4 Defining bold words, German

Guided Reading

While the majority of students read about animals in partnerships and independently, Mr. Matt selects a group of students to stay with him on the carpet for guided reading. Mr. Matt tries to read with all of his students in a small group setting at least once a week, and meets more often with the students who need additional support with reading. By supporting reading in small groups, Mr. Matt is able to differentiate his reading instruction to focus on a particular reading skill or strategy he has identified that the students need. His guided reading groups are flexible and change often so that his instruction is aligned to the specific needs of his students.

Today, Mr. Matt has pulled together a group of students who he has noticed need additional support with strategies to make sense of unknown words. He has noticed that these students often skip or mumble through words they are not sure about in their reading and when talking about their reading. He has found that it affects their comprehension. The focus on bold words and glossary definitions during the read aloud served as a helpful introduction for this guided reading focus on unknown words.

Mr. Matt begins by asking the students "What can you do if you are reading and come to a word you don't know?" "Look it up in the glossary!" Adrien answers enthusiastically. "Sure, we have just been talking about that. What else can you do?" Students suggest sounding it out and skipping it. Knowing that this group of readers often sound good but don't always understand what they read, Mr. Matt wants to make sure they focus in on comprehension strategies. With that in mind, Mr. Matt also suggests thinking about what might make sense and also re-reading the section to see if that helps provide more clues about what the word is. Mr. Matt makes a list on a small white board as the group comes up with ideas. "As you are reading here today with me, when you come to something you don't know, try one of these strategies. I'll leave the list right here." Mr. Matt passes out copies of the same rainforest book he had been reading during the read aloud to each student so they can continue reading independently. "I'd like you to continue to notice the bold words as you read as well," Mr. Matt instructs. Also, "If I tap on your book, read aloud to me." The students take the books and spread out a bit on the carpet to work on their reading strategy independently. Mr. Matt moves around to each student to listen in on their reading and takes notes on what he notices.

At the end of the guided reading time, Mr. Matt askes the students to scoot in together to talk about how it went. "Mila, I noticed that you got stuck on the word *approximately* and used some of the strategies we talked about. Can we all find it?" Mr. Matt helps the students turn to the page with the word *approximately* on it and point to the word. "Mila, can you tell us what you did?" Mila describes to the group how she tried to sound it out and then re-read it. The group talks about what the word could mean and decides that *about* is a good synonym. Mr. Matt has a few other students share and, before dismissing them, reminds the group about the list of things they can do when they get stuck in their reading.

Whole Group Reading Time Wrap Up

At the end of the reading time, Mr. Matt asks all of the students to come back to the carpet area. He had written the following sentence frame on the board: *I found the bold word* _____, *and it means* _____. He reads this to the students and explains that they will use this sentence to share about a word they found in their reading. Mr. Matt has found that providing sentence frames scaffolds discussion for the more reluctant speakers in the class. Students are instructed to pair and share about a word they found with a partner in either Spanish or English. Once students finish sharing with their partner, Mr. Matt pulls student names randomly out of a cup to share about bold words they had found with the whole group in English. By sharing with a partner first, all students have an opportunity to talk and are also better prepared to share with the whole group.

Mr. Matt then ends with the same question he asks daily at the end of reading time: "If my mom and dad ask what I learned in reader's workshop today, I would tell them … ?" Students eagerly share about vocabulary they had learned, how they knew about bold words and the glossary, and several share interesting facts about the animals they had read about.

Literacy Instruction that Effectively Supports All Students

Through this reading lesson, we see the ways in which Mr. Matt supports his students, who are all at different stages of language and literacy development, as they work to learn content, language and literacy. To begin, Mr. Matt organizes his instruction around integrated, thematic units of inquiry. Second, he engages students in a variety of instructional structures for reading, providing different levels of support throughout the reading time. Finally, Mr. Matt strategically provides multiple opportunities for translanguaging, or use of the student's home languages as a resource for learning. These three ideas are discussed below.

Teaching Language and Literacy through Meaningful Content

Rather than teaching reading skills and strategies, or English language vocabulary and structures in isolation, Mr. Matt teaches language and literacy through an engaging unit on the environment. As Freeman, Freeman, Soto, and Ebe (2016) explain, there are multiple benefits to this approach. To begin, students are able to develop language, literacy and content at the same time. Mr. Matt's third grade team works together to organize curriculum around specific Next Generation Learning Standards (NGSS Lead States, 2013; NYSED, 2017). As Table 13.1 shows, through this reading lesson, Mr. Matt is able to focus not only on reading standards, but additional language arts and science content standards as well:

Table 13.1 Next Generation Learning Standards addressed during reading lesson

Next Generation Learning Standards
English Language Arts Reading, Writing, Speaking and Listening: 3R5: In informational texts, identify and use text features to build comprehension. 3R7: Explain how specific illustrations or text features contribute to what is conveyed by the words in a text. 3W2c: Use precise language and content-specific vocabulary. 3W6: Conduct research to answer questions, including self-generated questions, and to build knowledge. 3SL1: Participate and engage effectively in a range of collaborative discussions with diverse peers and adults, expressing ideas clearly, and building on those of others. 3L4d: Use glossaries or beginning dictionaries to determine or clarify the precise meaning of key words and phrases. 3L6: Acquire and accurately use conversational, general academic, and content-specific words and phrases. **Science:** 3LS43: I can explain and provide evidence why my animal survives well in its habitat.

Through this approach, language is kept in its natural context and students have reasons to use English language and to read for real purposes. Students read about animals they were interested in for their research project. In addition, students learn the academic vocabulary of the content areas. In this case, the literacy vocabulary of the features of text the students are learning about (bold words and glossary) as well as the science content-specific vocabulary of different environments and the animals the students were reading about.

By organizing instruction around a unit of inquiry on the environment, Mr. Matt's students see the big picture for their learning, making instruction more comprehensible and engaging. Literacy time and science time are interrelated for the students so concepts and vocabulary are repeated naturally throughout the day. Mr. Matt is also able to differentiate the instruction for his students at different language and literacy levels while still engaging them in the same content. In addition to Mr. Matt providing different instructional structures for reading, students could select from a wide range of books with varying text difficulty for their research.

Providing a Variety of Instructional Structures for Reading

Through an interactive read aloud, guided reading, shared reading, and independent reading, Mr. Matt differentiated his reading instruction by providing his students a range of support during the reading lesson. Mr. Matt began his reading lesson with a whole group *read aloud* where he was able to focus the class on an exploration of key vocabulary while at the same time engaging all students in science content information about the rainforest, regardless of their reading level. During a read aloud, the teacher is responsible for the reading providing information about the topic and, in this case, also modeling how to focus on bold words and find them in the glossary. Following the read aloud, the responsibility for reading shifted from the teacher to the students with varying levels of support. Some students were provided a great deal of support during *guided reading* with Mr. Matt where they focused on specific reading strategies. Others were supported by peers in strategic paired, *shared reading* while others read *independently*. By planning for a range of instructional structures during the reading time, students are provided opportunities to increase their reading proficiency with just the right level of support.

Using Students' Home Languages as a Resource

While the target language of instruction during Mr. Matt's reading time is English, there were multiple ways in which he was able to strategically use translanguaging to support student learning. While there is no question that students in bilingual programs need dedicated time to develop each language, in this case Spanish and English, teachers can plan strategically for times when students can use all of their language for learning. For example, during this lesson, when the target language was English, students noticed cognates for key vocabulary about the environment. Listing cognates and talking about them helps students make connections between languages, strengthening both their language and content knowledge. As students found bold words in their animal books, Mr. Matt encouraged students to write the words in their home languages. This gave students another way to think about the word and to demonstrate that they knew what the word meant. In addition to reading in English about their animals, the class followed the same inquiry unit in Spanish class. During Spanish time, students read books and did research on the internet about their selected animal in Spanish to complement what they were doing in English. This gave these bilingual students an advantage during their research as they were able to access more resources to find the best information available in multiple languages about their selected animal.

Translanguaging can also serve as a scaffold for students who may need extra support as they learn a language. During the turn and talk at the end of the literacy lesson, Mr. Matt encouraged students to share with a partner in English or their home language. Several pairs shared in Spanish, the language in which they were more proficient. All students, regardless of their English language proficiency, had a chance to share what they had learned. By talking through their ideas in their home language first, they were able to organize their thoughts and engage in a kind of practice for what they would say if later called on to share with the whole class in English.

By providing students opportunities to use their home languages as a resource for learning, providing a variety of instructional structures for reading, and by teaching language and literacy through meaningful content, Mr. Matt's literacy instruction provided multiple opportunities for his multilingual students to be successful in their learning. Teachers, like Mr. Matt, who work with multilingual students at different stages of language and literacy development, need strategies for helping their students succeed in school. Through an analysis of Mr. Matt's literacy lesson, we are provided a variety of strategies for teachers to consider as they plan effective content, language and literacy instruction for their students.

Discussion Questions and Application

1. How does Mr. Matt support readers at various proficiency levels to comprehend the texts they need to read for their research? Discuss which instructional structures you regularly use in your reading instruction and describe an example of what it looks like in your classroom (e.g. read alouds, guided reading, shared reading, and independent reading).
2. What are some of the benefits for multilingual learners of organizing instruction around thematic units of inquiry? In what ways have you integrated curriculum in your classroom?
3. Explain how teachers can use students' home languages as a resource for learning, even when they don't speak their students' languages. Share examples of this.

4. Consider this quote: "Educators may talk about the importance of culturally responsive pedagogy, but how are teachers to enact such pedagogy if they do not systematically collect information about who their students are, the languages they speak, their cultural practices, their experience and the worlds that they know?" (García, Johnson, & Seltzer, 2017, p. 31). Discuss the ways that Mr. Matt got to know his students and built on their backgrounds and interests. What are the ways you do this in your classroom?

References

Celic, C. (2009). *English language learners day by day K-6. A complete guide to literacy, content-area, and language instruction.* Portsmouth, NH: Heinemann.

Freeman, Y., Freeman, D., Soto, M., & Ebe, A. (2016). *ESL teaching: Principles for success.* Portsmouth, NH: Heinemann.

García, O. (2009). Education, multilingualism and translanguaging in the 21st century. In A. Mohanty, M. Panda, R. Phillipson and T. Skutnabb-Kangas (Eds.), *Multilingual education for social justice: Globalising the local* (pp. 128–145). New Delhi: Orient Blackswan.

García, O., Johnson, S. I., & Seltzer, K. (2017). *The translanguaging classroom: Leveraging student bilingualism for learning.* Philadelphia: Caslon Publishing.

Garcia, O., & Wei, L. (2014). *Translanguaging: Language, bilingualism and education.* New York: Palgrave Macmillan.

NGSS Lead States. (2013). Next generation science standards: For states, by states. Retrieved from www.nextgenscience.org

NYSED. (2017) Next generation English language arts learning standards. Retrieved from www.nysed.gov/common/nysed/files/programs/curriculum-instruction/nys-next-generation-ela-standards.pdf

Chapter 14

Mensajes de los abuelitos
Multimodal Zapotec Literacy Development via the Assertion of Local Ontologies and Community-Based *Xkialnana* (Knowledge) in Oaxaca, Mexico: A Case Study

Steve Daniel Przymus, Felipe Ruiz Jiménez, and Virgilia Pérez García

Introduction

A challenge facing Zapotec teachers in multicultural bilingual schools in Oaxaca, Mexico, is a persistent colonial and Eurocentric system of national education curriculum in Mexico that places greater value on Western, White, monolingual, epistemological knowing-about knowledge over profound, community-based, traditional, ontological, Indigenous knowing—a knowledge that is vital to the maintenance of the Zapotec language and way of life. The chasm between the national curriculum driven by the Mexican Secretary of Public Education (SEP) and the community-based knowledge in Indigenous communities has been well researched by academics, some in collaboration with Indigenous teachers, as is the case with our chapter. McCarty (2006) documents how "asserting Indigenous literacies and education rights collide with larger bureaucratic texts" and how teachers can reclaim their pedagogical power and own literacies by "asserting their role as change agents and recentering the community-based mission of their school" (p. 2).

Francisco Antonio (2015) calls for a "decolonial" (ontological) way of thinking that values and legitimatizes Indigenous categories of thought (p. 1).

> Francisco Antonio contends that this can lead to decolonial education models, such as the community-based teaching approaches to literacy highlighted in our case study below, that contest normalized official school knowledge and advocate for a more diverse understanding of what knowledge is and can be at schools.
>
> (Przymus, Ruiz Jiménez, & Pérez García, In press)

This decolonial education model is in line with critical approaches to pedagogy and literacy instruction that act to achieve both educational and political means. In this vein, Freire (1993) states that

> To teach to read and write should never be reduced to the reductionistic, inexpressive, insipid task that serves to silence the voices of struggle that try to justify our presence in the world and not our blind accommodation to an unjust and discriminatory world ... Teaching literacy is, above all, a social and political commitment.
>
> (p. 115)

In this case study, conducted with two *maestros Zapatecos originarios* (native Zapotec teachers) in the *pueblo originario* (native village) of La Soledad Salinas, Oaxaca, Mexico, we describe multimodal literacy teaching methods. These methods derive from and honor community-based *xkialnana*/ʃkelna:nə/, local ontologies that work to develop Zapotec (and Spanish) biliteracy/identity development and in doing so challenge normalized/official/colonial knowledge acceptance at schools. We find, however, that the assertion of local ontologies through community-based *xkialnana* as a decolonial pedagogy is both difficult within the demands of meeting the requirements of the national curriculum and questioned by school personnel and even Zapotec-speaking parents, whose ideologies of educational success are heavily influenced and defined by meeting the benchmarks of epistemological knowing-about literacy knowledge, first in Spanish and then in Zapotec. This takes us to the second challenge, addressed in this case study; a challenge of language policy and planning.

Case Study

Escuela Primaria Intercultural Bilingüe: Ramón López Velarde
Escuela Primaria Intercultural Bilingüe: Luz y Progreso
La Soledad Salinas, Quiatoni Tlacolula, Oaxaca, Mexico

Context

Zapotec is the name of a family of 58 languages and Zapotec speakers, some 450,000 individuals, comprise the third largest Indigenous ethnic group in Mexico (Thompson, 2016). Most Zapotec speakers live in the two Mexican states of Oaxaca and Veracruz and the context of this case study is the Western Tlacolula Valley and the *pueblo originario Zapoteco* (native Zapotec village) of La Soledad Salinas, Oaxaca—situated two and a half hours south-east of the capital city of Oaxaca, a state in southern Mexico. Most residents, especially the youth, of La Soledad Salinas speak Spanish and although 99.25% are Indigenous and 87.71% speak Zapotec, according to Ethnologue, only

10% of the population in this region of Oaxaca is literate in Zapotec (Retrieved January 4, 2019 from www.ethnologue.com/language/zab; see also PueblosAmerica.com, Soledad Salinas, retrieved January 4, 2019 from https://en.mexico.pueblosamerica.com/i/soledad-salinas/).

Soledad Salinas has just over 3,000 inhabitants, and is served by one high school, one middle school, and three primary schools. Two of the primary schools share a campus with Luz y Progreso imparting classes in the morning (matutino) and Ramón López Velarde in the afternoon (vespertino). Luz y Progreso (Light and Progress in English) is a public bilingual, intercultural school, whose nine teachers serve 199 students. It is estimated that all but two to three teachers speak Zapotec, but the majority of instruction is in Spanish (all but one–two hours/per week) due to a lack of resources in Zapotec and ideologies of parents, critical that teaching in Zapotec will slow down their children's progress in Spanish. Co-author, Virgilia Pérez García (Viki) currently teaches first-grade at Luz y Progreso. Ramón López Velarde serves 213 students who attend this public bilingual, intercultural, elementary school in the afternoons. Of the ten teachers, seven speak Zapotec, but similar to the Luz y Progreso school, Zapotec instruction only occurs about one to two hours/week, usually on Thursdays. Co-author Felipe Ruiz Jiménez (Wihdxya) currently teaches third-grade at Ramón López Velarde. Both Wihdxya and Viki graciously share their perspectives, examples of personally created poetry and didactic materials, and examples of student work.

First Challenge: Contesting Normalized/Official Knowledge and Asserting and Valuing Local Ontologies in the Curriculum

The following poem written by Wihdxya makes visible the struggle between the requirements (and resulting ideologies) of the official national curriculum, influenced by Western, epistemological knowledge, and the valuing of local ontologies. Themes of pride, local knowledge, resistance, and strength flow through this poem that Wihdxya then used for Zapotec literacy development at school as a way of asserting and infusing local ontologies.

First, Wihdxya and the students read the poem together in Zapotec, then the students painted their understanding of the poem (see Figures 14.1 and 14.2 below).

"The above activity is an example of a teacher combining his love and his knowledge of poetry, his ethnicity, and teaching to in order to get his students thinking about and questioning their lives and sources of knowledge" (Przymus, Ruiz Jiménez, & Pérez García, In press). Another approach to developing Zapotec literacy via the assertion of local ontologies is the tapping into community-based *xkialnana* (knowledge), such as *mensajes de los abuelitos* (messages from grandparents).

Rehn nu	(My blood)
Ngach nak rehn nu	(I am made of yellow blood,)
Rehn nuu naka bee	(I am made of brown blood,)
Nkich nak rehn nu.	(and of course, I am made of white blood.)
Tson yee nak rehn ni nu duurehn nah	(Three colors that are found in my veins,)
Duu rehn ni naadz loh xdoa xi'ch.	(the veins that strengthen my heart,)
Xtiãz loh xdoa ni ranchina nah,	(A heart that beats with love,)
Ni riana xpecha,	(The love of brotherhood,)
Ni ranchina gichlyuh.	(The love for mother earth.)
Nah nak behn diidx zah, nah ranchi xtixa,	(I am the Zapotec that loves his language,)
Ranchi xkialnana, xkialnana ni bchial xkialbañ llob,	(One who loves his knowledge,)
Xkialbaña git, Xkialbaña bziaa, Bagoka chii mil ihdz nib a pschial gial mbahñ re.	(The knowledge of having discovered the food sources of corn, squash, and beans more than ten thousand years ago.)
Tson giahl mbahñ re bena tuhñ gehn ngiehx.	(Three foods that have strengthened brave warriors,)
Bena tuhñ behn gialnan, bena tuhñ behn nia.	(wise teachers of knowledge,)
Tuhñ nak behn nia, zek tuhn sonbahñzan na,	(men who transform into divine beings.)
ria bixtiil nada nlox tuhñ nguita,	(We, the Zapotec, are the divine beings;)
ria bixtiil nzebroka xbeelohna ni nana,	(that is why the White man has not been able to exterminate us)
lox xete ni nana, nex kaloxa ria xkichyuhn.	(those that think they know, but ultimately do not, because they destroy everything.)
Zehna xkial riena riopa lohxdoa nzäy mbahñ ni naka xi'n llob:	(Today my mind and my heart are alive with emotion because I am proud to be the son of the corn).
Xi'n llob ngach,	(Of the yellow corn)
Xi'n llob ngaa,	(Of the brown corn)
Xi'n llob nkich.	(Of the white corn.)
—Felipe Ruiz Jiménez (Wihdxya)	—Translated from Zapotec to Spanish by Wihdxya, from Spanish to English by Steve Przymus

Figure 14.1 Student painting 1

Mensajes de los abuelitos

Throughout our conversations, both Wihdxya and Viki stressed the importance of elders' knowledge. What is it that grandparents know and what can
students learn from them? This method for literacy development is important for both rejecting Western knowledge by not simply translating texts
from Spanish, but rather using authentic texts derived from local knowledge
and for preserving this knowledge so that it is not forgotten. First, students
are tasked with investigating a theme by interviewing parents, grandparents,
and neighbors. Second, they collaborate with these community members
and their parents to write their findings in Zapotec and in story form.
Finally, the students become authors by creating and presenting their own
books. Figures 14.3–14.6 are a series of photos showing a book produced in
Zapotec, by Viki's third-grade students in 2016–2017, which is a collection
of *mensajes de los abuelitos*. Learning from their grandparents' knowledge of
animals, students practice Zapotec.

Figure 14.2 Student painting 2

Mensajes de los abuelitos are also a form of educating students with community and family values. For example, other *mensajes de los abuelitos* gathered by students teach lessons, such as

- Don't sit on the corn, or you will fill with grains
- Don't lay down while eating tortillas, or you will get sick
- Don't sit by the corner of the table, you can get hurt

are forms of teaching children how to act, such as at the table, and behave well.

Other activities directly involve family members' participation at home and at school. After collaborating with parents and grandparents at home to document a skill or lesson in Zapotec, grandparents go to the school and give a demonstration, such as how to make *atole* (a traditional drink made from corn, sugar, cinnamon, and vanilla). In order to motivate the students, the elders involve some students in the demonstration, while others record

Figure 14.3 A collection of *mensajes de los abuelitos*

and take pictures of the demonstration. Later, some students do the demonstration by themselves, explaining to others how the elder performed the task, while the other students document the steps in Zapotec. This kind of community-based pedagogy achieves the goal of preserving local ontologies that contest ideas of official, Western knowledge, all the while preserving these same local *xkialnana*. Finally, these kinds of activities that involve the community beyond the school, act to raise the function, importance, and status of the Zapotec language, an effort that we address in the next section.

Second Challenge: Winning the Ideological and Pedagogical Battle for Zapotec Language Planning and Policy in Schools

Although there are 58 varieties of Zapotec, members of La Soledad Salinas all use the same, mutually understood variety. However, as is the case with many bilingual education contexts in the U.S., ideologies among many administrators, teachers, and even parents in Oaxaca exist of educational success being

Figure 14.4 *Mensajes de los abuelitos*, page 1

Figure 14.5 *Mensajes de los abuelitos*, page 2

Figure 14.6 Mensajes de los abuelitos, page 3

measured first by typical development in the dominant language. In Mexico the dominant language is Spanish. Both Viki and Wihdxya relayed stories of parents saying, "I've sent my kids to school to learn Spanish, why are you teaching Zapotec?" Parents have also expressed concerns that their children will become confused and not learn how to read and write well or will be slowed down in their literacy development in Spanish.

Instrumentalization

The community-based approach, shared above, has addressed some of these concerns, as through collaboration, parents and community members witness the function and value of preserving and teaching local knowledge. This approach is related to what Ruiz (2013, personal communication) calls "instrumentalization" of language or "creating conditions for its use and perceptions of its usefulness … in the many contexts in which it is used for significant functions-the family, community agencies, electronic and written media of communication, schools, churches, commercial centers, universities, etc." (Richard Ruiz, personal communication/lecture PowerPoint slides, September 2013). Both Viki and Wihdxya expressed sentiments during our conversations regarding, giving Zapotec importance at school, that can best be summed up with "*Para que tenga valor*" (So that it is valued). School-wide at Luz y Progresso, the Mexican national anthem is sung in Zapotec each Monday. Important announcements and signs are hung around the walls of the schools in Zapotec and it is encouraged that students help each other create, understand, and use the signs. I have observed other linguistic landscape efforts in other Zapotec communities of Oaxaca of placing Zapotec signs around town with messages such as, "Respect your elders."

Play is another way to make a language instrumental. Beyond the Zapotec integrated in poetry, Wihdxya also uses drama and has students write and perform their own readers' theater, based on Zapotec stories that Wihdxya tells them. Viki sings songs in Zapotec with her students, plays games in Zapotec, such as the classic Mexican game *lotería*, gives students Zapotec riddles, and creates guessing books, such as *Xwia Xwia* (What do you See?, see Figures 14.7–14.9).

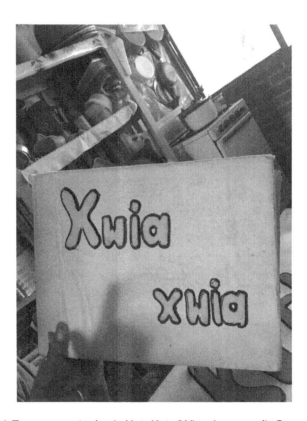

Figure 14.7 A Zapotec guessing book, *Xwia Xwia* (What do you see?). Cover

Figure 14.8 A Zapotec guessing book, *Xwia Xwia* (What do you see?). Page 1

Figure 14.9 A Zapotec guessing book, *Xwia Xwia* (What do you see?). Page 2

Playing with language or creatively using all of one's linguistic repertoire (translanguaging), such as a student at Luz y Progreso does here, "*Está bien maestros si pa ni ba bloxa ya puedo descansar?*" (Is it ok teachers *if I have finished* that I rest?), perhaps gives us direct insight into how students and teachers might leverage community knowledge and holistic language use, ubiquitous in Zapotec homes, for instrumental language and content development at schools.

Translanguaging

Translanguaging, the language practice and ability of multilinguals to utilize their full linguistic repertoire, which includes features of multiple named languages, but which are all part of an individual's sole linguistic idiolect (Otheguy, García, & Reid, 2015), is an important concept that deserves more investigation in the context of Zapotec literacy development. Based on my time spent with Wihdxya, Viki, their families, and participating in community events, I observed ubiquitous translanguaging. The seamless use of individuals' full linguistic repertoire, which sounds like the integration of the named languages of Zapotec and Spanish, is just a part of daily living, evidenced by Wihdxya using Zapotec to speak to his mostly Zapotec-speaking mother, turning to speak to me in Spanish, and at the same time using both named languages to communicate to his brother and adolescent son. I observed communicative interactions like this all across the community: in the tailor shop, in restaurants, and in people's houses, while sharing meals with their families. Although a quotidian part of life outside of schools, within the school walls, translanguaging, such as the student example above, is more of a contested practice. There is agreement among the teachers that with younger students it is OK to use both named languages in instruction and allow students to use both in the classroom, but that in order to develop "good" Spanish and "good" Zapotec, the languages should be kept separate in older grades during instruction and student use. Although recent literature in U.S. Spanish/English bilingual education has shown that students produce more language practice and develop greater bilingual content knowledge when allowed to translanguage (García, Ibarra Johnson, Seltzer, & Valdés, 2017; Przymus, 2016), language separation ideologies expressed above remain strongly influenced by the myth that what many call code-switching will lead to confusion and underdeveloped literacy in the dominant language at schools. However, as I refute this ideology, by citing the above research, I am aware that I am privileging Western, colonial epistemology over the local ontologies of this Zapotec community, the very problem that we wish to confront with this chapter. Although, I believe that translanguaging in instruction and use at schools, may have a positive impact on the current context of educational inequities among

Zapotec communities in Mexico, further research, driven by local Zapotec teachers and researchers, is needed.

Conclusion

"All across México, and specifically among Indigenous Zapotec teachers in Oaxaca, teachers are acting as change agents that honor and incorporate local ontologies and community-based *xkialnana* in the community schools where they live and teach" (Przymus, Ruiz Jiménez, & Pérez García, In press). Authentic, community-based literacy instruction can provide an alternative to the homogeneous approach outlined by the Mexican national curriculum (Meyer, 2016). Colonial nations have exerted political, cultural, and knowledge-based agency over Indigenous communities. What we have highlighted here is an example of how a community can enact the power of decolonial, community-based literacy instruction for rewriting the narrative of what knowledge counts (Przymus, Ruiz Jiménez, & Pérez García, In press).

Ideologies of the monolingual paradigm and of educational success being intrinsically linked to success first in the dominant language persist, however, and the creative solutions shared above and acknowledgement of the importance of allowing students to use their full linguistic repertoire (translanguaging) are important for dispelling the myths of bilingual confusion, and for shifting the view of continued literacy development in Zapotec from a language-as-problem to a language-as-resource orientation (Ruiz, 1984). Teaching in and about a language should always be much more than simply knowing-about the language. Teaching to read and write should always be more than just learning how to read and write. True knowing goes beyond simply knowing-about. *Knowing* is about experiencing, living, and being the language.

Discussion Questions and Application

1. What did you find most interesting, surprising, and/or new to you in this case study?
2. In what ways were the featured Indigenous teachers (co-authors) change agents in rewriting the narrative about what knowledge counts in Mexican schools?
3. How might the multimodal literacy development strategies highlighted in this case study be implemented in other contexts where minority groups advocate for the recognition and valorization of community knowledge in schools?
4. How are the concepts of instrumentalization and translanguaging related and in what ways might they be used to for more meaningful literacy development?

References

Francisco Antonio, E. (2015). *Los conocimientos comunitarios del pueblo Ayuuk y los contenidos escolares: Elementos para la construcción de una didáctica decolonial.* Ciudad de México: Ediciones Díaz de Santos.

Freire, P. (1993). *Pedagogy of the city.* New York: Burns & Oates.

García, O., Johnson, S. I., Seltzer, K., & Valdés, G. (2017). *The translanguaging classroom:Leveraging student bilingualism for learning.* Philadelphia, PA: Caslon.

McCarty, T. L. (2006). *Language, literacy, and power in schooling.* New York: Routledge.

Meyer, L. M. (2016). Teaching our own babies: Teachers' life journeys into community-based initial education in indigenous Oaxaca, Mexico Global. *Education Review, 3*(1), 5–26.

Otheguy, R., García, O., & Reid, W. (2015). Clarifying translanguaging and deconstructing named languages: A perspective from linguistics. *Applied Linguistics Review, 6*(3), 281–307.

Przymus, S. D. (2016). Challenging the monolingual paradigm in secondary dual-language instruction: Reducing language-as-problem with the 2-1-L2 model. *Bilingual Research, 39*(3–4), 279–295.

Przymus, S. D., Ruiz Jiménez, F., & Pérez García, V. (In press). *Mensajes de los abuelitos*: Reclaiming Zapotec ways of knowing and community-based biliteracy practices in Oaxaca, México. *Bilingual Review/Revista Bilingüe.*

Ruiz, R. (1984). Orientations in language planning. *NABE Journal, 8*(2), 15–34.

Thompson, I. (2016). Zapotec. *About world languages.* Retrieved from http://about worldlanguages.com/zapotec

Chapter 15

Literacy Learning in the UAE

A Case for Exploration: NorthStar International School, United Arab Emirates

Fatima Hasan Bailey

Cultural Context

The United Arab Emirates (UAE), is a young and industrious country, which is 47 years old. It is considered part of the Middle East, located in the Arabian Gulf peninsula. While Arabic is the official language, English, Urdu, and Hindi are also widely spoken. The UAE is an international hub for various economies and industries. The country comprises over 200 transient expatriate nationalities and ethnicities. Public and private schools are options for P-12 education. Expatriate families primarily enroll their children into private schools. Emirati Muslim families enroll their children in both private and public schools. Educators come to the UAE from around the world bringing diverse teaching expertise and experiences (O'Sullivan, 2015). Students who attend UAE schools, bring an array of cultural, linguistic and educational learning experiences.

Stating the Problem

Speaking, reading, writing, and comprehending in the English language is sometimes confusing for both non-native and native English speakers as it looks, sounds, and seems to be written differently in the UAE. In part, this is due to the various languages, nuances, and dialects spoken by students and teachers. Teachers and students often notice subtle differences of how English is spoken, written, and comprehended, especially those from certain countries such as the US, UK, South Africa, Australia, and the Philippines (Colón-Muñiz, SooHoo, & Brignoni, 2010).

Ms. Amira is a veteran first grade teacher in an P-12 international private school. She is multilingual. She is fluent in classical Arabic, English, Urdu, and French. Ms. Amira's class includes 22 students, with 12 boys and 10 girls in attendance. The school expects that the medium of instruction is English. During literacy activities and circle time, several students found themselves feeling disempowered, confused, and uncomfortable in front of peers.

Ms. Amira began to gauge and assess the situation. As a veteran teacher, she considers the results from the language skills inventory she conducted for all

22 students. She reviews and reflects upon their KG assessment/grade reports. She considers the results and observations yielded from the interactive language games that are set up in her class. Additionally, she learns that some of her students have attended different schools in the previous year, and have been exposed to different learning experiences (i.e. teacher led vs. student led) as well as curriculum (i.e. American, British, French, Indian, Arabic, etc.)

She observes that students could not comprehend language elements, short passages, parts of texts, or literary works because the words seemed different. Some of the words sounded different or were completely unrecognizable. Students would become confused and frustrated when reading words such as "apologize," "cracker," "color," "humor," and "center." The main reason being that previously, a majority of students learned these words differently as "apologise," "biscuit," "colour," "humour," and "centre." *Hence the question, "Miss Amira is it colors or colours?"* Ms. Amira is cognizant that there is an issue. She recognizes the dilemma that her students face and decides to do something about it.

Reaching and Teaching Students

Ms. Amira is committed to both "reaching and teaching" her students. Ms. Amira is committed to connecting with her students and communicating across cultural and linguistic boundaries. She identified that 85% of the multicultural students in her classroom are ESL learners and 15% of the students are ELL learners. The ESL learners are learning English as a second language, other students are learning and developing their proficiency of English language. The breakdown of the students' primary languages include: English, Arabic, Urdu, Hindi, Farsi, French, German, as well as Emirati dialect. She recognizes there are noticeable difference between American and British English such as vocabulary. There are hundreds of everyday words that are different. Ms. Amira recognizes that there is a dilemma in how her young learners face comprehension issues.

Ms. Amira considers herself to be a globally minded teacher, with an introspective outlook. She feels that it essential to recognize her students' backgrounds, experiences, perspectives, and needs. She is prompted to act and intervene, on a local level, i.e. in her classroom, a creative learning environment. Thus, Ms. Amira's operational framework for teaching and learning coalesces around culturally relating to students and reflecting on students' attitudes, knowledge, and skills. She strategizes approaches and develops ways, to scaffold and support students in their learning. Her practice shifts from marginalization to intervention. Her practice shifts from low to high impact. Literacy support and student engagement shift from language immersion and exclusion to language immersion and inclusion.

One challenge for Ms. Amira is ensuring that she is "reaching and teaching" students by honoring the cultural values and acknowledging the various perspectives of her diverse students Teachers should identify materials and employ a range of strategies to embrace, respect and promote the multicultural linguistic aspects, cross cultural values and diverse ethnicities of their students (Zhao, 2010). In total, 75% of her students observe Islamic tenets and principles. Story selection is a delicate matter in this part of the world and in this classroom. Choosing stories and books can be difficult as topics such as magic, tricks, etc. are controversial. The portrayal of gender roles, or stereotypes of Middle Eastern people must be considered. The use of music/rhythm is sometimes limited as well, depending on school policy. Teachers do not always give consideration to the different learning styles and multiple intelligences children possess (Van Roekel, 2010). One way to address this is through a balance of teacher- and student-led activities and structures. Teachers do not give enough consideration to teaching and reaching students by offering twenty-first-century fluencies to support student literacy (Crockett, Jukes, & Churches, 2011). Much of this work can happen through critically reflecting upon language and literacy practices, structures, and activities that are planned and that happen in classrooms.

Teacher-led Structures and Activities

Ms. Amira facilitates daily read alouds of various and interesting texts for students. Every morning she conducts whole group reading "circle time" on the carpet. She uses large print books and engages students. She changes the intonation in her voice. She stops at certain points, points out vocabulary including individual words, phrases, and idioms, and discusses their meanings with students. She asks student to respond to questions. She models and sets the pattern for students to follow. In an introductory reading lesson, she reads a simple passage from a fiction, non-fiction, or picture book. Students are provided with a digital display on the smartboard of the text being read, so they can follow along. She intentionally creates and builds a productive language learning environment through the use of innovative methods and technologies.

Student-led Structures and Activities

Ms. Amira provides students with an abundance of culturally relevant books, materials, and interactive activities such as games. She provides students with small group and "paired" activities, which student take turns at reading to their reading partner. She indicates written prompts at certain points in sections of text where they should stop to discuss what they have read and understood. These prompts help students to comfortably, freely and safely begin expressing their thoughts to peers. These prompts include: *I think ...; I noticed ...; I like the part where ...; I don't believe/think ...* Before beginning the lesson, students acquaint or re-acquaint themselves with certain expressions. Some days she allows students to bring an item from home that helps them build literacy and connect to the story. Students happily participate. They share their links and sometimes create a story to help others relate to the item they brought from home.

Implementing a Literacy Teaching Toolkit and a Student Literacy Toolbox

Ms. Amira recognizes that her students must develop literacy skills. She understands that her young students must learn to read for the purpose of understanding content. She is cognizant that there are impending factors that will impact her students literacy. She decides that there are ways that her students can enjoy the process of learning to read and develop their literacy. She creates and implements the use of a "student literacy toolbox" consisting of different tools, resources and materials. In their linguistic toolbox, students can select a tool in order to parse more complex texts. Students can access tools needed to identify and understand challenging vocabulary. They can "pull out their comfy charts," which are comparative word charts. If a student gets "stuck" or frustrated, they can use a tool to get them "unstuck," and help them move forward in their learning. The teacher hopes that if her students are aware in advance of word irregularities and vocabulary differences, and prepared to mitigate these difference, they are less likely to experience frustration, anxiety or discomfort; and move comfortably through the text.

Implementing Teaching Roles, Strategies and Approaches

Ms. Amira reflects on her role(s) to support student learning. She recognizes that teachers have a role in implementing strategies and approaches to support students understanding of what is going on in any given text. Teachers need tools to support a range of levels, abilities and reading interest. She decides to create and implement the use of a "literacy teaching toolkit." It allows her to scaffold student learning. In this toolkit, she will access a range of approaches, strategies and technologies to support students wrestling with understanding different writing styles and in confronting complex content. Additionally, she employs seven critical strategies and approaches to address the challenges her students face:

1. *Ms. Amira links literacy to real life experiences.* She provides students access to picture rich and culturally relevant books and other literary materials/media. She uses IT, and student movement from a literacy corner and literacy center that is set up in her classroom. She uses printed books that contains songs, rhythm, and music. She uses digital technology, audio-books and smart technology. Her literacy corner and center contain student-centered activities. She carefully arranged the literacy corner in her classroom. It is a student friendly, fun and engaging area that contains a collection of activities and materials (food menus, street signs, advertisements, etc.) designed to teach, reinforce, *and* extend reading comprehension skills *and* concepts. Her literacy center serves as an interest area that focuses on important and specific learning

goals set by the teacher. There are other opportunities for students to have one-on-one support, small group reading circles, and interactive games like Scrabble and Kahoot using I-Pads and MacBook Pros.

2. ***Ms. Amira models reading, language expressions and expectations.*** She reads texts of different lengths. She read sentences at a slow-to-normal speed, using an expressive tone. She allows think time after each sentence or paragraph for students to assimilate the material. She point to the words in the text as she reads them. This is particularly useful for Arabic speaking students who need to learn the left-to-right flow of English text. She points to the corresponding pictures as she reads the text. She shows students how to use picture dictionaries and illustrated short stories so that it all becomes more accessible to them and the reading material is gradually understood.

3. ***Ms. Amira facilitates developmentally appropriate practices (DAP) and differentiation.*** This teacher employs DAP appropriate techniques such as mime and gesture and the use of flashcards and pictures to help her students with understanding the unknown vocabulary and also in understanding the story. She differentiates the teaching and learning through product, process, content and learning environment. She provides colorful visuals and manipulatives such as flannel board pieces, props, puppets, and "realia." ESL and ELL learners especially benefit from any three dimensional objects you bring in to enhance the reading experience.

4. ***Ms. Amira monitors, verifies and assesses comprehension.*** She verifies comprehension of the story by asking students to point to items in the illustrations. She monitors and checks comprehension with simple yes/no and either/or questions at first, and then moves to fill-in-the-blank or who/what/when/where/why questions when students are more comfortable.

5. ***Ms. Amira is intentional, she strategically plans and acts.*** She employs intentional teaching strategies. She is deliberate and purposeful. She reads the same story on successive days. She pauses at strategic points. She points to corresponding illustrations. She invites individual students to supply the words or phrases they know. The teacher implements learning materials and resources to promote individual students' growth towards goals set by Ms. Amira.

6. ***Ms. Amira is creative, interactive and innovative.*** She, along with her students, acts out the story as they read it. She invites students to act along with her. When students are familiar with the story, she invites them to "read" along with her as she points to the words. If appropriate for younger students, she uses Big Books, as both text and illustrations can be easily seen. She presents text in a more creative and more imaginative way (i.e. using guessing techniques, adding warm-up activities that include sound, images or movements); younger learners are intrigued to read as they have guessed and also been involved in something that is both useful and pleasurable.

7. ***Ms. Amira is reflective, motivational and inspires her students to strive towards greatness.*** She provides feedback and positive reinforcement. She praises the emerging literacy of non-native students as well as the

Figure 15.1 Ms. Amira and child

Figure 15.2 Ms. Amira and child reading

literacy development of native students. She empowers struggling students. She celebrates milestones of students and acknowledges all of her students' efforts. The teacher provides positive reinforcement and praise for their effort, participation, and engagement. Students receive literacy awards, class dojo points, certificates and enjoy a host of end-of-term celebratory events and parties. Ms. Amira engages students, parents, and colleagues towards the national campaign launched in the UAE that promotes the culture of reading.

Concluding Thoughts

While the target language and medium language for instruction is English, this teacher recognizes that there are a myriad of factors that impact her students literacy development. She recognizes that students' schooling and literacy skills will vary dramatically. This teacher places the notion of "teaching and reaching her students" as a center point. She is keenly aware of the cultural context and underpinnings that impact students' experiences. Upon assessing and gauging the issues that her students face, she scaffolds her students. She becomes determined to preliterate students who are developing proficiency and literate those students whose native language is not English in ways that benefit students. As a globally minded teacher, who is reflective in her practice, she considers her roles in supporting student learning. She designs and implements a caveat of supportive structures, strategies and approaches which ultimately yield positive and favorable student learning outcomes with regards to literacy development.

Discussion Questions and Application

1. What did you find most interesting, surprising and/or thought provoking about this case study?
2. How does Ms. Amira support and empower her young learners at various proficiency levels?
3. Explain why teachers should employ innovative strategies to support readers in developing literacy and comprehension strategies?
4. Consider the work of a globally minded literacy teacher. Discuss challenges as well as opportunities that might be presented in a multi-lingual, multi-cultural, and diverse classroom. How might you address those challenges and opportunities, in order to support student learning and yield positive learning outcomes?

References

Colón-Muñiz, A., SooHoo, S., & Brignoni, E.G. (2010). Language, culture and dissonance: A study course for globally minded teachers with possibilities for catalytic transformation. *Teaching Education, 21*(1), 61–74.

Crockett, L., Jukes, I., & Churches, A. (2011). *Literacy is not enough: 21st century fluencies for the digital age.* Thousand Oaks, CA: Corwin Press.

O'Sullivan, K. (2015). Education reform in the UAE–Bringing private schools into the fold. *Journal of Teaching and Education, 4,* 311–320.

Van Roekel, D. (2010). Global competence is a 21st century imperative. Retrieved from www.nea.org/assets/docs/HE/PB28A_Global_Competence11.pdf

Zhao, Y. (2010). Preparing globally competent teachers: A new imperative for teacher education. *Journal of Teacher Education, 61*(5), 422–431.

Chapter 16

Literacy Learning in Spain

Marta Larragueta and Lorena de Poza Gutiérrez

Marta Larragueta is a PhD candidate on children's literature at Universidad Camilo José Cela, in Madrid (Spain). She has a Master's degree in International Education and Bilingualism and has been working for several years as a kindergarten primary teacher in different schools in Spain and the United Kingdom.

Lorena de Poza is a teacher of Hearing and Language and Therapeutic Pedagogy with a Bachelor's degree in Kindergarten Education. In 2015 she was awarded the Extraordinary Award in the Master's in Psychology and Educational Sciences Research from the University of León (Spain). She started her profession in Cantabria and currently works in a school in León.

Today, knowing a second language is perceived as an essential requirement in different aspects of our lives: working, travelling, meeting people from other parts of the world. In Europe, English is still the main choice to be taught as a second language and each country is developing and promoting different national and regional policies regarding that implementation. In recent years there has been a great effort in Spain to improve the English proficiency of the population and in schools in Spain, the early grades have been the main focus for English instruction.

This scenario has led to the implementation of various methodologies, some of which aim to use English as a tool to teach and learn other contents. This plan of action expects to integrate the second language in the daily life of schools, trying to turn it into a vehicle for academic communication. However, there are many teachers and families who see some drawbacks in the wide use of English with young learners; for example, there are claims that subject contents are often simplified and limited since they are not taught in the mother tongue, which makes comprehension harder. There are also issues with students' motivation when they have difficulty understanding what their teachers are trying to communicate to them.

Within this context, many kindergarten teachers are particularly concerned about the impact of bilingualism in other development areas. Moreover, the acquisition of English vocabulary in the early years is not always as adapted and playful as it should be if we expect the learning process to be meaningful for children. Different methods and materials have been applied for this purpose and nursery rhymes, games, flashcards and other materials are used to try to motivate students and engage them. However, there are still many teachers who do not feel confident enough with the approaches that are commonly used. So, a major cause of concern is how to engage the youngest students to learn a second language, while being able to plan meaningful and effective activities.

For this reason, an early elementary teacher, Lorena de Poza, started to research the different options available, seeking to find a suitable and effective way of catching her pupils' attention and helping them to learn new English vocabulary. Lorena is a hearing and speech specialist who has been working for more than four years in different schools in the north of Spain, usually in rural contexts. She thinks it is essential to engage students with meaningful and motivating activities in order to achieve significant and durable learning.

She is currently teaching in a small public rural school located in Cantabria, in the north of Spain, and works with children from 3 to 12 years old. She is especially focused on language development and is very interested in the role that picture books can have for vocabulary acquisition. Luckily, her school is also quite aware of the importance of literacy and literature in children's development and organizes activities to promote that area: intergenerational activities such as reading partners, a system of weekly book loans from the school library and specific time dedicated to individual and free reading at the beginning of every school day.

Before implementing a project to systematize the use of picture books to facilitate the development of language among the youngest students, Lorena de Poza implemented a short research to study the impact of two different methodologies. The first one was based on the introduction of vocabulary in contextualized situations through storytelling with picture books. The second one was based on a more decontextualized teaching of words based on different games such as bingo or memory, for example. She wanted to find out what kind of activity could be more effective for vocabulary acquisition in a kindergarten context.

Vocabulary Instruction in Contextualized and Decontextualized Settings

The main hypothesis that drives this research is that vocabulary is better learned when presented in a contextualized environment rather than in isolated activities. Children's literature has already been proved as a highly estimable resource for language development (Eller, Pappas, & Brown, 1988; Isbell, Sobol, Lindauer, & Lowrance, 2004; Sénéchal, LeFevre, Hudson, & Lawson, 1996), which makes an impact on children's progress in reading and language development in following years (Kaderavek & Justice, 2002). Stories engage students and rise their motivation and improve their attitude towards learning (Ghosn, 2002) and also allow learners to develop strategies such as predicting and hypothesizing to facilitate understanding (Castro, 2002; Ghosn, 2002). That is why they are a very frequent tool in kindergarten and primary classrooms where storytelling and reading aloud have shown to have positive effects in literacy development.

Within this context, picture books have been praised for their capacity to develop communicative and interpretative skills (Kachorsky, Moses, Serafini, & Hoelting, 2017; Pantaleo & Sipe, 2012) that are strongly related to the multimodal narrative that characterizes this kind of literature (Nikolajeva & Scott, 2006). Actually, they offer excellent opportunities for vocabulary acquisition thanks to their meaningful and natural context and the illustrated examples of new words (Ghosn, 2002). But how can we know whether they are more effective than other methodologies that are also engaging and motivating for children? How can we decide between picture books and other options, such as linguistic games and other playful dynamics?

There are 27 children attending Lorena's class of four-year-olds, of whom 20 are boys and 7 are girls. All of them are Spanish, though one girl's father is French and therefore her main tongue is French but she understands and speaks Spanish well. There are two students with special needs: one of them with language difficulties and the other with developmental delay.

Lorena de Poza has divided her class into two different groups to compare the efficiency for vocabulary acquisition of a contextualized methodology (picture books) and a decontextualized methodology (games such as bingo or memory, for example). She wants to examine the number of words learned with both approaches in order to be able to select one strategy or the other. Children, therefore, are randomly assigned to one of the two groups (with 13 and 14 students each) with the only consideration of allocating students with special needs equally in both groups.

Lorena has implemented the contextualized methodology with picture books in one of the groups and the decontextualized approach in the other, in order to compare the outcomes. She has applied the same test before and after the implementation of each method, so as to analyze the vocabulary acquired in each case. Afterwards she has analyzed data using a statistical software (Jamovi) and finally she has drawn the conclusions derived from the results.

In the contextualized group (CG from now) five picture books are chosen and read aloud to children: *Shadows* by Suzy Lee, *Oh!* by Josse Goffin, *Flashlight* by Lizi Boyd, *Journey* by Aaron Becker and *Flotsam* by David Wiesner. The teacher has decided to choose wordless titles and then invent a story herself, selecting six target words per book that will be evaluated in order to track and measure vocabulary acquisition.

Children are sitting on the carpet, in a semicircle and the book is read while showing the illustrations; questions to prompt hypothesis about the plot and the characters are asked while showing the cover before reading. There are no activities carried out after reading, apart from simple questions to learn whether children enjoyed the story or not. Each book is read three times per week, and each week is dedicated only to one of the books, so the whole project lasts five weeks.

In the decontextualized group (DG from now) the same target words chosen for the books are taught using different games and activities: flash-cards with words and drawings that children have to classify, differentiate, order and so on; memory and bingo games; shadow tasks using the smart board where students have to identify, link or name the element based on their shadow; mime activities where students have to dramatize the target words; activities involving movement where children have to find and catch words around the classroom for example. For this group, the number of sessions and the length is the same as in the CG group in order to offer students the same exposure to the new words.

Supporting Vocabulary Development with Picture Books

The evaluation of the vocabulary acquired by children, before and after the implementation, is conducted individually with each student. In order to take into consideration both passive and active vocabulary – what they can understand and what they can produce – children are told a word and asked to find it among different pictures and are also asked to name the pictures. These evaluations are planned on different sessions to avoid the interference between them. Moreover, children are asked more than once and in a different order the same vocabulary to avoid guessing.

All the collected data is analyzed by Lorena de Poza using Jamovi, a free statistical software; she applies the T-test to study whether the differences between the vocabulary learned with each methodology can be considered significant.

The results show that the use of a contextualized resource such as picture books has facilitated vocabulary acquisition in the class group Lorena was working with. In fact, for both passive and active vocabulary, children have significantly learned more words in the CG than in the DG. This shows that in this case at least, picture books have proved to be more effective than other games that can be as motivating as stories but may lack the necessary context that facilitate understanding.

These findings defend the importance of children's literature for language development in early years and coincide with other research conducted in the same direction (Castro, 2002; Eller, Pappas, & Brown, 1988; Ghosn, 2002; Isbell, Sobol, Lindauer, & Lowrance, 2004; Kaderavek & Justice, 2002; Sénéchal, LeFevre, Hudson, & Lawson, 1996).

Concluding Thoughts

Lorena de Poza is a teacher aware of the importance of language development in early stages and she wants to tailor her practice to her students' needs following the most efficient methodology. For that reason, she has decided to undergo a little research in her own classroom in order to compare two different approaches that are commonly used with kindergarten children. Lorena is already familiar with the use of picture books in educational contexts and she has been able to prove also their suitability as didactic tools for vocabulary acquisition with her group of four-year-old kids.

She has decided make use of five wordless books, creating the story herself so as to control the vocabulary she wanted to practice. Nevertheless, it could also be very enriching for young students to take advantage of the fantastic titles offered nowadays by the children's publishing market; in that case, it is necessary to bear in mind the complexity of text and illustrations, and how they can influence the process of learning new words (Larragueta & Ceballos-Viro, 2018).

Finally, after having checked the worthiness of picture books for vocabulary acquisition, it could also be illuminating to progress on the research related to the benefits offered by children's literature in terms of critical thinking and the development of communicative and interpretative skills. In that field there are already numerous studies that have shown positive results (Arizpe & Styles, 2016; Kachorsky, Moses, Serafini, & Hoelting, 2017; Pantaleo & Sipe, 2012).

However, children's literature is one of the various tools available for teachers to promote effective and engaging learning. How books are presented to students is a very important factor for the success of the activities and also the features of the materials should be considered. Therefore, there is still need for much more research, both from scholars and from teachers, in order to find the most suitable options for vocabulary acquisition.

Discussion Questions

1. Are we aware of the impact of our methodological decisions in the classroom?
2. What kind of training would teachers need to implement a project for language development based on children's literature?
3. In what other ways could we use picture books to promote spaces for the development of language or memory skills?
4. How do we select what kind of picture books are more efficient for vocabulary acquisition?
5. For the teacher in this case study, the main concern was how to engage the youngest students to learn a second language, while being able to plan

meaningful and effective activities. How does this case relate to your own instructional contexts? Can any of the activities presented here be implemented in your contexts?

References

Arizpe, E. & Styles, M. (2016). *Children Reading Picturebooks: Interpreting Visual Texts.* London: Routledge.

Castro, M. (2002). The Magic World of Storytelling: Some Points for Reflection. *Profile: Issues in Teachers' Professional Development,* 3, 52–54.

Eller, R.G., Pappas, C.C., & Brown, E. (1988). The Lexical Development of Kindergartners: Learning from Written Context. *Journal of Reading Behavior,* 20(1), 5–24.

Ghosn, I.K. (2002). Four Good Reasons to Use Literature in Primary School ELT. *ELT Journal,* 56(2), 172–179.

Isbell, R., Sobol, J., Lindauer, L., & Lowrance, A. (2004). The Effects of Storytelling and Story Reading on the Oral Language Complexity and Story Comprehension of Young Children. *Early Childhood Education Journal,* 32(3), 157–163.

Kachorsky, D., Moses, L., Serafini, F., & Hoelting, M. (2017). Meaning Making with Picturebooks: Young Children's Use of Semiotic Resources. *Literacy Research and Instruction,* 56(3), 231–249.

Kaderavek, J. & Justice, L.M. (2002). Shared Storybook Reading as an Intervention Context: Practices and Potential Pitfalls. *American Journal of Speech- Language Pathology,* 11(4), 395–405.

Larragueta, M. & Ceballos-Viro, I. (2018). What Kind of Book? Selecting Picture Books for Vocabulary Acquisition. *The Reading Teacher,* 72(1), 81–87.

Nikolajeva, M. & Scott, C. (2006). *How Picturebooks Work.* New York: Routledge.

Pantaleo, S. & Sipe, L. R. (2012). Diverse Narrative Structures in Contemporary Picturebooks: Opportunities for Children's Meaning-Making. *Journal of Children's Literature,* 38(1), 6–15.

Sénéchal, M., LeFevre, J.A., Hudson, E., & Lawson, E.P. (1996). Knowledge of Storybooks as a Predictor of Young Children's Vocabulary. *Journal of Educational Psychology,* 88(3), 520–536.

Web

Centre for Literacy in Primary Education, with the project "The Power of Pictures": https://clpe.org.uk/powerofpictures. They offer teaching resources and information about different teaching approaches in order to achieve quality children's literature at the heart of all learning.

Picture Books Cited

Becker, A. (2014). *Journey.* London, UK: Walker.

Boyd, L. (2014). *Flashlight.* San Francisco: Chronicle Books.

Goffin, J. (2007). *¡Oh!* Sevilla. Spain: Kalandraka.

Lee, S. (2010). *Shadow.* San Francisco: Chronicle Books.

Wiesner, D. (2012). *Flotsam.* London: Andersen Press.

Index

Note: References in *italics* are to figures, those in **bold** to tables; 'n' refers to chapter notes.

Made in the USA
Coppell, TX
06 May 2021

55158623R00154